TOURNAMENT

of

ROSES

THE FIRST 100 YEARS

by

Joe Hendrickson

Former sports editor, *Pasadena Star-News*

Drawing, in part, upon the work of

Maxwell Stiles

KNAPP PRESS　　•　　LOS ANGELES　　•　　1989

TOURNAMENT OF ROSES

Published in the United States of America by
The Knapp Press
5900 Wilshire Boulevard
Los Angeles, California 90036

Edited, designed and produced by
Knapp Western Publishing
a subsidiary of Knapp Communications Corporation
5900 Wilshire Boulevard
Los Angeles, California 90036

First published in 1971 as *The Tournament of Roses*

Edited by R. Kent Rasmussen
Production by Karen L. Sinrud
Copyediting by Katie Goldman
Publishing Director Richard Cramer

Library of Congress Cataloging-in Publication Data

Hendrickson, Joe.
    Tournament of Roses.

    Includes index.
    1. Rose Bowl Game, Pasadena, Calif.—History.
2. Tournament of Roses, Pasadena, Calif.—History.
I. Stiles, Maxwell. II. Title.
GV957.R6H42   1989   791'.6   88-8331
ISBN 0-89535-215-X

Contents

This is the updated edition of the first attempt by any writer to record the complete Tournament of Roses story from its beginnings to the present in its total makeup. It is not solely an account of the tremendous Rose Bowl games, but also a compilation of many of the happenings in the Tournament of Roses since the inception of this festival in 1890.

The story of the Tournament parade, the crowning of the Tournament queen, and the festive events leading up to the climactic Rose Bowl game represent a unique example of community cooperation and worldwide response.

The late Maxwell Stiles, sports editor of the *Hollywood Citizen News* at the time of his passing in 1969, left me much of the exciting story of those Rose Bowl games that dominated the New Year's Day scene up to the time the Pacific–Big Ten series began in 1947. His accounts have been augmented to complete the first full story of all seventy-five years of exciting gridiron action.

While the beauty of a queen such as Julie Jeanne Myers or the wholesome smile of a grand marshal like Shirley Temple cannot be equated with the symmetry of a winning forward pass from a Doyle Nave to an "Antelope Al" Krueger, there is a common tie in all that has made the festival great. Since 1890, this has been an operation of cooperation, spirit, hard work, and good will—and that is the story I have put on paper.

Stiles, a most competent newspaper-man for nearly fifty years and my fine friend, contributed a great deal of information to this story of the Tournament of Roses that merited permanent recording. Also I was aided by Sam Akers, the late publicist for the Tournament of Roses, and current publicist Bill Flinn.

Of considerable satisfaction to me are the words of my former editor at the *Pasadena Star-News,* Arnold Huss, who said of *The Tournament of Roses:*

You have captured the spirit of Pasadena's big day. You have put into the book warmth with touches of humor and an amazing amount of detail, not generally known to followers of the pageant.

To me, the opportunity to live and work in Pasadena through three of the ten decades in Tournament of Roses history has provided much personal satisfaction and appreciation for my good fortune. Life really has become a rose; some thorns along the stem, perhaps, but always with a beautiful flower atop.

The Rose Bowl game, the parade, the cooperation and joint effort that make this festival the finest in the world, represent the warm and positive side of American living. This is the spirit that can dispel impressions of discontent, unhappiness, greed, selfishness, and haughtiness that taint the American reputation in some countries and areas where the true inspiration and motivation of Americans is not understood or realized.

Joe Hendrickson
August 1988

This book is dedicated to each of the fourteen hundred members and staff of the Tournament of Roses Association whose united and unselfish efforts contributed to the success of Pasadena's one hundredth New Year's festival. The following men and women have charge of the 1989 celebration:

Ronald T. Aday, Arthur W. Althouse, Harrison R. Baker Jr., Delmer D. Beckhart, John H. Biggar Jr., John H. Biggar III, Otis Blasingham, James B. Boyle Jr., H. W. Bragg, Lorne J. Brown, Paul G. Bryan, Kenneth H. Burrows, John J. Cabot Jr., Robert L. Cheney, W. Robert Clark, Roy L. Coats, Harold E. Coombes Jr., Harriman L. Cronk, Millard Davidson, Thomas I. Delahooke, Gareth A. Dorn, C. Lewis Edwards, Don W. Fedde, L. Raymond Freer, Lawrence C. Gray Jr., W. H. Griest Jr., Stanley L. Hahn, Thornton H. Hamlin Jr., Frank Hardcastle, Gary K. Hayward, Ralph S. Helpbringer, Walter Hoefflin Jr., Lloyd D. Hopf, Esler H. Johnson, Frederick D. Johnson Jr., William S. Johnstone Jr., Donald Judson, Robert D. Kenney, Lathrop K. Leishman, Patrick A. Lejeune, Phillip R. Marrone, Thomas K. McEntire, R. Allan Munnecke, William H. Nicholas, Ronald A. Okum, Jon T. Pawley, Gleeson Payne, Edward J. Pittroff, Dick E. Ratliff, Roy W. Reeves, J. Randolph Richards, Michael K. Riffey, Donald A. Schroeder, A. Lewis Shingler, Thomas E. Smith, Fred W. Soldwedel, James N. Stivers, Gary L. Thomas, Michael E. Ward, Arthur D. Welsh, Edward Wilson and Carl E. Wopschall.

Staff

John H. B. French, Forest W. Foster, William B. Flinn, Julie Luna, Kristin Mabry, Gloria Meade, Richard A. Quattropane, Angela Rector and Robert Resendez.

Introduction

The 100th Year

The Tournament of Roses becomes one hundred years old on January 1, 1989. Granddaddy won't need a cane. He is still very agile, very healthy and very alert. In fact, he's never looked better. He feels so good he called in the carpenters to have them fancy up his home for another hundred years of life.

His birthday party will be a never-to-be-forgotten affair. It'll go on for four days—the entire New Year's weekend—as 1989 greets the world. It will truly be America's New Year's Celebration. Granddaddy's centennial isn't just Pasadena lighting up the sky; the whole nation is joining in.

Because New Year's Day falls on a Sunday in 1989, the Tournament will, for the fifteenth time, stage its festivities–its beautiful parade and glorious Rose Bowl football game–on Monday, January 2. This means the big show isn't just a one-day affair. From Friday through Monday, Pasadena can shout. And shout it will. Actually festivities went on throughout the previous year, starting with the unveiling of the Centennial Fountain at Tournament House in April 1988.

An estimated seven hundred people attended the kickoff which featured cannons, balloons, songs and a giant birthday cake. Mary Hart, star of television's "Entertainment Tonight" program, emceed the program, which introduced Ross Jutsum's official centennial song and Melanie Taylor Kent's official centennial poster. Pasadena mayor John Crowley and Los Angeles county supervisor Michael Antonovich made presentations to the Tournament, and in a speech before a conference on tourism, California governor George Deukmejian proclaimed "Celebration 100" as California's greeting to the world.

Other events scheduled for the preceding year included a Rose Bowl Hall of Fame dinner and a Rose Bowl Diamond Jubilee golf tournament at Brookside Golf Course in August, and a centennial celebration gala featuring past grand marshals, queens and presidents at the Pasadena Civic Auditorium Center in October.

California governor George Deukmejian, 1988 Tournament queen Ann Myers, and John H. and Mrs. Biggar

INTRODUCTION

By January 1, 1989, almost every American should know that the one hundredth Tournament of Roses and the seventy-fifth Rose Bowl game are being celebrated.

Heading the centennial is President John H. Biggar III, a Pasadena furniture executive. A Muir High School and Stanford University graduate, as well as an artillery officer during the Korean War, Biggar has served as a Tournament member since 1958, during which time he has chaired three tournament committees—decorating places, music and transportation.

To honor the Tournament's one hundredth year, President Ronald Reagan signed legislation making the rose America's national flower. At White House ceremonies, President Reagan was presented with a bouquet of roses by 1988 Tournament head Harriman L. Cronk and 1986 Tournament queen Aimee Lynn Richelieu.

As a prelude to the centennial, the Tournament offices in Tournament House in Pasadena were remodeled. Even the top Tournament staff members were given more significant titles. Tournament manager John "Jack" French was appointed executive director of the association. Forrest "Frosty" Foster became assistant executive director in charge of administration and membership. Public relations director William Flinn was named assistant executive director in charge of communications and marketing.

When Professor Charles Frederick Holder dreamt in 1889 that Pasadena should express its inspiration, he led the organization of the Tournament of Roses first held on January 1, 1890. Little did he realize the extent to which his creation would become a prime factor in the growth, importance and happiness of the entire area, as well as an event of world-wide significance. The Tournament of Roses, perhaps more than any other single event, has stimulated California's growth in sports, business and population.

Jim Murray, the humorous and perceptive *Los Angeles Times* columnist, points out that Southern California has problems such as smog, floods, fires, wind and fog 364 days a year, "but not," he says, "on New Year's Day."

That day dawns bright and clear, a stage setting for a Jeanette MacDonald–Nelson Eddy musical. Lush, sunny. Snow in the mountains. Orange blossoms blinking in sun. The trouble is that NBC televises this fantasy land into millions of homes, many of which have driveways full of snow or trees hung with icicles. The people there look up and see guys sitting here bare to the waist at a football game and girls dancing on the sidelines. The viewers look outside and it's Duluth out here. They say, "What in the world am I doing here? Mama, call Cross Country Van, pack the dishes and tell the postman to forward our mail to California."

There has been a claim that the Tournament of Roses parade and Rose Bowl game have caused millions of people to choose the Southland as their home. Coming with the people have been major league sports teams, skyscrapers, manufacturing plants, freeways—everything that fits into a humming metropolis. Pasadena grew from ten thousand people to a city of one hundred twenty-five thousand and now boasts of athletics, schools, churches, homes, business, science, art, engineering, attractive streets, parks and beautiful buildings.

Waiting in the wings during the 100th year celebration was Don W. Fedde, who will be president of the 1990 festival.

THE 1890s

MEDITERRANEAN OF THE WEST

1890
The Tourney of Rings

Charles Frederick Holder

Dr. Francis F. Rowland

Pasadena's graceful Valley Hunt Club, where gentlemen assembled, was a proper setting for the birth of the Tournament of Roses. In this peaceful setting a century ago, when Pasadena was a sleepy burg of 4,882 souls, Professor Charles Frederick Holder lifted a handful of newspaper clippings about the great New York blizzard of 1888 and addressed the club's members: "Gentlemen," he said, "I came from the East to this beautiful area for my health. I found it here. I also discovered happiness and beauty. In New York, people are buried in snow. Here our flowers are blooming and our oranges are about to bear. Let's have a festival and tell the world about our paradise."

A willing listener was Dr. Francis F. Rowland. He said he liked the professor's idea and added, "My wife has just returned from a festival of roses in Nice, France. Let's call our festival 'The Battle of Roses.'" Several other members chimed in: "We will be the Mediterranean of the West."

Thus was the Tournament of Roses born. The members of the Valley Hunt Club voted that on the first day of 1890 they would mount a parade of decorated carriages and stage an afternoon of public games on the "town lot" east of Los Robles between Colorado and Santa Fe.

When the big day arrived, the young men of Pasadena competed in footraces, tug-of-war matches, jousts, and a strange event called the "tourney of rings." This was an old Spanish game in which horseback riders with long lances tried to spear hanging rings while riding at top speed. In fact, it was the tourney of rings, coupled with a large display of roses that prompted Professor Holder to say, "Now

we have the name we want—the 'Tournament of Roses.'" The name stuck.

Although 1890 was the first year of the famous Army-Navy football rivalry, football games were still many years in the future for the Tournament of Roses. In 1890, C.V. Howard won the first Tournament of Roses sports event ever—a 100-yard footrace. For his 11¼-second effort, Howard received the Pickwick Cup, donated by Pickwick House. Howard was versatile: he also won the mile race in 5:40. Most novel of the 1890 races was an orange race. Each contestant picked up a line of fifty oranges placed two feet apart and put them into a basket. Bob Collingwood won the event and received a whip for a prize. In the quarter-mile pony race, Clayton Raymond aboard Dr. Rowland's Elsie nosed out Capt. A. B. Anderson aboard Fairy. Raymond received a silver watch. Anderson's second prize was a complete set of Charles Dickens's literary works.

Newspaper ads invited citizens to watch the promenade and games as they picnicked under giant oak trees. A wagonload of ripe oranges was distributed. Oranges didn't carry the day, however. Youngsters scattered rose petals along the dirt road that was then Pasadena's main street.

Dr. Rowland and Professor Holder led the first parade riding on their favorite mounts. The carriages were decorated with flowers. Valley Hunt Club members led their hounds on leashes. The theme of the affair was "A Time to Remember"—a theme repeated when Bob Hope was grand marshal in 1969.

Professor Holder later recalled that after parade entries had been judged, C. D. Daggett reached the grounds in a carriage so beautifully decorated he would have won first place if he had arrived on

Dr. Rowland leads the first parade in 1890

Eighty years after the first Tournament, Tournament manager Max Colwell recalled the message given to Pasadenans in the original Tournament of Roses: "Go home, pick your natural flowers and turn them into displays." The policy set in the beginning is the policy that has survived and expanded to its present magnificent splendor. "That," said Colwell, "is one of the wonders of our festival. The founders knew what would succeed. The same idea has always prevailed."

time. Daggett later was to distinguish himself as Tournament president, as grand marshal, and as the person who first proposed staging chariot races as a major attraction.

More than three thousand people attended the tournament and the *Pasadena Evening Star* gave it a smash review: "The greatest festival of similar nature ever held in the country."

1891
Dead of Winter

The first Tournament of Roses showed a cash profit of all of $229.30. In staging the 1891 festival, Valley Hunt Club members urged their fellow Pasadenans to join the parade along with club members. A prize was offered for the best decorated carriage.

"Who will say that Life, Liberty and the Pursuit of Happiness is not more desirable in Southern California than elsewhere on earth!" exclaimed the official

announcement of the Tournament. B. Marshall Wotkyns was president of this second festival.

To impress upon Easterners the stunning beauty of Pasadena on January 1, the Valley Hunt Clubbers called their 1891 festival "Dead of Winter." It was held at Devil's Gate Park to accommodate picnickers. A major feature was the appearance of the Monrovia Town Band, the first musical organization ever to participate in the Tournament of Roses.

"I think we have something started," said Dr. Rowland, who was to serve as parade grand marshal seven times—more than anyone else in the event's history. Equally enthusiastic in their response were other members of the Valley Hunt Club, who were dedicated to "the hunting of the jackrabbit, fox, and other wild game with horses and hounds."

The 1891 line of march started on South Orange Grove Avenue, virtually

B. Marshall Wotkyns

Frank C. Bolt

Charles D. Daggett

the same site used today, and led to Devil's Gate, a wooded amphitheater in the northern part of Pasadena where the games were held.

The modern parade route on Colorado Boulevard, which 1979 grand marshal Lathrop Leishman recommended should be renamed Tournament Boulevard, had much colorful history.

In 1874, the year Pasadena was founded and sixteen years before the first Tournament parade, Colorado Boulevard was the scene of a robbery committed by the feared outlaw Tiburcio Vasquez, who was in the midst of outrunning a posse. Vasquez and his men held up the farm wagon of three early settlers, from whom they got little beyond some watches. The victims were so slow in giving up their possessions, Vasquez grew infuriated and shouted, "Hurry up, can't you see the sheriff is coming after me?" Before the posse came within gunshot range, the outlaws dug their spurs into their horses, raced across the Arroyo Seco, site of the Rose Bowl today, and escaped into the mountains.

These were the same San Gabriel Mountains in which gold was first discovered in California. Northern California's goldfields later became more famous for gold because the findings there were larger.

1892
The First Flower Children
The 1892 parade produced an edict from the Valley Hunt Club in paid newspaper advertisements that "every man, woman, and child plus horse and carriage should be decorated with flowers." This celebration was returned to the east-central part of the city.

On this very same New Year's Day, an event was taking place in New York Harbor which was to have much to do with the future influx of people into Southern California: Ellis Island opened as the nation's primary receiving station for new immigrants. By the time it closed sixty-two years later, twenty million people had passed through it. The Tournament president for this and the following year was Frank C. Bolt.

1893
It Might Have Been the "Orange Bowl"
The name of the festival nearly became the "Orange Tournament" in 1892 when a severe winter caused a shortage of roses. The *Daily Star* campaigned to call the Pasadena fete the Orange Tournament whenever there was a shortage of roses, so there would be "no misnomer attached to our great celebration." However, when warm weather brought out plenty of blossoms before the 1893 event, the idea of changing the name was dropped.

1894
Unnatural Acts?
Reviewing stands were built for the first time along the parade route in 1894. Perhaps a step-up in public interest was precipitated by the 1893 decision to permit female equestrians in the parade to wear "bifurcated skirts"—what today might be called "culottes." The "bifurcated skirts" also precipitated the Tournament's first public debate on accepted style and fashion. In the first three parades, women rode sidesaddle. Opponents of the new way argued it wasn't a "natural, graceful and becoming act."

The 1894 parade represented growth from the few teams decorated with flowers and greens to a parade of many classes with six-in-hand and four-in-hand

The first "floats": prize-winning decorated carriages in 1890 and 1891

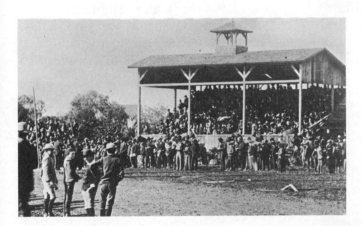

Two scenes from the 1890 festival: The first Tournament Games (above); Jennie Graham at the reins (right)

turnouts, double and single teams, and equestrians. Floats also were entered by organizations. The Columbia Hill Tennis Club, the Valley Hunt Club, and Hotel Raymond had the first float entries.

1895
Bringin' in the Rain

Then came a historic decision by members of the Valley Hunt Club. "We have grown to the extent the staging of this festival is more than we as a club can handle," said President Daggett in 1895. He was right. The parade had become so big that the incline-railway man, Thaddeus S.C. Lowe, had seven entries alone. Included were a single rig, four pairs, a four-in-hand and a six-in-hand.

The Valley Hunt Club also was finding that staging the festival was costly. Club members decided there was less risk in sticking to their hunting. Although 1895

marked the Valley Hunt Club's last parade, their present home still remains in the parade's formation area.

It rained steadily a week before the 1895 event. Many women refused to ride in the parade. Wettest of all were the young high school girls, whose dainty white gowns were soaked and stained, while their heads were protected only by marguerite petals. Through all this confusion, there was at least one float which seemed right at home. San Pedro's Chamber of Commerce entered a full-rigged brig with spectacular masts and rigging on a sea of flowers which read, "San Pedro to Pasadena." One wag quipped, "It took a day like this to get a full-rigged brig this far up the San Gabriel." All this water might have been more welcome later that year on the East Coast, where the American yacht *Defender* was to sink England's attempt to

If the Tournament founders had wanted a new sport to provide excitement, they might have turned to Dr. James Naismith, who was busy inventing basketball in 1891 in Springfield, Massachusetts. Perhaps it was significant that at the same moment Walter Camp was writing the first rule book for football. In it he defined such matters as the eleven-man team, the line of scrimmage and the quarterback position.

A decorated brougham typifies an entry in the 1895 parade

win the America's Cup trophy, proving, for the seventh consecutive time, that Britannia did not always rule the waves.

1896
The Association

This was to be a big year in the world of sports. The modern revival of the Olympic Games began in Athens, Greece, and the first public golf course in the world opened in New York City. Meanwhile, in Pasadena a public subscription campaign raised $595 to underwrite the expenses of the 1896 Tournament of Roses. At a public meeting, the Tournament of Roses Association was formed with Edwin Stearns as its first president. Nature gave the world a hint the Tournament of Roses Association would cause a stir in the years to come. Clouds of dust harassed the 1896 proceedings—a subtle harbinger, perhaps, of Big Ten running teams to come.

Little did the citizens realize, as they petitioned for better sprinkling of the streets to prevent more such dusty disturbances, that the second great rain in the history of the Tournament was to strike Pasadena in 1899. It has been Pasadena's good fate that rain has troubled the festivities only nine times in its one-hundred-year history—in 1895, 1899, 1906, 1910, 1916, 1922, 1934, 1937 and 1955.

Communities from outside Pasadena joined in the Pasadena parade in 1896 when the city of South Pasadena had an official entry.

1897
Enter Los Angeles

In January much of America turned its attention toward Alaska, from which the news of gold discoveries in the Klondike was just arriving. In March heavyweight

Chariot racing in the pre-football era

champion "Gentleman Jim" Corbett was knocked out by Bob Fitzsimmons, and in April the first Boston Marathon was run. Things were quieter in Pasadena, where chamber officers gave a yell during the Rose parade: "Pasadena, Pasadena. What's the matter with Pasadena? She's all right." The Los Angeles Chamber of Commerce entered its first float.

1898
On the Threshold of War

"We have started to achieve the goal of our founders and the cities around us are beginning to join in making our festival one of national interest," said President Martin H. Weight when, in 1898, he welcomed reporters from large eastern newspapers who came West for the first time to bring the story to their readers. A month later the nation's press would be focusing its attention on the East, after the American battleship *Maine* was blown up in Havana, Cuba. Despite the heavy burden the ensuing Spanish-American War placed on the nation, President William McKinley told officials of the festival to carry on. The twelve thousand citizens of Pasadena, just ten percent of what the population is today, cheered

College football made a major change in 1898, increasing the value of a touchdown to 5 points—up from the 4 points awarded since 1884. Conversion scores, on the other hand, were reduced from 2 points to 1. The next major rule change in scoring came in 1912.

McKinley's blessing, but the high school band of Whittier wasn't so happy. It couldn't make the twenty-mile trip to Pasadena to appear in the parade because every rig had been rented by the stables of Southern California and there were none left for the trip.

By contrast, twenty miles were nothing to G.A.W. Haas, who rode a bicycle from New York to Pasadena. And once he arrived in town, he simply kept right on going, riding his cross-country bike in the parade.

1899
Wash Out!

When a rainstorm struck in 1899, Tournament officials displayed their first example of collective cool by waiting until 3:45 in the afternoon for the skies to clear. Although the downpour made Colorado Avenue a sea of mud, the parade finally started—and eventually finished. The sports events, however, were called off. On the bright side, a Pasadena rain out once again seemed to bode well for the U.S. entry in the America's Cup competition, in which *Defender* was to turn back another British challenge later that year. It was also the year that James J. Jeffries won the heavyweight boxing crown from Bob Fitzsimmons, who had taken it away from Jim Corbett just two years before.

THE 1900s

CHARIOTS

Robert Gaylord pilots a horseless carriage in 1901

Herman Hertel

F. B. Weatherby

1900
Post Card Profits

When President Herman Hertel made a deal with the Vitascope Company granting that firm exclusive rights to film the 1900 parade, the Tournament of Roses was brought "live" to audiences throughout the United States. Though shown days, weeks, even months, later, Tournament parade scenes became a motion-picture favorite in many cities. Newspaper coverage increased also, as did the number of visitors to Pasadena.

The end-of-the-century parade attracted fifty thousand visitors, who came with a Fourth-of-July spirit. Every five minutes a trolley car from Los Angeles rolled in with men and boys clinging to its sides and roof.

The 1900 festival also was famous for having the Tournament's first distinguished parade guests—General William Rufus Shafter, commander of the American forces in Santiago de Cuba during the Spanish-American War, and Brigadier General Harrison Gray Otis, newspaper publisher and war veteran.

Unnoticed at the time, one of the Tournament standard bearers accompanying herald Paul Heydenreich was sixteen-year-old George Patton Jr.—later famous as a World War II general.

Hertel's term as Tournament president also was significant because he proposed that money be raised to obtain a permanent site for sports activities. After $2,043 was raised from selling post cards with parade pictures, Patton Field (no relation to George) was leased and renamed Tournament Park.

1901
Before They Invented Smog

"The automobile is here to stay. Let's let automobiles appear in our parade," said President F.B. Weatherby as the 1901 festival approached. "But," he added, "they must appear in the rear of the parade so they don't scare the horses!" Five chugging, flower-bedecked automobiles then entered the competition. Things have never been the same since.

Automobiles were not accepted with total enthusiasm. One Tournament official compared autos unfavorably with horse-drawn vehicles: "The pesky things stand there puffing like a frosty force pump and the flowers seem to have caught on by accident."

An annual parade feature in these years was competition for the best float between Throop Polytechnic Institute, a private school founded in 1891 and now known as the California Institute of Technology, or Caltech, and Pasadena High School. Throop had the best of it for several years until Leroy Ely, who later become principal of Pasadena High, took over the designing and decorating of high school floats and soon developed the Tournament's first truly elaborately conceived entry, drawn by six horses.

To inspire more women to enter, the Tournament this year advertised: "Ladies who wish to ride in the parade will be welcome and they will be furnished escorts by contacting F.E. Burnham and Ed Braly."

1902
Football Comes (and Goes)

Up until 1902, the Tournament's sports events did little to attract visitors. People came to Pasadena primarily to see the parade; they regarded the sports events merely as sideshows to their afternoon picnics. One Don Arturo Bandini had indeed won some local fame as an expert in the tourney of rings. A Duarte tug-of-war team had defeated a strong-armed group from Pasadena. There had been bicycle and running races, picnic style. Riverside defeated Santa Barbara 4–1 in polo. But none of this received much attention in the *Chicago Tribune* or the *New York Times*.

Under the new Tournament administration of James B. Wagner, the idea of staging a football game as the major sports attraction came to the fore. "We are national in everything but a sports attraction that will get people in the icy North and East talking," said President Wagner when he took over leadership of the Tournament.

Coach Fielding H. Yost's University of Michigan football team had won ten straight games and outscored its opponents 501–0. "Let's match our best against them. Stanford will test them," agreed other Tournament members. The invitations to the two teams were extended and accepted, and the game was scheduled to be played at Tournament Park after the parade on the first day of January, 1902.

New Year's Day turned out to be hot and dusty. After the parade, people started to head for Tournament Park, which was located on part of what now is the athletic field of Caltech, then known as Throop Polytechnic Institute. The city was decorated in blue and gold, the official colors adopted by the Tournament.

Maj. Gen. William Rufus Shafter, Mayor G.D. Patten and Brig. Gen. Harrison Gray Otis in 1900

Blue and gold pennants were everywhere. The colors so closely resembled the maize and blue of Michigan that Stanford followers became miffed. Stanford fans began to tear down the pennants and streamers, some shouting, "Those colors we hate—they are too much like the University of California's."

It soon became evident that Tournament Park's one thousand seats wouldn't be enough. The two teams had ridden tallyhos in the parade, an introduction that stimulated the enthusiasm of many to see them "push and pull each other" on the field.

Tallyhos, 1901 automobiles known as Victorias, and farm wagons carried people on the narrow road to Tournament Park. Hundreds came afoot, kicking up dust. It was Pasadena's worst traffic snarl to date. For hours the crowd waited for the lone gate to Tournament Park to open. There was one policeman, H.L. Van Schaick, and a few ticket handlers in charge of controlling the mob. Finally, at two o'clock, Van Schaick climbed to the top of the high board fence and shouted: "Ladies and gentlemen: May I have your attention! You are to line up single file and march through the gate in an orderly manner!"

About twenty lines formed, however, and each claimed it had the right to go

When Indians sold Manhattan Island to Dutch settlers for $24, the bargain turned out to be not much more profitable than the purchase of Tournament Park. Fourteen "country acres" at Wilson Avenue and California Street were purchased for $6,300; the amount that was needed beyond the post card profits was borrowed at 5% interest. The land, deeded to the city of Pasadena with the proviso that it would be available each January as a disbanding area for the sporting events, eventually was sold by the city to the California Institute of Technology for $650,000.

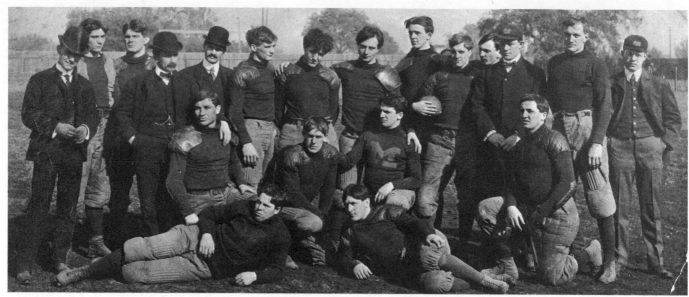

Michigan's point-a-minute football machine before the 1902 game

James B. Wagner

through the gate first. The snarl was checked temporarily when the gate was closed. But a boy was hoisted to the top of the fence and he wriggled over. Another followed. And another. Then came the stampede. It was estimated that eighty-five hundred people managed to squeeze into the park to witness the game between Michigan and Stanford— the first football game in Rose Bowl history.

Intersectional Experiment: Michigan 49, Stanford 0

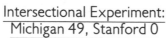

The Michigan Wolverines couldn't pierce the Stanford line early in the game, so a punting duel developed between Michigan's Sweeley, who kicked twenty-one times, and Stanford's Fisher, McGilvray and Traeger. Finally, Michigan's great star, Willie Heston, wrote his name into Rose Bowl history. He broke away for a 21-yard run that put Michigan on Stanford's 8-yard line, from which fullback Neil Snow charged over to score the first touchdown in Tournament of Roses history.

While Heston was Michigan's superstar, with nearly 200 yards gained, there were other greats in the game. Michigan had Dan McGugin at left guard; he later was famous as coach at Vanderbilt. The

Wolverines' left end, Curtis Redden, scored two touchdowns on 25-yard punt returns. Sweeley stood out with his punting. Al Herrnstein, a great ball carrier, won the respect of Stanford, and fullback Snow scored five times.

Stanford's lineup included tackle Bill Traeger, later to become Los Angeles County sheriff, and left guard W. K. Roosevelt, a second cousin of President Theodore Roosevelt. Early in the game, Roosevelt hobbled over to R.S. Fisher, the Stanford captain, and said, "Something is broken in my leg."

"Stay with it!" snapped Fisher.

"You bet I will," replied the Stanford guard with true Rooseveltian grit. He dragged himself back to the line of scrimmage and played fifteen more minutes, until he finally left the game with a broken leg and fractured ribs.

Despite the great courage of the outmanned and outnumbered Stanford players, Michigan eventually rolled up a 49–0 advantage on eight 5-point touchdowns, one 5-point field goal, and four 1-point conversions. It thereby extended its winning streak to eleven games on the season, which it won by the combined score of 550–0.

One of the first newspaper stories reporting on a Tournament of Roses foot-

12

Stanford football team on the eve of the first Tournament of Roses game

ball game also was one of the funniest. The *Pasadena News* compared the game to the South African War, which was then nearing an end:

"Several thousand Dutchmen and Britishers engage in several years of bloody fighting for the possession of a government and don't get an encore. Twenty-two college striplings argue for an hour over the progress along the ground of an inflated pig's hide, and law-abiding citizens bounce up and down on the seats of their trousers, while demure maidens hammer plug hats sown over the ears of their escorts with parasols."

1903
Polo and Navajo

The stampede of fans before the Tournament's first football game may well have contributed to the decision to abandon intersectional football games after just one try. In any case, President Charles Coleman and his aides had difficulty in negotiating for teams. Nobody on the West Coast wanted to take on the Michigan powerhouse. The 1903 festival thus reverted to the old format of general sports events, the main attraction being a polo match which only drew two thousand spectators.

Coleman did, however, succeed in

bringing one big new attraction to Pasadena during his lone year at the helm. A large group of Arizona Navajo set up camp at Tournament Park, where they drew hundreds of curious people. Needless to say, they were also a popular feature of the parade.

The Hotel Green float in the 1903 parade, a four-horse tallyho all red and green with flowers, was filled with attractive young women in big red picture hats and dainty summer gowns. As they passed the reviewing stand, each woman released a red toy balloon from under her parasol, dotting the sky with small red balls.

The women of Hotel Maryland were disappointed at losing first prize to Hotel Green. They showed their true feelings the next year by intoning,

We want the prize,
We want it bad,
And if we fail,
We'll feel sad.

Apparently the chanting worked, as they won in 1904.

1904
"Ben Hur"

When Charles D. Daggett took over the 1904 presidency, he convened the Tournament committee and declared, "Gen-

The Tournament's first football game was almost aborted by a minor crisis. When the Tournament offered the fifteen or so Michigan players only $2 a day as meal money, Charles Baird, the team's graduate manager, replied, "We won't come unless we can go comfortably and in reasonable style. We want $3 a day meal money." The raise was granted.

Michigan's Neil Snow

Stanford's 49–0 loss to Michigan in 1902 has been equalled, but never surpassed, as the worst drubbing in Tournament of Roses history. It could have been even worse. The year the game was played, touchdowns counted only 5 points. If the modern system of point scoring—instituted in 1912—had applied, Michigan's margin of victory would have been 55–0! On the plus side, Stanford beat the odds by a point. In its previous ten games, Michigan had *averaged* 50 points a game.

tlemen, our beloved founder, Mr. Holder, has a wonderful idea. I will let him tell you about it.''

Holder arose and said, ''You have read the best-seller, *Ben Hur*. That book gives us the idea we need for our festival. Let us stage a true Roman chariot race. It will make modern history.''

Tournament members cheered. They hadn't dreamed anything so exciting could be a part of their great festival. The world had to take notice now. Ed Off, a courageous man who was director of the Tournament, said, ''Yes, the world will notice. And I will race.'' And race he did.

The 1904 race featured two authentic double-wheeled Roman chariots with four-horse teams lashed together. A hush fell over the sixty-five hundred spectators just before the start. Off, the novice with more enthusiasm than experience, and Mac Wiggins, a veteran horseman from El Monte, stood precariously in their fragile chariots. The latter's professional horsemanship proved too much for the amateur. The race was no contest. Off lost, but he returned the next year more determined than ever.

The chariots were a big hit, but they weren't the only crowd pleasers in 1904. Automobiles wcrc still a novelty, and driving was a tricky matter. To compare skills in handling the iron monsters, elimination speed contests were held. The contestant who drove a given course at a speed closest to four miles an hour won a pair of women's gloves as a prize. There also was an exhibition of control between horse-drawn vehicles and automobiles, in which each was driven at high speed and stopped at a signal.

1905
Enter the Queen

While the rest of the world concerned itself in 1905 with such matters as the Russo-Japanese War, formation of the NAACP, Albert Einstein's newly published special theory of relativity, the beginning of Ty Cobb's professional baseball career and other matters, Pasadena remembers its 1905 Tournament of Roses for two reasons: Ed Off nearly lost his life in a wild chariot race, and the Tournament named its first Rose Queen—Hallie Woods.

Woods, chosen by her Pasadena High School classmates, may have been a queen, but she had to work. She made her own gown and helped decorate the float upon which she rode in the parade. That year's parade, in fact, was full of surprises. Bugler Ernest Crawford, for example, astounded spectators by wearing an outfit in which leggings, coat and hat were made entirely of flowers.

Harry Zier's automobile set the stage for future floats. Designed as a barge, the big touring car was covered entirely with a boat-shaped frame so that not a bit of the running gear was visible. As if seated at the oars, the chauffeur and his friends sat amidst white carnations, dotted with red.

When the temperature reached seventy-six degrees by mid-morning, nervous parade officials moved the automobiles from the rear to the very beginning of the parade to prevent their radiators from boiling over while they maintained the slow pace of the horse-drawn vehicles. The fire department rig was placed at the end of the parade so it would be in a position for a quick getaway if necessary.

Ed Off went into the 1905 chariot race with memories of 1904, determined to make good. This time he was matched against the widely known hotel man, D. M. Linnard. The popular Off got away to an early lead, but found his steeds unmanageable. Apparently infuriated by gopher holes in the track, they roared around the curve; Off lost all control.

Men shouted for the horses to stop, women screamed and held handkerchiefs to their faces, expecting at any moment to see the daring rider dashed to the ground and crushed to death beneath the horses. But as it has done so often, fortune smiled on the Tournament of Roses. A horseman astride a big bay came out of nowhere to attempt the rescue. The crowd of twelve thousand roared its approval when he halted the runaway.

Following his narrow escape, Off attempted to bow before Queen Woods, who had viewed the scene from the royal box, but he collapsed into the arms of the man next to him.

1906
Two-Dozen Ladies in Waiting

The indefatigable Off returned to the chariot races a third time in 1906. He actually managed to win a heat against another rider, but his horses wouldn't stop after crossing the finish line and he was injured. He must have finally decided that chariot racing wasn't for him. This ended his career as a charioteer, but not his love for the Tournament. After having risked his life to make the Tournament a thrilling affair, he was rewarded for his dedication with the post of

Ed Off, the persistent charioteer

Queen Elsie Armitage with the largest court in Tournament history

Former Civil War general Lew Wallace's novel *Ben Hur: A Tale of the Christ,* first published in 1880, was a best seller in the late nineteenth century. Several silent film versions of the story were made in the early twentieth century. The two best-known film versions—those of 1926 and 1959—are perhaps most famous for their chariot-race scenes. Wallace himself died in February 1905; it is doubtful he ever saw the Tournament of Roses chariot races his novel inspired.

1907 Tournament president, succeeding Edwin D. Neff.

The picnic-like atmosphere of the 1906 event featured the concession of T.H. Cook of Los Angeles, who was granted the right to conduct a stand that featured "fortune-telling birds, magic fish pond, and a doll race." Cook had to pay a $10 license fee. L. H. Lancaster had the food concession. He could sell sandwiches, soda water and lemonade on condition that he provide first-class sandwiches with meat and butter for ten cents, a good cup of coffee with cream and sugar for five cents, and cigars at the same price and quality as downtown.

The 1906 queen, Elsie Armitage, will go down in history as the queen with the largest court—twenty-four ladies-in-waiting. Altadena High School had the eye-stopper in that year's parade—a float representing a large man-of-war sailing on a sea of flowers.

The tranquility enjoyed in Pasadena was not to last throughout the state. Just three-and-a-half months later a devastating earthquake nearly leveled San Francisco, four hundred miles to the northwest.

1907
Horse Thieves

The biggest excitement in 1907 came when horse thieves raided many of the stables and stole many rigs before they could be hitched for the parade.

Joan Hadenfeldt Woodbury, at the age of thirty-five, became the first of two queens in Tournament history who was married when chosen. At the time, her husband was managing the Maryland Hotel. She was also the first officially to be called the "Queen of the Tournament of Roses." She lived until 1969, reaching age ninety-seven—the greatest age yet reached by a former queen.

1908
Airships and Whales

The festival of 1908 is remembered for many things. It was the first year parade officials had to be concerned about the height of wires above the parade route. Wires had to be elevated to let one high float pass. Another float, created by the Pasadena Merchants Association, got caught in the car tracks along Colorado; one flowery wheel had to be removed and a wheel of another color substituted to permit the float to continue. Redondo Beach entered a most unusual float in the parade—a mammoth floral whale that spouted carnation perfume twenty-five feet in the air and opened a geranium-lined mouth. The Redondo Beach whale was forty-one feet long, and its mouth was eight feet wide. The mouth opened and closed as the huge creature wallowed down the street like a great denizen of the deep. Green magnolia leaves, twenty thousand of them, made the

The danger and thrill of early chariot racing

Mayor Thomas Early and the city council ride a spectacular 1908 float

If American sports fans were disappointed by the dropping of football from the Tournament of Roses in 1903, they had plenty to cheer about that year when major league baseball inaugurated the World Series. Boston (AL) beat Pittsburgh (NL), five games to three. The World Series was not played the following year, but it returned permanently in 1905.

whale look as though it had just left the water. Members of the Redondo Arrowhead Club, all in whaling costumes, marched beside the float carrying strings of freshly caught fish from the bay.

It was indeed becoming a new age of spectacular floats. Redlands, famed for its orange groves, presented an orange twenty-seven feet in diameter, created from three thousand ripe oranges. Altadena High School entered an airship thirty-five feet long.

In 1908 the trolley line traffic from Los Angeles to Pasadena was so heavy it caused a temporary breakdown; there wasn't enough "juice" to operate so many cars. More than a hundred cars were on the rails between the two cities at the time. It was estimated that a thousand automobiles creaked into Pasadena—enough to cause the first traffic jams on Pasadena's quiet streets.

Chariot race rivalry reached a high point of intensity when a driver named Michel duclcd C.C. West in the finals. They were neck and neck down the stretch, West on the pole. Near the finish line, Michel drove in front of West, knocking down two of his opponent's horses. West was winner on a foul.

1909
Stagecoach Holdup
"We have sent thousands of posters to railroads for distribution in depots all the way to the East Coast telling about

Although the Rose Bowl was still in the Tournament's future, 1906 was a significant year in football history. The forward pass was legalized in the game, and the National Collegiate Athletic Association (NCAA) was founded.

While Pasadenans enjoyed their festival, future Arizona senator Barry Goldwater was born in Phoenix on the first day of 1909. He had to wait until his seventy-eighth birthday to see a team representing his state play in the Rose Bowl.

1908 float of Alhambra, "The Gateway to the San Gabriel Valley"

our festival," said President Carey as the 1909 festival neared. The holdup of a stagecoach was re-created as part of the show that year. A crowd of twenty thousand saw the chariot races won by C. C. West for his sponsor, Lucky Baldwin.

Individual floats became ever more spectacular. In 1909 E.W. Knowlton used five hundred American Beauty roses to decorate a two-seated surrey drawn by two Arabian horses. Walter Raymond, owner of Hotel Raymond, decorated his automobile to resemble a huge seashell.

THE 1910s

FOOTBALL FOREVER

Ezra Meeker, pioneer traveler who crossed the continent with an ox team by the old Oregon Trail in 1852 and repeated the trip in 1906, was a special attraction in 1910, driving an ox cart in the parade.

1910
It Never Rains in California

During the first decades of the twentieth century the Tournament of Roses groped for a formula that would establish it indelibly as first in all festival activities—both parade and sports. While the parade confidently evolved from primitive carriages and crudely decorated automobiles to magical and stunning flowered floats that became increasingly mechanized, Tournament sports promoters fumbled about, trying everything from footraces and tug-of-war contests to polo matches and chariot races.

Mother Nature decreed that the twentieth anniversary festival in 1910 was to be a wet one—so wet that the chariot races had to be postponed a week. Tournament founders Holder and Rowland were grand marshals of the parade, which couldn't start until noon.

Dr. Rowland attracted attention aboard Prince Arthur as he led the parade. The magnificent horse wore a collar of red and white carnations, and tied to its front ankle was a garter of red and white ribbons.

1911
The Return of the Queen

By 1911, when Frank G. Hogan took over the Tournament presidency for a year, the population of Pasadena had grown to over thirty thousand people.

"We haven't had a queen for two years. I think the practice should be revived," said Hogan, who came up with an idea for public voting for the queen: anyone who joined the association could vote for the queen. Under this new system, Ruth Palmer was elected queen for the 1911 festival. A second parade, a night affair, was staged by the "Komical Knights of the Karnival with King Kidder and Kween Karmencita."

1912
An Air King

By 1912, one hundred and fifty thousand people were in Pasadena to see the parade as Edward T. Off returned to the presidency for a two-year term. Off did not have a queen for his court, but he did have the king of the airways. C.P. Rodgers, who had made an epic flight from the Atlantic to Pasadena, was named king of the festival. He flew over the entire parade route and dropped rose petals from the sky.

The promotion departments of the leading railroads already were taking advantage of the Tournament's drawing power as a travel attraction. The Salt Lake and Santa Fe lines printed folders claiming, "The Tournament of Roses is like nothing else in the sun . . . it is a fiesta impossible to accomplish anywhere else in the world . . . it is Pasadena's New Year's gift to mankind."

Harrison Drummond and Jean French—the first king and queen

Once again, the chariot races were the festival's top sports attraction. However, when the chariots of Albert Parsons and C.E. Post bumped in a nerve-tingling collision, sports fans began to suspect that chariot racing was becoming far too dangerous. Tournament officials themselves recognized that the results were not significant anywhere but in Pasadena and the news stories were brief. What was more, the sport had become too expensive. First prize was seldom over $1,000, yet it was estimated by E.J. Levingood, a long-time competitor, that it cost $5,000 to train a team of horses for the event. Only Lucky Baldwin among the horse breeders had enough money to afford such a luxury.

1913
Kings, Queens, Ostriches and Elephants

"What our festival needs is both a king and a queen," said the creative Off in 1913. Jean French was named Tournament queen and Harrison P. Drummond became king.

Interest in chariot racing was waning, and it was the animal races that began attracting more interest. That year featured an ostrich race and a race between an elephant and a camel at Tournament Park. The animal races were memorable. One of the ostrich riders was thrown from his mount in front of the judging stand. When he attempted to capture the bird, he was kicked across the racecourse. For fifteen minutes the ostrich kicked and scattered a half-dozen men until it was captured. The elephant grabbed an early lead in its race against the camel, but stopped twenty feet from the finish line, refusing to budge. His rider finally jumped off and goaded him across the line from the rear.

1914
Flowered Floats

R.D. Davis became president in 1914, with Mabel Seibert Loughry reigning as queen and Dr. F.C.E. Mattison as king. By now the horse-drawn floats were rapidly disappearing from the parade, and big cities like San Diego and Portland were entering floats.

The outstanding feature of the Tournament's twenty-fifth parade was the entry of Mrs. Anita Baldwin McClaughry's—Lucky Baldwin's daughter: a huge white peacock mounted in an oak tree. The float used thousands of lilies of the valley, orchids and white roses. Throughout the country the press raved that this was the most beautiful float in history.

The Knights of the Rose, a booster group of fifty-four men in scarlet coats, riding horseback, made their first appearance. Although the United States hadn't yet entered the impending world war, thoughts of war and peace were evident. The Pasadena High School float had Helen Marie Neilson as the goddess of liberty with her arms extended to the soon-to-be-warring nations of Europe.

1915
Chariots Expire

In 1915 Lucky Baldwin's daughter, Mrs. McClaughry, again entered a stunning float, the Santa Anita "Dove of Peace"—a gigantic floral bird with more than five hundred lilies of the valley, five thousand hothouse Killarney roses, five hundred sprays of Stevia serulata, and a thousand sprays of maidenhair fern. The bird was twenty-six feet long with an eleven-foot wingspread. The parade's grand marshal was M.S. Pashgian, an equestrian who had ridden in a dozen parades and who would ride in eighteen more before retiring.

College football rules again changed in 1912. The fourth down was added to the game, and dimensions of the playing field and end zones were standardized for the first time. Six points were awarded for a touchdown—up from 5. There would not be another change in scoring rules until the introduction of the 2-point conversion in 1958.

Anita Baldwin's famed peacock float

During the 1971 Tournament, Kathy Howie and Kathy Parker claimed they were the first women in Tournament history to drive a float; however, some locals quickly produced evidence to prove that Edith Wright had piloted the Eagle Rock float in 1916. However, it was agreed by all that Howie and Parker were the first women to pilot a float while concealed in a compartment underneath the float.

While chariot enthusiast Edward Off continued to praise his favorite sport as the greatest entertainment since Rome ruled the world, the 1915 festival under the presidency of J.B. Coulston marked the last of the chariot races. Pasadena was still unsure what its festival formula should be. The 1915 parade featured the land of make-believe—fairy tale characters and animals such as elephants, camels, lions, tigers and leopards. The Tournament also began another era without queens, this time for eight years.

"We'd better go back to football," advised cofounder Dr. Rowland, the ever-present councillor, and 1916 president Lewis H. Turner agreed as he set up a committee to land for Pasadena the biggest football game that could be sched-uled—"so Pasadena can give the newspapermen from coast to coast something exciting to write about."

1916
Football Forever

If the chariot races accomplished anything lasting, they provided an impetus to build wooden stands at Tournament Park, to the point that there were twenty-five thousand seats for football fans by 1916. The solitary 1902 game had earned a profit of $3,161.86, and President Turner and his aides—men like W.L. Leishman who were coming forth with far-reaching football vision that eventually was to lead to the construction of the modern Rose Bowl—had hopes of a solid financial enterprise when they invited Washington State and Brown to play the 1916 game.

A heavy rainstorm held the football crowd to seven thousand and the Tournament lost $11,000 staging the game. To add insult to injury, even at that early date, there was complaining that the East's best team hadn't been secured. The Tournament had tried to get Syracuse, but that New York school balked at the prospect of so long a trip. Discouragement might have thwarted the football dream right then and there, but men like Turner, Leishman and others retained their vision.

In 1916 the Tournament honored its cofounder, Dr. Rowland, by naming him grand marshal on the occasion that marked his retirement from the festival's active leadership. This was his seventh time in this role—a record no other grand marshal has even approached.

The only event not dampened by rain in 1916 was the annual Tournament ball held in the evening. It was customary in

Continued on page 31

PASADENA
Tournament of Roses
PICTORIAL
1937

ROMANCE IN FLOWERS

FRANK E BROWN

PASADENA

Located at the foot of the San Gabriel Mountains in the San Gabriel Valley, seven miles northeast of Los Angeles, Pasadena is entered by four major freeways and is served by the Burbank, Ontario and Los Angeles airports.

While Pasadena is best known as the home of the Rose Parade and Rose Bowl game, it is also home to the Jet Propulsion Laboratory, the California Institute of Technology, the Norton Simon Museum, the Huntington Library, the Pasadena Playhouse, Ambassador College, Pasadena City College, Fuller Theological Seminary, Ambassador, Beckman and Pasadena Civic auditoriums, five radio stations, the *Pasadena Star-News* newspaper, Huntington and St. Luke's hospitals, the Pacific Asia Museum, the Pasadena Shopping Plaza, historic Pasadena City Hall, Gamble House, Wrigley Mansion and rose gardens, the soon-to-be-rebuilt Huntington Hotel, Parsons Company and the offices of many other corporations.

Nearby are Santa Anita race track, Dodger Stadium, Occidental College, California State University at Los Angeles, Descanso Gardens, Griffith Observatory, San Gabriel Mission, Los Angeles County Arboretum, Mount Wilson Skyline Park and Heritage Square.

The city of Pasadena was officially four years old when the Tournament of Roses was born in 1890, by which time it had a population of 4,882. Midwestern settlers founded the community in the early 1870s and called it "Indiana Colony" after their homeland. When a post office was established in 1875, the government insisted the settlement be renamed—apparently to avoid confusion with the state of Indiana. After failing to find a suitable Spanish place name, the settlers looked back to the Mississippi Valley for an appropriate word from the Chippewa language. They eventually abbreviated a long Chippewa word meaning "valley between the hills" or "crown of the valley." Even now Pasadena is often known as the "Crown City."

Over the past century the city has grown into a community of over 130,700 people. The Tournament of Roses has played a major role in Pasadena's development into a cultural, business, educational and residential center of world-wide repute.

Pasadena benefits from the annual Tournament through over $500,000 in direct revenue from the festival's net profits and an estimated $68,000,000 from the economic impact of the event. A survey conducted in 1983 estimated hotels, restaurants, stores, tranportation facilities, markets, amusement centers, the labor force, theaters and many other segments of the economy were the recipients of this income, most of it from visitors.

In the decade from 1970 to 1980, more than $400,000,000 was invested in building contruction in Pasadena, including many new office buildings limited by city statutes to eleven stories high. The figures for 1980–1990 are expected to be even more.

Pasadena often is described as the city of parades. The Rose Parade, of course, is best known. But the Centennial parade in 1986 was a three-hour review of the stages in the city's growth. And in the 1980s, the Doo Dah parade was originated by Peter Apanel and developed into an annual late autumn attraction that attracts crowds as big as three hundred thousand. It is designed to spoof the Rose Parade—a phenomenon the Tournament of Roses politely accepts. In fact, in the early days of the Tournament's existence, members of the organization known as the Knights of Karnival made fun of their own organization by tooting and prancing in the city streets on New Year's Eve in clown costumes.

A Pasadena landmark: The Rose Bowl entrance

Beautiful "Sent with Love" FTD float, 1988

Pasadena's magnificent City Hall

Pasadena has two sister cities, Ludwigshafen in Germany and Jarvenpaa in Finland. Officials from these cities attended the 1988 Tournament festivities.

Ethnically, the city is composed of 54.7% whites, 20.2% blacks, 18.3% Hispanics, 5.2% Asians and 1.6% others, according to the 1980 census.

The Rose Bowl

It's the king of the bowls, the first bowl site, the largest and the mecca of collegiate football.

In 1987, the U.S. Department of the Interior through the National Park Service designated the Rose Bowl for the National Register of Historic Places.

The Rose Bowl stadium was constructed in 1922 by the Tournament of Roses, which gave the property to the city of Pasadena in return for perpetual right to use it for the annual Rose Bowl game. The Tournament also has financed stadium enlargements and improvements.

The stadium was built during the term of Tournament president J. J. Mitchell with former president W. L. Leishman spearheading the project. The architect was Myron Hunt. The original stadium was an open-ended horseshoe with fifty-seven thousand seats, built for $272,198. The money was raised through ticket subscriptions.

The stadium measures 880 feet from north to south rims, and 695 feet from east to west rims. It has seventy-seven rows of seats, divided into twenty-eight sections, and twenty-eight entrance tunnels. There are forty-six thousand theater-type seats with backs and armrests; the remainder are aluminum benches. The press box seats 377. The playing surface is natural grass. The Bowl once had an asphalt track, which was removed to widen the playing surface for soccer.

The first official Tournament of Roses game in the stadium—and thus the first true "Rose Bowl" game—was played on January 1, 1923. Since 1923 there has been a Tournament of Roses football game on the first or second day of every year except in 1942, when the game was moved to Durham, North Carolina, because of fear of Japanese attacks on the Pacific Coast.

Many other football games have also been played in the Rose Bowl. At one time, Pasadena's Caltech played its home football games in the Rose Bowl—which is only fair, since the original Tournament of Roses sports competitions were staged on what is now the Caltech campus. Occasional football games have also been played there by California State, Los Angeles, and Pasadena City College teams. Muir and Pasadena high schools have played their annual "Turkey Tussle" game on Thanksgiving Day in the Bowl. It has been the site of four National Football League Super Bowls—1977, 1980, 1983 and 1987. It has been the site of twenty-three Junior Rose Bowl games played for the national junior college football championship, as well as five Pasadena Bowl games matching eastern and western small-college champions. Since 1982, UCLA has made the Rose Bowl its home field, and the Army–Navy game was played there in 1984.

The stadium has also housed many non-football athletic events, such as cycling during the 1932 Olympic Games and soccer during the 1984 Olympic Games. For part of their brief history, the North American Soccer League's Los Angeles Aztecs played in the Rose Bowl.

Other events staged in the Rose Bowl include track meets, rock concerts, Fourth of July circus and fireworks shows, car shows, off-road motor rodeos and, of course,

Rose Garden at Tournament House

above: enlarging the bowl to increase capacity, in 1932

below: Original Rose Bowl construction, 1922

the monthly flea markets, where as many as thirty thousand bargain hunters sort through wares offered by more than fifteen hundred vendors.

There are several acres of no-fee parking facilities outside the stadium fence, some of it paved. Soccer fields outside the stadium and adjacent Brookside Golf Course are used for additional parking. A feature of the fenced area surrounding the stadium is the rose garden dedicated in honor of Lathrop Leishman, past president and grand marshal.

Because of the huge television contract, there is an emphasis each year in making the bowl's playing field attractive, with the names of the competing schools painted in the end zones. This work has been done for eighteen years by Phil Ishizu, who also has painted the rose in the center of the field freehand. Volunteers from the Pasadena Junior Chamber of Commerce have aided field supervisor Richard Gonzales in the overall field preparation.

Harlan Hall, *Pasadena Star-News* reporter and Tournament publicist in 1922, named the Rose Bowl. He was influenced by the oval construction of the stadium, and he said the choice of the word "rose" was a natural.

The stadium facility was developed in several stages. In 1922, the rocky and heavily shrubbed Arroyo Seco on the northwest side of the city was chosen as the site for construction. The initial stadium was horseshoe-shaped with the south end open. It seated forty-seven thousand people.

The south end was enclosed in 1932 to raise the seating capacity to seventy-six thousand. Both sides of the stands were made the same height by increased concrete construction that increased the seating to 83,677 in 1932. End zone seating was enlarged to lift the seating capacity to 100,807 in 1949. Subsequent changes increased the capacity to 104,696 by eliminating field-level chair boxes and replacing them with aluminum seats that also were installed throughout the stadium, forty-six thousand of them with backs. To make the stadium field regulation-width for international soccer matches in the 1984 Olympic competition, it was necessary to cut into the curves of the stands, thus reducing seating capacity to 103,553.

Other improvements through the years have included a large press box with elevator, periodic enlargement of dressing rooms, and the installation of a powerful new lighting system.

Manager of the stadium for the city is Barbara Barrett, who directly reports to Dave Jacobs, director of community services. The stadium has three full-time maintenance employees and an office staff.

Radio and Television

One of the most significant developments in Tournament of Roses history has been the growth of television and radio exposure.

It was the dream of the Tournament of Roses originators that Pasadena's festival focus national attention on the wonders of sunny Southern California. Because of the modern capacity of radio and television to bring the live story everywhere on the globe, the exposure has exceeded all dreams. The Tournament can now be seen by almost the entire world each New Year's Day—one reason it ranks first among all community pageants.

The first radio broadcast of the Rose Bowl game in 1926 was announced by ex-Olympic sprint star Charles Paddock on Pasadena station KPSN. NBC carried the first network radio broadcast of

Crowd awaiting start of parade

The Rose Bowl from the air

the game in 1927 with Graham MacNamee and Bill Munday the announcers. Famous radio announcers to follow MacNamee for the NBC network included Don Wilson, Ken Carpenter (1933–39), Bill Stern (1940–46), Al Helfer and other voices.

Lathrop Leishman recalled early negotiations with Lew Frost, NBC vice president in charge of West Coast operations: "Our radio broadcasts started out noncommercial," he said. "I recall telling Frost 'You couldn't pay us enough money.' When NBC offered $50,000 for the radio rights of the game while the Tournament was asking $60,000, the negotiations broke down, with the Tournament giving away the early broadcasts without commercials."

When television came along, the Tournament took bids on a year-to-year basis. Radio, at the time, was commanding about $100,000 yearly. CBS came up with a television bid of $210,000 and got the contract for a year. Then Tom Gallery, representing NBC sports events, outbid the rival, and long-range contracts started to be the vogue. The Tournament remained with NBC until 1988, when the rights reached over $11 million a year. A major development occurred in June 1988, when the ABC network purchased the rights to broadcast the next nine Rose Bowl games for a total fee of $100 million. The Tournament had turned down NBC's request to restructure the remaining two years of its contract with the Tournament.

Although announcer Don Lee described float preparation for the 1939 parade on TV station 6XAO of Los Angeles, the first game telecast was carried in Los Angeles in 1948 by KTLA with Bill Welsh describing the action.

NBC had only four play-by-play announcers over thirty-six years, with Mel Allen announcing the first national Rose Bowl game telecast for NBC in 1952. Allen continued through 1963, followed by Lindsey Nelson (1964–67), Curt Gowdy (1968–79) and Dick Enberg (1980–88). ABC is expected to assign veteran play-by-play announcer Keith Jackson to the 1989 game.

The parade was first televised on local television in 1947. KTTV initiated the first network telecast in 1951. The first color telecast was in 1961 and the first satellite telecast to bring the game live to foreign countries was in 1968. By 1988, three American networks and several local stations were televising the parade, which was also seen in forty other countries with a worldwide audience estimated at four hundred million people. The football game was seen in thirty countries with an audience of three hundred million.

Although the networks do not pay for rights to televise the parade because the event is staged on public streets, they earn millions from commercials on both the parade and game telecasts.

Historically, the New Year's Day games have received huge audiences. The Rose Bowl ranked second in the ratings competition in 1988 (a 16.5 Nielsen compared to a 20.8 for the national championship Orange Bowl game between Miami and Oklahoma which followed). But the Rose Bowl almost annually has led in the Nielsen count. Rose Bowl games have accounted for nine of the top ten bowl telecasts of all time.

the early days to stage the ball at the conclusion of the New Year's Day activities. This was, evidently, an era when folks had more stamina.

The Tournament of Roses parade was in its twenty-seventh year before bathing beauties first appeared on a float. The young ladies, in "natty and alluring" bathing suits, rode on the Ocean Park float. What were those "alluring" suits like? They were all-black, full-length arm-and-bloomer suits.

A New Tradition Begins:
Washington State College 14, Brown 0

It was very cold and wet at kickoff time when Washington State (6–0) faced visiting Brown (5–3–1). Brown's highly rated all-American, Fritz Pollard, was handicapped by the wet cold, netting a mere 40 yards on the day. Washington State's victory was due largely to a hard-charging line that dominated in the mud-covered field.

Howard Angus in the *Los Angeles Times* described State's victory over the Rhode Island team: "The western backs, with five and six men ahead of them, literally tore the right side of the Brown line to shreds during the last half when all the scoring was done. Boone, Dietz and Bangs, the Washington State backs, were practically unstoppable. It was seldom that they didn't reach the secondary defense before being downed. The interference caught the Brown men amidships and the men carrying the ball tore on, dragging two tacklers through the mud."

Referee Walter Eckersall praised State's Carl Dietz for hitting the line faster than any back he had ever seen. A young Brown guard named Wallace Wade did a noble job trying to bust up State's interference, but he, too, was trampled after a great effort. This wasn't the last the Tournament saw of young Mr. Wade, however. In later years he was to lead five Alabama and Duke teams into the Rose Bowl as a coach. Dick Hanley, another man who went on to a great coaching career at Northwestern, also played in the 1916 game for Washington State.

Perennial equestrian M.S. Pashgian in 1915

Lewis Turner

Perhaps no team "took home" more from its experience of coming to Pasadena than Washington State. While practicing in the Los Angeles area for the 1916 game against Brown, each player made $100 a day working in the Hollywood film *Tom Brown of Harvard.* It was rumored that they pooled their earnings to bet on themselves and went back to Pullman with big loot.

1917
Going International

The 1917 parade took on an international dimension when hotels from Yokohama and Manila joined with American cities to enter massive floats. D.M. Linnard was president and Dr. C.D. Lockwood was grand marshal. It was a beautiful day with the temperature at eighty-six degrees.

A model impersonating Hawaii's King Kamehameha III escorted a float from the Mid-Pacific Carnival Association of Hawaii. "Kamehameha" rode horseback in full war costume and feather headdress. The float, an outrigger canoe formed of marigolds, smilax and white carnations, was manned by four bronzed oarsmen and thirteen Hawaiian women who threw thousands of pink and white carnations to the cheering crowd.

A True Test of Power?
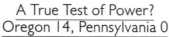
Oregon 14, Pennsylvania 0

The West earned national respect in football when Oregon defeated Pennsylvania, 14–0. Whereas Brown had been regarded as a second-rate eastern team the previous year, Penn, with a 7–1 record, was considered a true power from the part of the country where the best football was thought to be played.

The crowd of twenty-five thousand got its first thrill in the football game when Howard Berry of Penn got off a 50-yard punt early in the game. Punts of that distance were unheard of in the West in those days. The fans watched the ball soar with something of the same awe that marks the viewing of a moon shot today.

Oregon's backfield brothers, Shy and Hollis Huntington, soon proved their own worth. Penn got the early breaks, however. A penalty saved Penn when Shy Huntington intercepted a pass and ran it

back 25 yards. Penn recovered its own blocked drop kick by Berry to retain possession and then drove to the shadow of the goal. It seemed ready to smash the ball into the end zone when—in the words of *Los Angeles Times* writer Harry Williams—"an error of judgement" turned the game around. Instead of continuing the power drives, Penn's Quigley ran to the right with two men providing interference. Oregon's left end, Mitchell, threw him for a 10-yard loss, forcing a drop kick from the 29 which Quigley muffed as the Oregon line charged him.

This unexpected development vanquished Oregon's stage fright and

Brown's Fritz Pollard

sapped the morale of heavily favored Penn. Berry later failed to convert 41- and 36-yard drop kicks for Penn, further depressing the easterners. Oregon meanwhile drove to its first score in the third period, a 70-yard push after Shy Huntington intercepted a Penn pass. The Huntington brothers made the big gains, with Shy passing to right end Tegeret in the corner of the field for the score. The next touchdown came after another interception by Shy, with Johnny Parsons breaking away 42 yards to the 1-yard line, where Berry caught him from behind. Shy then rounded end to score.

Penn's quarterback was Bert Bell, who later gained fame as president of the National Football League. One of the Penn tackles was Lou Little, who later coached Columbia to a Rose Bowl win. Oregon's two strong tackles, Beckett and Bartlett, outplayed Little in the 1917 thriller that forced eastern sports writers to admit good football had arrived west of the Rockies. Coach of this Oregon team that first established western football on the national scene was Hugo Bezdek, who came back in 1918 with the Mare Island Marines and in 1923 with Penn State.

1918
Waving the Flag

B.O. Kendall served the first of two terms as Tournament president in 1918; his grand marshal was Dr. Z.T. Malaby. Patriotism was the parade motif. Warship, tank and flag floats, plus marching units representing patriotic groups, dominated the parade.

President Kendall; A.L. Hamilton, chairman of the Pasadena City Commission; and William H. Veddar, chairman of the Pasadena Red Cross, offered to President Woodrow Wilson to call off the parade. The president replied he couldn't see how such a celebration would hurt the government's war activities, and suggested that the country's normal life should be continued.

A quarter of a million spectators—the largest crowd to date—watched the parade on another eighty-six-degree New Year's Day. In accordance with Secretary of Commerce Herbert Hoover's meat-conservation edict, it happened to be a "meatless day," so the traditional hot dogs gave way to tuna, minced egg and various meatless sandwich concoctions.

College Football on Hold:
Mare Isl. Marines 19, Camp Lewis Army 7

Throughout the country, many colleges and universities suspended football during the war, but military trainees were permitted to perform on camp teams as part of their rugged preparation for war. Kendall and his associates asked the military to provide a football match in order to keep the Tournament's new sports tradition alive and to help take the nation's mind off the developing hardships of the world war that America had just entered.

W.L. "Fox" Stanton, for many years identified with Caltech in Pasadena, returned to Tournament Park on his former campus as coach of the Camp Lewis team. But his men were dominated by Hugo Bezdek's Marines, which featured "Jap" Brown at quarterback and Hollis Huntington—in his second-straight Tournament game—at fullback.

Clyde Bruckman summarized the Marines' 19–7 win in the *Los Angeles Examiner*: "The mystic maze which Hugo Bezdek brought down from Mare Island in the disguise of a football team won as they were expected to win before a crowd of twenty-five thousand fans. They won because they had the better

Back in 1916, college nicknames weren't as formal as they are today. Washington State didn't have an official nickname until it adopted "Cougars" in 1919. Before then, its teams were variously known as "Farmers," "Indians" and "Redskins."

The First World War era proved a turning point in American college football. Two years after the Tournament of Roses inaugurated the tradition of post-season intersectional contests, the 80,000-seat Yale Bowl opened in New Haven, Connecticut. The first of the great modern football stadiums, it was in fact a direct inspiration for the Rose Bowl, which opened five years later.

Japan's 1917 entry—the first international float

George Halas of Great Lakes Navy

team, the smoothest working combinations, led by Jap Brown, whose generalship throughout the struggle was superb. Always it was Brown and Hollis Huntington when the Marines made a drive. A year ago it was Shy Huntington who created a hero role, but yesterday it was brother Hollis who wrote his name large. Like a devastating tank he ripped through the entanglements of the Army defense. It was Hollis the unstoppable who carried the ball through the heart of the Army line. He made more yards than Hoyle has rules. He didn't have any more use for interference than a snake has for corn plasters. He was as easy to stop as a porcupine.''

Army backs Romney and McKay were praised for performing great deeds behind a ''line that leaked Marines.'' Proof that football was toughening military personnel for war was offered in the Marine team's feat of playing the entire

game without a substitution after right end Hobson went out with a shattered ankle on the first play of the game.

The Marines' Ambrose booted a 31-yard field goal to give his team a 3–0 lead. Romney ran end for 6 yards to put Army ahead. Passes to Beckett and Sanderson set up a 5-yard sprint by Brown that put the Marines ahead to stay at 9–7. A 32-yard run by Sanderson and a Huntington buck scored again, and Ambrose added a 33-yard field goal.

1919
War Games

B.O Kendall's ''war term'' was completed in 1919 when America celebrated the end of World War I with the theme ''Victorious Peace'' in the Tournament parade. The sun seemed to smile on the occasion. While much of the nation was blizzard-bound, it was a warm, beautiful day in Pasadena. Returning servicemen

TOURNAMENT
OF ROSES

New
Years
Day
1916
Midwinter Floral Pageant

FOOTBALL

BROWN UNIVERSITY
—vs—
STATE COLLEGE OF WASHINGTON
Pasadena - California

Taylor

Les Barnard of the Great Lakes Navy team recalled admiring Northwestern's Paddy Driscoll when he practiced field-goal kicking for the Navy team. "He would stand on the 50-yard line and drop-kick one ball through one goal post, then turn around and drop-kick another ball through the goal post on the other side of the field."

Navy's "Wasp," Paddy Driscoll of Northwestern

teams of that era, they nevertheless contained some exceptional talent. Les Barnard, of the Great Lakes Navy team, for example, became a great Minneapolis high school football coach before retiring to Orange, California. Another Navy star was George Halas, the founder of the Chicago Bears, who helped pioneer the National Football League. It was he who caught Paddy Driscoll's 45-yard touchdown pass. He also returned a pass interception 77 yards. He later often said that playing in the Rose Bowl was one of the greatest thrills of his life. Charley Bachman, later famous as football coach at Michigan State, played in the strong Navy line.

More than twenty-seven thousand spectators watched Northwestern's Driscoll, "The Wasp," lead the Great Lakes Navy team to a 17–0 victory over the Marines. As Navy's quarterback, the Wasp passed for 77 yards, completing four of eight throws, including one for a 45-yard touchdown; caught a pass which set up another touchdown; rushed for 34 yards from scrimmage; drop-kicked a 30-yard field goal; averaged 43.5 yards on six punts, including 50 and 60 yarders; and returned nine punts for 115 yards.

were guests of Pasadena.

"Welcome Home" signs were prevalent in the city. The flower crop was especially abundant, giving the floats a beauty that elated everyone. For the second time, service teams provided the football.

The Wasp Packs a Sting:
Great Lakes Navy 17, Mare Isl. Marines 0

While the makeshift service teams were not in the same class as the best college

THE 1920s

BIRTH OF THE MODERN BOWL

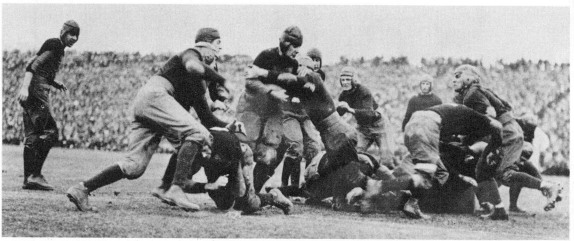

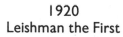
Harvard avenges the Ivy League, edging Oregon in 1920

W.L. Leishman

1920
Leishman the First

A Connecticut tailor who had become a community-minded Pasadena entrepreneur ascended to the Tournament of Roses presidency in 1920. He was William L. Leishman—an impeccably dressed, richly imaginative and hard-working person blessed with foresight and interest in community good.

The name Leishman is a significant one in Tournament history. William L. Leishman inaugurated a new policy when he became president. The head of the Tournament had always ridden a horse at the front of the parade, but Leishman became the first president to ride in his own car. Leishman's car was decorated by women of the Eastern Star, and the driver in the 1920 parade was his son Lathrop, who was himself destined to be Tournament president nineteen years later. Lathrop's own sons, William and Robert, are active "Men in White" volunteers today, while Lathrop continues his contribution as a member of the Rose Bowl Football Committee.

The Tournament Park stands needed repairs during W.L.'s presidency. A former lumberman, Leishman knew the patchwork couldn't go on forever. "Son," he told Lathrop one day, "I am going to take you to my home town, New Haven, and show you the kind of stadium we should have here someday for our football games. When I go to Harvard to make a gold football award, we'll take a look at the Yale Bowl."

Lathrop accompanied his dad on the long railroad journey east, where they saw the first great modern stadium built for football—Yale's eighty–thousand–seat Yale Bowl. He recalls the many meetings his father later held in the family living room with architect Myron Hunt and builder William A. Taylor. He would peek through the keyhole and hear thrilling talk about a huge concrete stadium in Pasadena. "Right then my interest in what today is the Rose Bowl was born," he remembers. "Dad always said Arroyo Seco, then just a barren area of rocks, was the place to build it." Such descriptions bring to mind talk in the late 1980s of football, gravel pits and a place called Irwindale.

The parade of 1920 was historic for more reasons than the switch of the president from horse to automobile. That year the Salvation Army Band made its first appearance. This band has appeared in the parade every year since—the longest record of continuous participation.

The 1920 parade held a special meaning for women of the Women's Christian Temperance Union. January 1920 was the month that the Eighteenth Amendment—prohibition—took effect. To celebrate the success of their long campaign against alcohol, the WCTU entered a float with the word "Victory" emblazoned on its side.

Prohibition did not, however, dry up the enthusiasm of Big Bear Lake Tavern, which entered a float containing a great mound of snow surrounded by pine boughs and cones. Two pretty young women sat on a toboggan surprising viewers by pelting them with real snowballs. An even bigger surprise was the live bear cavorting in the snow.

By 1920, the Hotel Raymond entry was the only float still drawn by a team of horses; everything else was now mechanized. Attendance reached two hundred thousand spectators.

Revenge of the Ivy League: Harvard 7, Oregon 6

After two years of Rose Tournament contests among service teams, a true college football monarch, Harvard's mighty Crimson, came to Pasadena to take on the University of Oregon—whose nickname "Webfoots" was still some years in the future. Harvard had compiled an 8–0–1 record, while outscoring its opponents 222–13. Only a 10–10 tie with Princeton marred its season. Oregon's 5–1 record included a solitary loss to Washington State. A former Tournament

game player, Shy Huntington, coached the Oregon team. One of his star players was his brother Hollis, who piled up 122 rushing yards in his third Tournament Park game.

Harvard won a well-fought struggle, 7–6, avenging the Ivy League losses suffered by Brown and Penn. Coach Bob Fisher had Walter Camp's All-America selection Eddie Casey in his backfield, but it was speedy Fred Church who scored the touchdown and Arnold Horween who kicked the point that outscored the drop-kick field goals by Oregon's Steers and Manerud.

Church, who had replaced Ralph Horween in the Harvard backfield, broke away in the second period, a 12-yard sprint in which he outran his interference. When he reached the end zone near the corner, he cut sharply toward the goal posts and crossed the goal line in the center of the field—a smart piece of work, because the kick for point had to be made from a spot directly opposite the spot where the touchdown was made. Thus Arnold Horween's kick was made easier.

In October 1969, the Boston Harvard Club held a fiftieth anniversary dinner for the little group of survivors of Harvard's great 1919 team—the only Harvard team to play in the Tournament of Roses. The players recalled that although Yale was traditionally Harvard's most bitter rival, Yale players refused to reveal any secrets about the Harvard team to Oregon. The East was represented by Harvard, Yalies decided, and there must be vindication for the Ivy League.

Old-timers from Harvard like R. Minturn "Duke" Sedgwick, the great left tackle, recalled that a few days before the game Douglas Fairbanks gave the Harvard players a tour of the movie set

The smallest player ever to appear in the Pasadena classic, 128-pound Skeet Manerud, came within a foot of making a 25-yard drop kick that would have given Oregon a victory over Harvard in 1920. The kick looked so good that the manual-scoreboard operator hung a big "9" for Oregon next to Harvard's "7," while Harvard players banged their helmets to the turf in frustration.

At the Harvard team's fiftieth anniversary reunion, "Duke" Sedgwick recalled an Oregon play in which the quarterback lay prone on the ground, as though injured, while teammates clustered around him. When a teammate asked, "Are you all right?" he handed the ball to a back who ran down the field with it.

Harvard's Eddie Casey

What made Cal's "Wonder Team" so wonderful? Numbers tell the story. In eight games Andy Smith's Golden Bears *averaged* 62 points while outscoring the opposition 499–14. Their biggest win was a 127–0 dismemberment of nearby St. Mary's College. Their opponents weren't all hapless. Washington State's *only* loss was to Cal—a 49–0 shellacking. Cal's Tournament foe, Ohio State, was no slouch, either. In seven games it rolled over opponents by an aggregate score of 150–20.

where he was making a picture. He and Charlie Chaplin subsequently accepted invitations to sit on on the Harvard bench during the game. Sedgwick remembered also that Jack Dempsey sat in the Harvard cheering section at the game. Sedgwick was heavyweight boxing champion at Harvard, so Dempsey's attendance meant a great deal to him.

1921
Standing Room Only

A hundred floats adorned the 1921 parade, among them the Pasadena Elks Lodge float—a freight train in miniature composed of a locomotive, tender, box car and caboose. The luncheon clubs of Pasadena Rotary and Kiwanis also had floats for the first time.

However, the big news of the day was the 41,500-person crowd that filled up Tournament Park. President Leishman and his aides looked at the mob and W.L. turned to the man who was to be the next year's president, J. J. Mitchell, and remarked, "We can't go on much longer like this. Soon there won't be enough lumber in the city to seat them. We've got to get our new stadium started."

"The Wonder Team":
California 28, Ohio State 0

California's first "Wonder Team" gained a decisive triumph over Ohio State, 28–0, beginning the swing of the West Coast pendulum southward. Until this game it was believed that the Pacific Northwest—which had provided all the western college Rose Tournament teams since 1916—was the sole stronghold of western football.

Coach Andy Smith's California team came in with an 8–0 mark; J.W. "Doc" Wilce's Ohio State team was 7–0. The passing combination of Harry "Hoge"

Workman to All-American Pete Stinchcomb established State as the favorite, but California supporters were wild about a young man named Harold "Brick" Muller.

Charles Paddock, the great American Olympic sprinter, wrote for the *Pasadena Star-News,* "Muller did everything a great end should do. He covered punts so swiftly, he often beat the ball to the receiver. He caught every pass that was thrown to him. His passing, too, was phenomenal."

To make his point, Paddock described a trick play in which Muller caught a lateral behind the line from Pesky Sprott and then completed a long spiral to Bro-

Brick Muller of California's "Wonder Team"

die Stephens in the end zone. The play uncorked when fullback Archie Nesbet pretended he was injured. Then, in unison with his mates, he suddenly jumped into the line as the center, not the fullback. This bewildered Ohio State, which stood up and watched. Nesbet snapped the ball to Sprott, who flipped it back to Muller, who then relayed it to Stephens.

The actual length of Muller's pass provoked one of the great sports debates of all time. Maxwell Stiles did considerable research to conclude that the pass actually traveled 53 yards, in contrast to the Spalding record book figure of 70 yards.

1922
A Bowl Is Built

When J. J. Mitchell became president in 1922, William L. Leishman concentrated on efforts to assure the construction of the bowl in Arroyo Seco. Money appeared to be the big problem, but when forty thousand people braved a heavy rain to see California take on Washington & Jefferson, the game showed a gross profit of $17,000. The obvious popularity of football made future financing of the stadium less difficult.

The game may have ended in a draw, but there was no deadlock about what Pasadena was going to do about a stadium. While the city acquired the Arroyo Seco land, the Tournament agreed to raise money for construction. Once the stadium was built, the Tournament would deed it to the city, and the city, in turn, would lease it back to the Tournament for ninety days each year.

The entire original stadium, a great horseshoe open on the south end with fifty-seven thousand seats, cost $272,198.26. The Tournament financed the project by offering two hundred and ten box seats for ten-year periods at $100 each. Another five thousand seats were sold for five-year periods for $50 each. Football may not have changed much, but economics have.

Harlan Hall, whose nickname was "Dusty," dusted off a name that was to become historic: the Rose Bowl. He came up with the idea while he was a *Star-News* reporter loaned out to the Tournament to serve as press agent.

Two Dead Presidents Come to Life:
California 0, Washington & Jefferson 0

Such was W&J's limited reputation as a football power that one anonymous sports writer wrote, "All I know about Washington and Jefferson is that they are both dead." He probably ate his words after the tiny school got through the game. W&J certainly came to life in the game; the team never even made a substitution. The game—the last major football battle ever staged at Tournament Park—was played on January 2 because New Year's Day fell on a Sunday.

W&J was no soft touch on the football field. H.G. Salsinger of the *Detroit News,* who witnessed W&J beat up on Detroit University in its last regular-season game, tipped off the fact that California hadn't contracted to play a humpty and told how Coach Earle "Greasy" Neale had to telegraph the players to come back to school when the Pasadena bid was accepted.

Cal's Brick Muller was suffering from boils and carbuncles on his neck and a knee injury which prevented him from starting the game. When he came into the game in the second quarter to replace Bob Berkey, he was met by a chorus of seemingly awed W&J voices.

"So this is the great Brick Muller!" said little end Herb Kopf of the visitors. "We are deeply impressed. We are humble in

Ohio State's 1921 appearance in the Rose Bowl was to be the last for a Big Ten team until the conference first signed its present pact with the Tournament of Roses in 1947. Since 1947 no team from outside the Big Ten or the Pacific conference has played in the Rose Bowl game.

With an enrollment of only 450 men, Washington & Jefferson was the smallest college ever to play a Tournament of Roses football game. W&J didn't have a formal nickname before it came to Pasadena, though its teams were informally called the "Presidents." W&J's participation in the Tournament itself attracted national attention and made the nickname stick.

In later years, W.L. Leishman and his son, Lathrop, study plans of the Rose Bowl

The original 57,000-seat Rose Bowl cost $272,198.26 to build. By contrast, Florida's recently constructed Joe Robbie stadium cost nearly $100 million for 75,000 seats. The average cost per seat in Robbie stadium was around $1,333, compared to the Rose Bowl's average seat cost of just under $5.

Hugo Bezdek

the presence of the great Muller. May I introduce myself?''

Sawed-off Kopf strode up to Muller and wiped his muddy hands on his jersey. Then all the W&J players did the same thing while the rain beat down on the playing field. *Liberty Magazine's* Norman Sper said he had been in Greasy Neale's hotel room the night before when the coach had planned the mud-rubbing episode with Captain Russell Stein. It was all part of a plan to confuse Muller and take him out of the game.

Paul Lowry, a *Los Angeles Times* writer, credited tackle Stein with the strategy that stopped California's attack. "He spoiled every play started by California," wrote Lowry. "His method was as simple as it was effective. He sensed the play and simply flopped on the ball. The play was off then, and Cal had to try it all over again."

When it was over, all California had to show for its efforts was 49 net yards rushing, no yards passing and two first downs. W&J netted 137 total yards and earned eight first downs. They also ran for a touchdown that was called back on an offsides penalty. The score was a dull-looking 0–0, but it was, all in all, not a bad showing for two dead presidents against the latest "Wonder Team."

1923
The "Rose Bowl"

As William L. Leishman proudly stood on the turf in the new Rose Bowl horseshoe anxiously waiting for the Penn State team to appear for its game with the University of Southern California (USC) on January 1, 1923, he remarked, "Some day this will be a complete saucer like the Yale Bowl. The way people are jamming up the roads trying to get here today, I know we will have to expand."

Leishman's prophecy came true in 1928 when the open south end of the structure was closed, adding another nineteen thousand seats to make the capacity seventy-six thousand.

Washington & Jefferson's Erick Erickson carries the ball against California in the mud-sodden 1922 game—the last at Tournament Park

USC won the first Tournament of Roses game played in the Rose Bowl in 1923. It did not, however, win the first football game played in the new bowl. That honor went to California. The undefeated 1922 Cal team won the Rose Bowl's very first college football game the previous October by a score of 12–0. The loser? USC—which thus has the double distinction of winning the first Rose Bowl game and losing the first football game in the Rose Bowl.

Pasadena was a proud city during the 1923 Tournament. It was celebrating the fiftieth anniversary of its founding, and, of course, the new stadium symbolized the city's growth.

Tournament president Mitchell named Hollywood film star May McAvoy queen. Her pictures were popularly attended in theaters everywhere; hence thousands came to Pasadena to see her in person during the parade. The crowd viewing the parade was estimated at three hundred thousand. "We brought in one hundred thousand people ourselves," said an official of Pacific Electric Railway.

While all of this was going on in 1923, a lad named Max Colwell was the Pasadena High School correspondent for the *Pasadena Post*. It was Colwell's job to report parade descriptions of the school floats for the newspaper. Little did he know then that this would lead to his becoming the successful manager of the Tournament of Roses many years later.

Though Penn State had been chosen the previous April to represent the East in the Rose Bowl's first New Year's attraction, the team still couldn't get to the game on time. In fact, Penn State had troubles from the moment that undefeated California, the Tournament's first choice to represent the West, refused to play them. Southern California—whose only loss had been at the hands of California—was the substitute selection, as well as the eventual 14–3 winner.

USC, with a season record of 8–1, was coached by Elmer "Gloomy Gus" Henderson. Penn State, 6–3–1, was coached under the iron hand of Hugo Bezdek, who was making his third Pasadena appearance. He had led Oregon to victory over Penn in 1917 and Mare Island over Camp Lewis in 1918.

Bezdek will be remembered for his late arrival in keeping his 1923 Rose Bowl date and a subsequent argument and near fist fight with Henderson for keeping the Trojans waiting. Hugo

Gloomy Gus Henderson

In 1973, thirteen members of the 1923 USC Rose Bowl team celebrated a fifty-year reunion. Golden anniversary Trojan players who returned to see Johnny McKay's national champions destroy Woody Hayes's Ohio State team were Reg Dupuy, John Riddle, Ralph Cummings, Eddie Leahy, W. F. Boice, "Chief" Newman, Phil Tiernan, Gwynn Wilson, Paul Didrickson, Leo Calland, Dick Emmons, Jim Purcell and Chet Dolley.

hadn't liked it that newspapermen insisted upon watching his practice sessions.

"I'll let you in the first few minutes of each practice, but no pictures," said Bezdek, who suspected someone wanted to pass along his secrets to USC.

A *Los Angeles Examiner* photographer refused to be denied. While Bezdek roared, "My team cannot be photographed in formation," the photographer placed his camera on the sideline and stood beside it with his hands in his pockets. However, each time the Penn State team came within range, his right foot moved just enough to click the shutter. Penn State pictures thus filled the *Examiner* sports page the next day.

The game was scheduled to start at 2:15 p.m., immediately after dedication ceremonies on New Year's Day, but the Penn State bus didn't arrive on the scene until 2:30.

Gloomy Gus waited by the Penn State dressing room while his team squirmed in its quarters.

"Where have you been?" Henderson roared at Bezdek when Penn State finally arrived. When Bezdek pleaded a traffic jam, Gus retorted, "You tried to stall so we would get itchy. Furthermore, you wanted the sun to lower, believing you'd have a better chance when it's cool."

Bezdek called Henderson a liar, and Henderson said he was full of "bunk," which inspired Bezdek to suggest he remove his glasses. Just when it appeared fists were ready to fly, listeners stepped between them.

Glendale's prize-winning peacock float in 1923

"We're not going to come out on the field until all those people back on the roads who paid to see the game are in their seats," said Bezdek.

The game didn't start until 3:05, and it finished when the sky was becoming so dark that sports writers and telegraph operators had to strike matches to complete their stories.

The Birth of the Bowl:
USC 14, Penn 3

Penn State took the lead when "Light Horse" Harry Wilson mousetrapped his way for several large gains to set up a field goal by Mike Palm. Leo Calland, the Trojan captain, then shifted his defense to stop the Penn State attack.

USC had to survive the disappointment of a freak mishap before it took command offensively. Fullback Gordon Campbell powered the ball downfield following recovery of a fumble. Then Roy "Bullet" Baker advanced the pigskin to the 1-yard line. While the huge crowd held its breath to witness the inevitable touchdown, the center snap did not reach the Trojan ball carrier, but sailed in the other direction, landing in the end zone. A Penn State defender fell on the ball for a touchback.

Coach Henderson explained what happened in a story he wrote for the *Examiner:* "Lindley, playing center for USC, ordinarily snaps the ball directly back of him. This time the play called for a sideways pass-back to a backfield man who was crouched close to the line of scrimmage near the right end of the line. Lindley snapped the ball in the correct direction, but as our line heaved forward, the pigskin hit someone's heel and careened over the Penn State goal line."

USC steadily battered the easterners after that, however. Howard "Hobo" Kin-caid, one of the greatest blockers ever to play in the Rose Bowl, led Gordon Campbell and Baker to steady gains. Baker was a bulldog with the ball, but USC needed a freak play to score.

USC did more than throw the football to get its touchdown. It threw a man! The ball was thrown by Bullet Baker. The man was thrown by himself. The man was miniature Harold Galloway.

When USC's ground attack was stopped on the Penn State 10, Baker threw a flat pass to the left, never more than shoulder-high, but it was far from the intended receiver. From nowhere, it seemed, a human meteor—Galloway—flew through the air. He skidded along, looked up, and saw the ball coming to him. It fell into his arms as he was hit on the 2-yard line. He was knocked out, but he held the pigskin in a death grip. Two plays later, Campbell scored on a delayed buck. Campbell and Baker took turns punching for the second touchdown.

1924
The First Sweepstakes

W. F. Creller became Tournament president in 1924. His parade featured two parts—the usual colorful floats in one section, and the Elks Lodges of California in the other section. The Grand Exalted Ruler of the Elks, James G. McFarland, was a distinguished visitor.

"Our most stunning float annually should be selected to set it apart from the rest," said Creller, and the Sweepstakes prize was initiated. Glendale's entry was the winner that year, an achievement often repeated in the years that followed.

The Tournament discovered its role as a football promoter was getting difficult, especially with various members of the

Larry "Moon" Mullins, a future Notre Dame star, made the first long run of his career in the Rose Bowl, immediately *before* the 1924 Navy-Washington game. After crashing the gate, the South Pasadena kid was chased the length of the field by policemen as the crowd cheered wildly.

association having favorites at team-selection time. A significant decision was reached by President Creller and his board of directors. They would let the colleges control the administration of the Rose Bowl game, a policy practiced successfully ever since.

Re-enter the Military:
Washington 14, Navy 14

The United States Naval Academy became the only military academy team ever to play in the Rose Bowl when it accepted a bid to play in the 1924 game before the football season even started. It proved itself fully worthy of the invitation during the 1923 season by compiling a 5–1–2 record, while outscoring its opponents 154–48. Ironically, Navy's sole loss was to Penn State—the previous year's eastern representative in the Rose Bowl.

Washington, which wasn't named western representative until early December, finished the 1923 season 10–1 while amassing a 284–44 scoring advantage. Its sole loss came at the hands of California—which had turned down the

Tournament's invitation to be western representative against Penn State the previous year.

The 14–14 tie was history making for several reasons: Navy completed its first fourteen passes; the tackling was so savage that Alan Shapley of Navy and Elmer Tesreau of Washington had to be carried off the field; and Les Sherman of Washington kicked two conversions with a broken toe. Tesreau went into the game with his leg heavily taped because of a serious outbreak of boils. His coach, Enoch Bagshaw, tried to keep him out of the game but he refused to remain idle.

Maxwell Stiles wrote that Washington had "no right to win this game. Navy outplayed the Huskies by a rather wide margin." The Midshipmen outgained the Huskies, 362 yards to 202, and got fifteen first downs to Washington's nine.

1925
The Four Horsemen

In 1925 the American Legion was honored in the parade with its national commander, James A. Drain, present.

Massed colors led the American Le-

Only 40,000 people attended the Navy-Washington game because Navy—which got its game cut in tickets—made the mistake of distributing thousands of them among the fleet harbored in Long Beach. The fleet admiral ordered the fleet to sea the day before the game. Hundreds of undistributed tickets were offered to the public by a sound car circling the stadium.

Sleepy Jim Crowley breaks free for Notre Dame against Stanford in the 1925 classic

gion division, which was loudly cheered along the parade route. In contrast to the youthful step of marching World War I veterans, a group of old-timers from the Grand Army of the Republic rode in a special car with their fife-and-drum corps. A lone marcher, J. V. Fickes, represented the Spanish-American War. To qualify as a "floral exhibit," Fickes trimmed his old knapsack with posies.

The parade was a whopper—three hours of floats and marching units. The Sweepstakes prize went to Aimee Semple McPherson's Angelus Temple float, which broke Glendale's hold on the Sweepstakes with what was estimated to be the most costly float ever built up to that time. The float, representing radio broadcasting of the gospel, cost around $4,000 to construct. Today many floats cost more than thirty times that figure. A radio tower of snow-white carnations stood atop a miniature replica of the Angelus Temple in Echo Park. From it was broadcast a New Year's greeting.

The Salvation Army entered its first float in Tournament history. Its band, of course, had been marching since 1920 in the festival.

Pasadena had its second married queen that year, Mrs. Margaret Scoville, who had been Pasadena Christmas Mother and was asked to continue for the Tournament festivities.

"Pop" vs. "Rock":
Notre Dame 27, Stanford 10

The 1925 Tournament of Roses will forever be best remembered for the presence of Notre Dame's coach Knute Rockne, its Four Horsemen and its great undefeated gridiron machine.

The fifty-three thousand spectators came early to see Rockne match wits with Stanford's great coach, Glenn Sco-

bie "Pop" Warner. They did not go home disappointed. The Irish won, 27–10, over Stanford, which also entered the fray undefeated, although tied once by California.

Stanford took the first lead on a 17-yard place kick by Murray Cuddeback. The crowd believed in the invincibility of Elmer Layden, Jim Crowley, Harry Stuhldreher and Don Miller. But the throng also had faith in Ernie Nevers of Stanford. Could Stanford's great blond-haired ball carrier counter the dread Raiders of the Apocalypse?

Rockne started his "shock troops" but quickly jerked them because Stanford had so much fury. A fumble of the only pass from center that had come back to the Four Horsemen, a bobble by Miller, was recovered by Stanford's right tackle, Johnston, to set up Cuddeback's kick.

Shortly thereafter, Notre Dame took over on its own 20-yard line. The thousands looking on wondered when the Four Horsemen would start to ride.

So it was when Adam Walsh, the Hollywood High School boy who had come home as captain and center for the Irish, bent down over the ball. The light cavalry behind him shifted into the Notre Dame box. Stuhldreher barked his signal. Into the big Red line Layden lashed with the sting of a whip. Layden was not like Nevers, the bone crusher. Elmer was slithery and slender, fast, agile and smart. He weighed only 165 pounds, not much for a fullback. Layden stabbed sharply and rapidly, but drew no blood.

Stuhldreher again barked signals and Notre Dame shifted in unison. This time it was Sleepy Jim's turn, and Crowley was far from sleepy. He swung to the left side of Stanford's line with great speed. His escorts, Miller and Layden, picked him up. Each of the Four Horsemen

Knute Rockne

Pop Warner

Notre Dame's Four Horsemen: Don Miller, Elmer Layden, Jim Crowley and Harry Stuhldreher

Jim Crowley, one of Notre Dame's fabled Four Horsemen, later recalled an incident before the 1925 Rose Bowl when Knute Rockne almost sent him and teammate Ed Huntsinger back to Indiana after catching them buying Christmas cards just before curfew. When Huntsinger recovered a fumble and ran for a touchdown early in the game, Crowley ran up to his buddy and said, "Isn't it a good thing Rock didn't make us go home?"

blocked as well as ran. No matter who had the ball, before him three galloping shadows carved out a path.

Out of the line came others to join the convoy set up for 155-pound Crowley. There were Chuck Collins and Ed Huntsinger, Joe Bach and Edgar "Rip" Miller, John Weibel, Noble Kizer and Walsh.

That moment may have presented the most beautiful bit of downfield interference ever seen in Rose Bowl history. Crowley hadn't gone 10 yards before the crowd, electrified, was on its feet. There they went—the Four Horsemen and the Seven Mules! Rockne's raiders were on the prowl! The raid was on!

Somebody at last brought Crowley down on the Notre Dame 49. The 27-yard run had seared Stanford's defense.

Two plays later, Crowley made another first down on Stanford's 39 after a cutback away from Ted and Harry Shipkey—the brother combination on the left side of Stanford's line. Stuhldreher then passed to Miller, to the 20-yard line. Miller shook off tacklers to skirt left end to the 9.

Led by Ted Shipkey and Johnston, the Stanford line held, and on fourth down Ted Shipkey rushed Stuhldreher, who was trying to pass. The ball glanced sideways off the Irish quarterback's fingers and was grounded. Time was taken out for Stuhldreher, who had his ankle taped. Later it was learned that a bone or two had been fractured. But these players refused to let injury keep them out of the action. Playing in the Rose Bowl game, Jim Lawson had one leg in a brace and Ernie Nevers had both legs so tightly bandaged after his recovery from two broken ankles that the circulation was all but shut off.

Following a short Stanford punt, Notre Dame took over again on the enemy 32-yard line. The Four Horsemen zoomed to the 7 as the quarter ended. Two plays later, Layden hit center for the touchdown, the only score that Notre Dame earned on straight, rushing football. The extra point try was blocked, so the score was 6–3.

Soon Layden set Stanford back on its heels with a punt that traveled 72 yards over the Stanford goal line. Nevers then started hammering. He became a crashing wild man. Following up a 14-yard end-around gain by Lawson, Nevers punched the ball to Notre Dame's 31. On fourth down and 6 to go, quarterback Solomon called to Nevers to throw a flat pass to the right, intended for Ted Shipkey. Nevers did not get protection. Layden sensed the play. He streaked in front of Shipkey and pulled off a volleyball play. The pass was too high for him. Instead of trying to intercept it cleanly, he tapped it toward the Stanford goal line. Layden then ran under the ball as it came down 5 to 10 yards away and caught it. Aided by the blocking of Huntsinger, Layden sped 60 yards down the sideline to score, and Crowley kicked the extra point to make the score 13–3.

Stanford came right back. The bulling rushes of Nevers, the end sweeps of Ted Shipkey, and some amazingly accurate passes by Nevers advanced the ball deep into Notre Dame territory. Warner was pulling a fast one on Rockne. The Irish had been expecting straight power, for which the Warner system was famous. Stanford, however, mixed things up, with Lawson and Shipkey end arounds a real trouble for Notre Dame.

Nevers hit Solomon for a 25-yard gain, and Solly was off for an apparent touchdown when he was dragged down from behind by Notre Dame's Collins. Walsh then recovered James Kelly's fumble on the 17 as the half ended.

Cuddeback narrowly missed field goal kicks from the 32- and 45-yard lines before Layden's 50-yard punt was lost in the sun as Solomon tried to catch it.

The ball slipped through Solomon's hands and seemingly was transformed into a greased pig. Solly slapped at the "animal," grabbed at it, and tried to fall on it. Each time the "pig" got away. Just as Solly thought he had it cornered and was about to put salt on its tail, he saw a pair of hands reach down out of the sun.

The hands belonged to Ed Huntsinger, and Huntsinger belonged to Notre Dame. He picked up the "pig" by the throat and hotfooted 20 yards into the end zone. Crowley's kick made it 20–3.

Nevers then had his greatest moments. He intercepted a Stuhldreher pass and was brought down on the Irish 39. He then blasted for steady gains, each time with Walsh's arms wrapped uselessly around him. Finally, Ed Walker rifled a pass to Ted Shipkey for the touchdown, and Cuddeback kicked the extra point. Notre Dame 20, Stanford 10.

In the fourth quarter, George Baker intercepted Crowley's pass and ran it to the Irish 31. Nevers carried half the Irish team on his back to the 18, after Ted Shipkey had fought around end for 5. Nevers bulled for a first down on the 6. On the fourth down, Nevers was stopped on the goal line. Did he score? The play was to be argued about for years.

After being denied a touchdown, Stanford battled back, only to have Crowley intercept a Nevers pass on Notre Dame's 10. Layden punted out, and Stanford threatened once more. Nevers tried the flat pass again, received little protection, and Layden reached up for an easy interception. Elmer raced 70 yards for the game's final touchdown. Crowley's kick made it 27–10. Stanford outgained Notre Dame in yardage, 298 to 179. But it was the scoreboard that had the only numbers that mattered.

1926
Jinxed?

President Harry M. Ticknor's 1926 Tournament of Roses became historic for several reasons. That was the year of the first radio broadcast of a Rose Bowl game, with Pasadena sports writer and ex-Olympic track star Charlie Paddock doing the announcing. Only the year before the first Wirephoto had been transmitted from a Rose Bowl game. Miss America, Fay Lanphier, was named Tournament queen.

Several tragic incidents gave Ticknor reason to believe his parade was jinxed. First, police officer John Fox suffered a wrenched back and spinal injuries when he was knocked down and trampled by a horse during the procession. Then fifty-one-year-old Mrs. C. W. Bowen, who was watching the parade from atop a building at 127 West Colorado, fell twenty-

Stanford's Ernie Nevers

Downtown Pasadena during the 1925 parade

Harry Ticknor

Alabama's Johnny Mack Brown

five feet to her death as the parade went by. And, in the worst tragedy in Tournament history, 2 women died and 236 people were injured when part of a wooden viewing stand collapsed on the corner of Madison and Colorado.

A coroner's jury found that the accident occurred because of improper construction of stands and carelessness in inspection. Strict construction rules were adopted for the future, including insistence on all-steel frames for all bleachers along the parade route.

The Age of Dixie Begins:
Alabama 20, Washington 19

Alabama launched the Rose Bowl's "Age of Dixie" with a one-point victory over Washington acclaimed by many as the Rose Bowl's greatest game. Both teams came into the game with sensational records. Washington had won ten games, tied one and outscored its opponents, 459–39. Alabama was 9–0 after outscoring its opposition, 278–7.

Alabama stars included Johnny Mack Brown, "Pooley" Hubert, Grant Gillis and three solid linemen named Buckler, Holmes and Jones.

Washington stayed in the game mainly because of the running brilliance of George Wilson, described by Maxwell Stiles as the hardest running back developed on the West Coast. Wilson played only thirty-eight minutes because of injuries; however, during that short time, Washington scored three touchdowns and gained 300 yards. During the twenty-two minutes Wilson was on the sidelines, Washington gained only 17 yards and failed to score. Wilson wound up the day with 134 yards alone in fifteen carries, and he completed five passes for 77 yards. He was also a terror on defense, and one of his punts traveled 62 yards.

The game matched Wallace Wade as Alabama coach against Enoch Bagshaw of Washington. While such accepted experts as Paul Lowry of the *Times* astutely rated the game as a duel between Wilson and Hubert, both All-Americans in his opinion, Wilson himself praised Brown. "That Mack Brown was all they said of him and more," declared Wilson. "He

Wallace Wade advises his Alabama players along the sidelines

Alabama passes against Washington

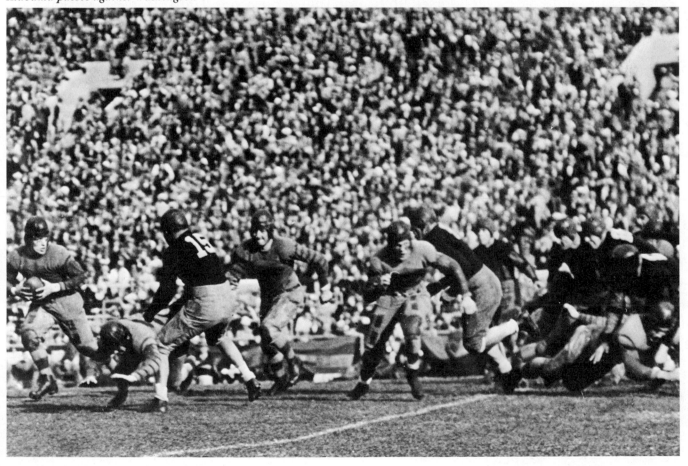

Dick Hyland carries for Stanford against Alabama in 1927

Wallace Wade

Washington's George Wilson

was about the fastest man in a football suit I have ever bumped up against. Hubert was good too.''

George Varnell, head linesman, who also was a Seattle newspaperman, said, ''Johnny Mack Brown has the sweetest pair of feet I have ever seen.''

Brown gained 15 yards around end on the first running play of the game. Wilson stopped the drive by intercepting Hoyt Winslett's pass, and Washington slashed 54 yards for its first touchdown with Harold Patton driving the final foot. George Guttormsen's extra-point try failed and Washington led, 6–0.

Wilson was knocked out tackling Winslett on a Statue of Liberty play. Bravely he remained in the game and got off a 62-yard punt that set up a second Washington touchdown after he had made the longest run of the day, for 32 yards. Wilson's pass to substitute end Cole scored the touchdown. The play that was eventually to mean defeat for Washington then occurred, as Guttormsen's drop kick hit the crossbar and bounced back.

After Wilson was knocked out a second time and forced to leave the game,

Alabama got going in the second quarter. However, Louis Tesreau, Wilson's replacement, made a great tackle of Brown on the last play of the half to thwart a possible Alabama touchdown catch and keep the half time score 12–0.

Alabama stormed over the goal line early in the third quarter after a short Tesreau punt, with Hubert and Brown ripping for big gains. Hubert went over and Buckler added the point.

Brown then caught a long pass from Gillis and raced the final 25 yards for a touchdown. Buckler converted a place kick again, Alabama went ahead, 14–12.

Ennis of Alabama recovered Louis Tesreau's fumble on the Husky 38. Brown caught a Hubert pass on the 3 and stepped into the end zone, but Buckler's extra-point try was blocked.

When Alabama threatened to score again, Coach Bagshaw sent the previously injured Wilson back into the game. This stimulated Washington, and the Huskies took the ball on downs on their 12-yard line. Wilson launched a resurgence by running 17 yards out of punt formation. Patton made a long run and Wilson started passing and smashing for gains, his 27-yard aerial to Guttormsen producing a touchdown. Cook, a reserve, received the call to try the extra point this time, and his kick was good, to bring Washington within a point of Alabama at 20–19. After an exchange of interceptions, the game ended.

1927
Flowers, Songs and Silk Pants

Oscar Hammerstein's and Richard Rodgers's *Flower Drum Song* would have found a welcome place in the 1927 Tournament festival, whose theme was "Flowers in Song." Every float portrayed some famous song. Newspapers of the day reported that the sight of women's legs proved shocking to some spectators.

Czechoslovakia was the first foreign government to enter the parade. Beverly Hills won the Sweepstakes Trophy with a float called "Sitting on Top of the World," with film star Madge Bellamy gracing the entry. A western movie star, Hoot Gibson, rode his horse alongside.

Even the football players added style to the Tournament when the Stanford team showed up wearing silk pants!

Another Battle of the Undefeated:
Stanford 7, Alabama 7

Once again the Rose Bowl staged a contest between two undefeated teams. Stanford came to Pasadena with a 10–0 record, which included a 41–6 thrashing of powerful California, and Alabama had a 9–0 record and a 241–20 scoring advantage.

While the 1927 Tournament may not have had a queen, it did have a king of tricks. He was "Tricky Dick" Hyland of Stanford, who got the block of the day from the goal posts. When Hyland scooted into the end zone while returning a punt, a pursuing Alabama player ran

smack into the posts and knocked himself out. This helped Hyland escape.

Wallace Wade was tricky, too. The great Alabama coach, destined to bring Alabama and Duke teams to Pasadena four times before getting beaten, came strategically prepared.

Braven Dyer, for years a leading writer for the *Times,* told the story of how Alabama got its tie by securing the ball on Stanford's 14 as a result of a blocked kick, relying on straight power to get into the end zone, and then using trickery to assure the extra point.

"After the touchdown came Herschel "Rosy" Caldwell's part in the drama," wrote Dyer. "What with our recent one-point margin games in these parts, we confess that we felt downright sorry for Rosy as he got ready to try for the lone digit. However, Alabama had made sure of the shot some time earlier, Coach Wade giving the boys a play which ought to work. Getting their signal in the huddle, the Crimson athletes went up into the line. Captain Barnes hesitated a moment, stood up and then repeated his signals. Stanford naturally relaxed a bit. The Redskins took their eyes off the ball to watch Barnes. Just as the Cards let down, Gordon Holmes, Alabama center, shot the pigskin back to Winslett. Caldwell kicked it between the posts. Rosy wasn't rushed, and Stanford didn't come near blocking it."

Stanford wound up with a 305–98 yard edge in total yardage, but the final score was 7–7.

Ted Shipkey, Stanford's All-American end, wound up with very impressive statistics. He carried on two end arounds, one of them for 23 yards. He caught five passes. He recovered two fumbles. He was a defensive fortress. In two Rose Bowl appearances, he accumulated

Freddie Pickard

There were just three tie football games in the first seventy-four Tournament of Roses games and all three were played within a space of just six years: 1922, 1924 and 1927. Since 1927, there have been sixty-one consecutive Rose Bowl games without a tie.

twelve catches, scored two touchdowns, and saved many—against very tough opposition (Notre Dame and Alabama). Maxwell Stiles rated Shipkey's bowl work among the greatest ever.

1928
Salvation of a Goat
Pasadena had a mighty parade in 1928, a parade that excitingly carried out the theme "States and Nations in Flowers." The parade covered almost five miles. Glendale's float was a sensation—an eighty-five-foot smoke-breathing dragon.

Harriet Sterling, Tournament queen, played the role of Statue of Liberty aboard her float, and the Pasadena Pigeon Club float released pigeons at intervals from wooden cages, much to the delight of youngsters.

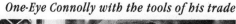

The Fickle Finger of Fate:
Stanford 7, Pittsburgh 6
The 7–6 victory by twice-beaten Stanford over previously undefeated Pittsburgh is a story of a coach's faith in one of his athletes. Frankie Wilton had been the goat of the game the year before because his punt was blocked to give Alabama a tie. That was just the beginning of Wilton's growth of capric horns. During the 1927 regular season, another of his fumbles had enabled USC's Trojans to beat the Indians.

Wilton must have thought himself ready to be put out to pasture permanently after fumbling in the second half of the 1928 Rose Bowl game to set up Pittsburgh's touchdown. Jimmy Hagan of the Panthers scooped it up and ran 17 yards to score. Although substitute Stanford tackle Walt Heinicke blocked the extra-point try by Pittsburgh's Booth, the 6 points on the Pittsburgh side of the scoreboard looked very big.

Wilton felt deep depression over the fact he again had made the mistake that was costing his team the Rose Bowl game. His only thought of hope must have been, "If only Pop Warner will let me stay in the game, maybe I can do something to make up for what I have done wrong."

With seventy thousand people watching in the newly enlarged stadium, Warner stuck with his disconsolate young man. Pop proved to be a real pop. He didn't send in a substitute for Wilton when Pittsburgh kicked off to Stanford in the third quarter with the Indians needing to rebound from a 6–0 deficit.

Biff Hoffman's running, catches by Sims and Worden, a timely 4-yard scamper by Wilton, and a guard-around trick run by Seraphim Post gave Stanford a first down on the 8. Three shots—Hoffman, Wilton, Hoffman—made 6 yards. It was fourth and 2 for a touchdown. Spud Lewis, at quarterback in place of Murphy, called a play in which Hoffman threw a short flat pass to Sims on the line of scrimmage. Sims got possession of the

Gate-crashing star One-Eye Connolly, who always insisted there wasn't a prominent sports event in America that he couldn't sneak into, was thrown out of the 1928 Rose Bowl seven times in twenty minutes. When he got in, he went up to radio sportscaster Graham MacNamee and shouted into the mike, "I'm here—I want Tex Rickard to know his fights aren't the only shows I attend."

One-Eye Connolly with the tools of his trade

Rose Queen Harriet B. Sterling as the Statue of Liberty in 1928

ball, tried frantically to find a way through the Golden Panthers, and suddenly was jolted into fumbling.

The ball bounded to the left . . . then to the right . . . and then the cosmic forces of the universe squared the books with Wilton. The Stanford player took the ball away from three Panthers and blasted into the end zone for the tying touchdown.

Hoffman kicked the extra point giving Stanford a 7–6 win and Warner a magnificent reward for keeping his faith in a depressed boy. Even Pittsburgh's coach Jock Sutherland—who had just seen his team's perfect season come to an end—admired the way his adversary stayed with a kid when he was down.

The following year's game was to call for what may have been an even greater act of faith of a coach in a player.

1929
Wrong Is Right

Tens of thousands of college and professional athletic contests are staged throughout the country every year. Most are quickly, permanently and deservedly forgotten. Every so often, however, something happens in a game which not only is remembered, but assumes mythic proportions. Such an event happened in the 1929 Rose Bowl game.

To put it simply: California's Roy Riegels got hold of the ball and astounded seventy thousand people by carrying it 65 yards toward *his own* goal line. This spectacular goof—one of the best-remembered events to occur in sports history—has made the name "Wrong-Way Riegels" legendary. Indeed, Tournament President Leslie B. Henry was later fond of saying, "When I headed the Tournament of Roses, the event really became famous. Roy Riegels ran the wrong way."

Many things happened during Henry's one-year term in the Tournament office besides that famous navigational error. The first post-parade exhibit of floats was staged at the Pasadena City Hall. Today this public viewing of the moving wonders of the flower world is one of the most popular features for Pasadena visitors at Victory Park, which is located near Paloma Street and Sierra Madre Boulevard where the parade concludes.

By 1929, twenty-two grandstands had been constructed along the Orange Grove and Colorado parade route and a record crowd of eight hundred fifty thousand watched the parade.

The California–Georgia Tech football game attracted a crowd of seventy-one thousand. The resulting $270,000 gate enabled the Tournament of Roses to pay off the Rose Bowl mortgage.

Glendale and Beverly Hills staged a battle for parade Sweepstakes honors that rivaled the football classic for intensity in the late twenties and early thirties. Beverly Hills won the award in 1927 and

1928, but Glendale sprang forth with the "Lady of Shalott" in the 1929 parade. It presented a castle of yellow and red mums plus a barge carrying a woman surrounded by banks of pink, red and yellow roses. The stream was created with white sweet peas. Beverly Hills came back to win in 1930, only to see Glendale make a comeback in 1931.

The sun was so hot that year it melted all the snow on the Camp Baldy float, but the Baldy youngsters came prepared. They threw papier-mâché snowballs at the crowd.

The Never-to-Be-Forgotten Game: Georgia Tech 8, California 7

The University of California came to Pasadena with a 7–1–1 record to face the undefeated Georgia Tech Yellow Jackets in the often-discussed 1929 game.

The score was 0–0 in the second quarter when a pass from California halfback Benny Lom to his other halfback, Barr, slipped through the latter's finger tips on the goal line. The ball went over to Tech on the 20-yard line. "Stumpy" Thomason of Tech made a nice gain around left end, but he fumbled when hit by Lom. The ball bounced into the hands of California center Roy Riegels on the Yellow Jacket 35-yard line.

Riegels headed for the Tech goal, then suddenly wheeled to elude Thomason and started in the opposite direction toward his own goal line. Instinctively, other California players began to take out Georgia Tech players, laying them low all over the field. California blocking was superb, so magnificent in fact, that nobody put a hand on Riegels.

Then Lom sensed something was wrong and took off after Riegels. He yelled at the top of his voice for his teammate to stop, but the roar of the crowd

California's immortal Roy Riegels

made it seem impossible for Riegels to hear anyone. Lom overtook Riegels near the goal line. He grasped the runaway with a desperate reach that connected with Riegels's wrist on the 1-yard line. With one mighty twist, just in time, Lom swung Riegels around. But before Riegels could head back in the correct direction, he was knocked to the earth by Tech's Frank Waddey on the 1-yard line.

This forced California to call for a punt to get out of trouble. Lom tried to kick out from deep inside his end zone, but Tech's Vance Maree, a giant tackle, leaped high to block the ball with his hands. The last man to touch the ball as it bounced out of the end zone was California's Breckenridge. Referee Herb Dana ruled the play a safety, giving 2 points to Georgia Tech.

The next day the *Times* reported on Riegels's reaction to his mistake, which produced the margin of California defeat. It said that he was heartbroken, but that he had no excuses to make. He had

Riegels carries the ball 65 yards—the wrong way

Riegels ponders the mistake that was to haunt him the rest of his life

Forty years after his famous "wrong-way run," Roy Riegels advised young people: "I gained true understanding of life from my Rose Bowl mistake, I learned you can bounce back from a misfortune. . . . At first it bothered me any time I heard the words 'wrong way,' but what happened doesn't bother me any more. . . . There isn't so much I remember about the historic play except that I would like to correct one misconception. I *did* hear Benny shout as I neared my goal line. So I slowed down as I looked back at him. He would never have caught me if I hadn't."

been merely mixed up in his directions; the first moment he knew anything was wrong was when Lom grabbed him.

After the game, Georgia Tech's All-American center Peter Pund, who played opposite Riegels, said, "That was a tough break for Riegels. But don't ever get the idea he isn't a wonderful center. He is the best center I have played against all year. He's a battler, and he never quit. Some boys might have folded up under the situation, but Riegels didn't. I admire him for it."

Coach Nibs Price and his California team had to solve a unique backfield alignment devised by Tech coach William Alexander. The Tech quarterback stood with his back to the center. He received the ball between his legs and tossed it to his backs for straight and split bucks. Some people called it the "crap-shooters formation."

Lom might have been famous today for winning the game, not for stopping Riegels. He recovered a fumble by "Father" Lumpkin, the Tech fullback, and ran 60 yards for a touchdown. The play was called back because referee Dana said he blew his whistle before the fumble.

At another moment during the game, the air went out of the ball on a California punt and the ball was awarded to Tech near the line of scrimmage. It wasn't Cal's day.

Georgia Tech took an 8–0 lead in the third quarter when Warner Mizell gained 30 yards around right end and Thomason broke through left tackle and reversed his field to go 15 yards for a touchdown. Thomason's conversion attempt was low and wide.

Historians hardly bother to record that Riegels blocked a Tech punt to start California on a drive that was climaxed by a long pass from Lom to Captain Phillips, a short clutch pass from Lom to Leland "Lee" Eisan, and then a scoring pass from Lom to Phillips. Barr kicked the extra point, but California still lost, 8–7.

THE 1930s

THE   HOWARD   JONES   ERA

1930
A Band Emerges

A pickup band made up of alumni and ROTC students was playing "Onward Christian Soldiers" at Pasadena Junior College (PJC) when a director named Audre Stong decided to shake things up.

"What our school needs is an all-student band trained for marching and concert," said Stong, who borrowed instruments, solicited volunteers to patch up old uniforms, and recruited music-minded students to "blow the depression out of our lives."

That was in late 1929; by January 1, 1930, Stong's group felt qualified to make an appearance in the Tournament of Roses parade. When the Caltech band failed to make an appearance that day, PJC's band won the hearts of Tournament officials by volunteering to split up and form two bands—one filling the PJC spot, the other subbing for Caltech.

Stong had trained his performers well and they were very popular in the 1930 parade—so pleasing that a few months later parade chairman Charles Cobb extended the official invitation to Stong and his student musicians to become the official Tournament band.

"We put a lot of tricks into our marches, and we developed ten-minute concerts for the many pauses in the parade," said Stong, who retired as director twenty years later and died in 1978. "A highlight of our experiences came in 1931 when we did the entire half-time show in the Rose Bowl," said Stong. "We had a large book the height of the goal posts, and we turned the pages of Rose Bowl history as we enacted the Tournament highlights. For years we represented the visiting teams when they came to the Rose Bowl, and we made many trips to other cities as the Tournament of

C. Hal Reynolds

James Rolph

Roses representative."

Radio was on a coast-to-coast network basis by 1930, and newsreels made Pasadena a major stop.

C. Hal Reynolds served the first of his two years as president in 1930. Holly Halsted reigned as queen, and Mayor "Sunny Jim" Rolph of San Francisco was brought in to be grand marshal. Reynolds then enunciated new policies of bringing in celebrities to serve as grand marshal and making the parade longer.

The tenure of Reynolds also introduced a new policy of queen selection. Before that time, women had been chosen as queens because they were prominent. For example, Fay Lanphier (1926) had been Miss America and May McAvoy (1923) was in the movies.

Harlan Hall, the secretary of the Tournament, and his committee wanted as queens young women who had a keen interest in the Tournament, whose families had been pioneers in early Pasadena, and who had been working closely with the board of directors. Holly Halsted, a Pasadena High School grad and UCLA student, worked for the Tournament of Roses about three years before becoming queen.

Beverly Hills won the Sweepstakes prize for its "End of the Rainbow" entry, depicting a huge heart opening under a dazzling, multicolored rainbow.

Glendale's consistently winning floats in this era were designed by L. H. Chobe. While preparing for the 1930 parade, Chobe's health failed and he underwent a serious throat operation. Nevertheless, he managed to work out the design, communicating with his associates with notes when he became unable to talk. Just before the float "Gold Rush of '98" was ready to move, Chobe's doctor told him he couldn't travel under any circumstances; however, the doctor relented and personally drove him to Pasadena under police escort. Chobe returned home, happy after learning Glendale had won its fifteenth gold cup as theme winner. Ten days later he passed away.

The Jones Boys:
USC 47, Pittsburgh 14

The 1930 Rose Bowl game is remembered mainly because it introduced Howard Harding Jones to the bowl world. When his great high-scoring team trounced Dr. John "Jock" Sutherland's previously undefeated Pittsburgh team, 47–14, it marked the first of five victorious teams Jones was to take to the bowl.

USC's star was "Racehorse Russ" Saunders. On the first scrimmage play of the game, Toby Uansa, one of four Pitt All-Americans, cut between Francis Tappaan, USC's left end, and left tackle Bob Hall. Behind a wall of interference, Uansa broke into the open and streaked toward the Trojan goal line. Saunders, knocked down at the start of the play, got up to give chase in one of the more thrilling footraces in Rose Bowl annals. Saunders caught Uansa on the USC 14-yard line to bring to a halt what was already the Rose Bowl's longest run from scrimmage, 69 yards.

"Let us pray," implored a USC cheerleader.

Another USC star, Ernie Pinckert, answered this Trojan prayer by knocking down a fourth-down Pittsburgh pass to end the threat.

Saunders then started raising his arm. He completed a 55-yard pass play to Harry Edelson for a touchdown. A 25-yard pass to Pinckert scored again. Swivel-hipped substitute quarterback Marshal Duffield ran the score up to 26–0 at halftime before Saunders returned to connect with Edelson for another touchdown. Three Saunders passes and three touchdowns: that was good percentage. Saunders was also true with his next two passes, to run his completion streak to five, even though they didn't produce touchdowns.

"I want to praise Saunders for picking their defense apart," said Jones after the game. "Their great fullback Pug Parkinson played close to stop our running, and Saunders passed over him. Saunders is as good as any back I have ever coached."

USC's Russ Saunders

1931
The South Rises Again

Glendale returned to the Sweepstakes pinnacle in the 1931 parade, with its float depicting "The Olympic Games," which were to come to Los Angeles in 1932. The float, made of chrysanthemums, depicted a discus thrower and a runner. The touching factor in this Glendale triumph was the fact that the float was designed by the widow of L. H. Chobe, the great designer who had died earlier in the year.

General C.S. Farnsworth rode a pure-blooded Arabian stallion named Jadaan which had been ridden by silent film star Rudolph Valentino in several films. The queen was Mary Lou Waddell.

Dr. Albert Einstein was honored by the Tournament, but remained in seclusion and watched the parade from the private office of a bank president. Nevertheless, he later said, "This was one of the most delightful days I have experienced."

Just in time for the 1931 football game, the last of the construction wood was removed from the Rose Bowl and the stadium's seating capacity was increased once again—this time to eighty-six thousand people.

Gen. C.S. Farnsworth

At the annual Rose Queen Luncheon for the 1979 Tournament, Holly Halsted Balthis, the 1930 queen, eyed May McAvoy Clearly, the 1923 queen, with a sharp, appraising eye, and remarked, "I am glad she appears to be healthy. I am not anxious to become known as the oldest living queen of the Tournament of Roses."

Babe Hollingberry

Washington State's coach, Babe Hollingberry, came up with the bright idea of outdoing the Crimson of Alabama in 1931 by having his players appear on the field dressed in red from head to foot. Their helmets were red, their jerseys were red, their pants were red, their socks were red, their shoes were red and—by dusk— their faces were red. The Crimson Tide won, 24–0. The Cougars burned their uniforms before returning to Pullman.

The Tide Rushes In:
Alabama 24, Washington State 0

The Washington State Cougars and Alabama Crimson Tide came to the 1931 Rose Bowl game with almost identical credentials. Both teams had won all of their nine games during the regular season, and their cumulative scores were very similar. Alabama had outscored its opponents, 247–13, and Washington State had had a 218–32 point edge. The Rose Bowl thus figured to be close.

Alabama was a cold, skilled machine. Coach Wallace Wade shifted his lineup around to get the best combination for every possible situation and quarterback Jimmy "Hurry" Cain called a variety of bewildering plays. Alabama scored three quick touchdowns and added a field goal. Washington State got only as far as Alabama's 1-yard line.

Glenn "Turk" Edwards and Mel Hein gave Washington State plenty of "oomph" in the line, but the Cougar backfield, especially on defense, was not up to reaping Hurry Cain. Monk Campbell spun away from Cougar tacklers as if they were kittens. Fred Sington of Alabama, an All-American tackle every pound of him, dueled Edwards every minute, although West Coast writers concluded Edwards was master this day.

Cain averaged 46 yards on six punts, truly a great kicking performance.

The victory was Alabama's third straight in the bowl. Over the next nine years, another five southern teams played in the Rose Bowl. It truly was an Age of Dixie.

1932
Olympic Games

The Tournament story went out to all parts of the world in 1932 when short-wave radio broadcasts of the activities were initiated. It was fitting that the world should receive the descriptions of the beautiful floats because, in the year that the Olympics were held in Los Angeles, the parade theme in Pasadena was "Nations and Games in Flowers."

William May Garland, who played an important role in the Los Angeles Olympics effort, was the grand marshal. Tournament president starting a two-year term was D.E. McDaneld. A UCLA freshman, Myrta Olmsted, was chosen to ride in the parade as queen of the Tournament's salute to the Olympiad.

Each float represented one of the fifty-seven countries participating in the Olympic games. The Sweepstakes winner was San Marino's float, a tribute to Australia in the form of a barge drawn by a huge floral lyrebird.

The South Returns:
USC 21, Tulane 12

Howard Jones's great USC team lost its 1931 opener, but as the season progressed, the tempo of crushing Trojan victories increased to the point where Troy beat Georgia, 60–0, in its final game. Along the way, the Trojans ended Notre Dame's twenty-five-game winning streak, 16–14, to qualify as the western representative in the 1932 Rose Bowl against Bernie Bierman's Tulane team, which had an 11–0 record.

Overall, Tulane and USC had compiled almost identical cumulative scores during the 1931 season. Tulane outscored its opponents 338–35, while USC ran up a 342–40 advantage. Again, the Rose Bowl figured to be close.

The Trojans had six men who were named on one or more All-American teams—tackle Ernie Smith, guards Johnny Baker and Aaron "Rosy" Rosenberg, *Continued on page 71*

TOURNAMENT OF ROSES

PASADENA CALIFORNIA
NEW YEARS DAY 1913

MIDWINTER FLORAL PAGEANT
ROMAN CHARIOT RACES

THE TOURNAMENT

Pasadena's "White House," a beautiful mansion originally built by chewing gum magnate William Wrigley Jr., is the home of the Tournament of Roses, the most successful community festival organization in the world.

Founded in 1890 by Professor Charles Frederick Holder and Dr. Francis F. Rowland, the Tournament Association now consists of fourteen hundred members, eight hundred of whom actively volunteer their services as "men in white," to stage the annual Rose Parade and Rose Bowl game. Members must live within a fifteen-mile radius of the city of Pasadena.

Heading the organization is the Tournament president who functions in that capacity for one year after serving first as a committeeman, then committee chairman, then on a board of directors, and finally on the nine-member executive committee. There is an automatic progression in the latter group to the presidency.

Twenty-nine committees annually named by the president perform the duties of staging the parade and game, and naming the Tournament theme for the year and the grand marshal, who is the titular head of the festival.

The Tournament's permanent manager, appointed in 1981 and heading a staff that performs the administrative duties, is Jack French. His top aides are assistant manager Frosty Foster and public relations director Bill Flinn. A Tournament of Roses Foundation was formed in 1987 to assist Pasadena in charitable ways from funds derived through individual and organization gifts.

But the Rose Bowl football game is the source of revenue that finances all Tournament expenses incurred by both the Tournament and the city of Pasadena in staging the festival. Under the terms of an agreement between the Tournament and city, all net revenue is shared, leaving no assessment to the taxpayers of Pasadena.

Based on average figures, which may vary, the breakdown is:

The game produces $15,000,000 gross revenue, over $11,000,000 from television rights and $4,000,000 from ticket sales and concessions. Game staging expenses are $500,000, leaving $14,500,000 net revenue.

Under terms of the pact between the two competing collegiate conferences and the Tournament, the Big Ten and Pac-10 each receive 42 1/2 percent, with 15 percent going to the Tournament of Roses. This amounts to $2,175,000 to the Tournament and $6,162,500 to each of the conferences. From the latter amount, after conference expenses are deducted, each member school annually receives approximately $500,000

According to the pact between the Tournament and the city of Pasadena, each reports its income and expenses from the festival and game. Tournament gross revenue is $2,175,00 from the game and $800,000 from other sources such as membership fees, grandstand parade profits, program and other sales, making a total of $2,975,000. The city's revenue is about $500,000 from hotel taxes and other sources such as concession fees. Combined revenue is $3,475,000.

The city reports expenses for policing, traffic control, cleanup and stadium maintenance at $700,000. The Tournament reports expenses of $1,975,000, which includes full operation of all Tournament activities, staff and maintenance for the year. Thus total expense becomes $2,675,000. Subtracted from the revenue figure of $3,475,000, the Tournament activities for the year show a net plus of $800,000. This is split with $400,000 going to the Tournament and $400,000 to the city for its general fund.

Men in White

President Fred Soldwedel in the 1987 parade with wife Donna

The Tournament gives approximately $200,000 of its balance to the city for stadium improvements each year. The remaining $200,000 is placed in the Tournament reserve fund.

The above financial figures are compiled from an average year and can vary annually according to increased revenue or expenses, the latter increased in 1988 due to extremely higher insurance rates.

How to Become President of the Tournament of Roses

1. Apply for membership in the Tournament of Roses after finding two Tournament members to act as sponsors. Pay minimum annual dues of $25.

2. Serve eight to ten years as an aide on various committees and then as a committee member.

3. Perform so credibly as to be named a committee chairman by the Tournament president.

4. After several years of chairmanship of various committees, be named by the executive committee to the twenty-three-member board of directors.

5. Within a ten-year span on the board of directors, be invited to become a member of the nine-man executive committee.

6. Move up the executive committee ladder, one step each year, ascending to the presidency in nine years. So far, the process requires from twenty to thirty years of service.

7. Serve one year as president, then phase out by sitting one year on the executive committee and two years on the football committee before retiring as a life director.

Tournament Presidents

1890	Charles F. Holder
1891	B. Marshall Wotkyns
1892	Frank C. Bolt
1893	Frank C. Bolt
1894	Charles Daggett
1895	Charles Daggett
1896	Edwin Stearns
1897	Edwin Stearns
1898	Martin H. Weight
1899	Martin H. Weight
1900	Herman Hertel
1901	F. B. Weatherby
1902	James B. Wagner
1903	Charles Coleman
1904	Charles Daggett
1905	Charles Daggett
1906	Edwin D. Neff
1907	Edward T. Off
1908	George P. Carey
1909	George P. Carey
1910	George P. Carey
1911	Frank G. Hogan
1912	Edward T. Off
1913	Edward T. Off
1914	R. D. Davis
1915	John B. Coulston
1916	Lewis H. Turner
1917	D. M. Linnard
1918	B. O. Kendall
1919	B. O. Kendall
1920	William L. Leishman
1921	William L. Leishman
1922	John J. Mitchell
1923	John J. Mitchell
1924	W. F. Creller
1925	W. F. Creller
1926	Harry M. Ticknor
1927	Harry M. Ticknor
1928	Harry M. Ticknor
1929	Leslie B. Henry
1930	C. Hal Reynolds
1931	C. Hal Reynolds
1932	D. E. McDaneld
1933	D. E. McDaneld
1934	George S. Parker
1935	C. Elmer Anderson
1936	C. Elmer Anderson
1937	Cyril Bennett
1938	George S. Campbell
1939	Lathrop K. Leishman
1940	Harlan G. Loud
1941	J. W. McCall Jr.
1942	Robert M. McCurdy
1943	James K. Ingham
1944	Frank M. Brooks
1945	Max H. Turner

Mayor and Mrs. John C. Crowley ride early car

1946	Charles A. Strutt
1947	William P. Welsh
1948	Louis R. Vincenti
1949	Harold C. Schaffer
1950	Drummond J. McCunn
1951	L. Clifford Kenworthy
1952	Leon Kingsley
1953	William H. Nicholas
1954	Harry W. Hurry
1955	Elmer M. Wilson
1956	Dr. Alfred L. Gerrie
1957	John S. Davidson
1958	J. H. Biggar Jr.
1959	Stanley K. Brown
1960	Raymond A. Dorn
1961	Arthur W. Althouse
1962	H. Burton Noble
1963	Stanley L. Hahn
1964	Hilles M. Bedell
1965	Walter R. Hoefflin Jr.
1966	J. Randolph Richards
1967	Henry Kearns
1968	H. W. Bragg
1969	G. L. "Tige" Payne
1970	C. Lewis Edwards
1971	A. Lewis Shingler
1972	Virgil White
1973	Otis Blasingham
1974	Edward Wilson
1975	Paul G. Bryan
1976	Ralph Helpbringer
1977	Carl E. Wopschall
1978	Harrison Baker
1979	Arthur Welsh
1980	Frank Hardcastle
1981	Millard Davidson
1982	Harold Coombes
1983	Thornton Hamlin
1984	Donald Judson
1985	James Boyle
1986	Frederick Johnson
1987	Fred Soldwedel
1988	Harriman L. Cronk
1989	John H. Biggar III

**Father & Son
Tournament Presidents**
Biggar: John H. (1958) &
   John H. III (1989)
Davidson: John S. (1957) &
   Millard (1981)
Leishman: William L. (1920–21)
   & Lathrop (1939)
Turner: Lewis H. (1916) &
   Max H. (1945)
Welsh: William P. (1947) &
   Arthur (1979)
Wilson: Elmer M. (1955) &
   Edward (1974)

Rose Bowl Tickets: Who Gets Them

The biggest question in Pasadena and elsewhere as each Rose Bowl game approaches is: How does one get a ticket?

The game is a sellout every year with attendance around 103,500. Only 3,500 tickets are available to the general public. Recipients are selected by a drawing of postcards which must be mailed to the Tournament of Roses. Usually over 30,000 requests are mailed in.

The remaining 100,000 tickets are distributed as follows:

In an agreement between the Pac-10 Conference, the Big Ten and the Tournament of Roses, the host Pac-10 receives 53,700, of which about 43,000 go to the school playing in the game. The school distributes its share to students, season ticket holders and alumni. Another 5,000 tickets are evenly divided among the other nine Pac-10 schools. The media purchase 3,500, and the remainder go to the Veteran's Administration, Pac-10 office, game officials and the football program publishers.

The Big Ten receives 22,400 tickets, of which about 20,000 go to the school playing in the game. Another 1,800 tickets are divided among the other nine schools in the conference, while the remainder are distributed by the Big Ten office.

The Tournament of Roses Association is allotted about 23,900 tickets, in addition to the 3,500 earmarked for the public drawing. Each of the 1,400 members of the Association may purchase four tickets. The remaining 18,000 or so tickets are available to Tournament officers, city directors and key city officials, game management, parade participants, float sponsors and selected organizations, including the Big Ten Club of Southern California.

How do scalpers and travel agencies get tickets? There is no formula except they must get them

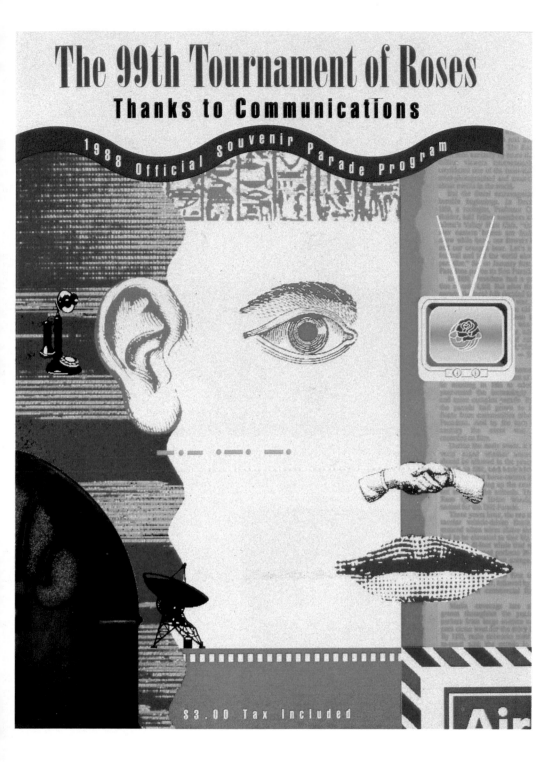

The 99th Tournament of Roses
Thanks to Communications

1988 Official Souvenir Parade Program

$3.00 Tax Included

the same way the rest of the public does. The key is to know somebody who has them. Reportedly, travel agencies and scalpers buy tickets from students and others willing to sell them for a profit. Who does the dealing will never be known, but somehow the scalpers and agencies get tickets that can command $200 to $500 on the open market.

Tickets to the 1920 game were 65 cents. In 1955, the price went up to $5.99. The odd figure was the result of an internal revenue rule that no ticket could sell for an even $6. It had to be one cent less or one cent more. By 1967, tickets sold for $7. They increased often after that By 1981, prices reached $25. Tickets for the 1988 game were $38.

The Biggest Service Club Luncheon in the World

The annual Kiwanis Kickoff Luncheon, usually held the day before the Rose Bowl game, tops the list of events that are supporting features of the Tournament of Roses. A box lunch affair, this event attracts four thousand people who come to hear the players, coaches and dignitaries—the largest service club luncheon in the world.

Other major Tournament events include an equestrian show, a high school bandfest, a dinner sponsored by the Big Ten Club of Southern California, the Queen's breakfast sponsored by the Pasadena Junior Chamber of Commerce and the President's breakfast sponsored by the Pasadena Chamber of Commerce.

halfback Ernie Pinckert, and quarterbacks Orv Mohler and Gaius Shaver.

Tulane didn't play dead for the great Trojans. Wop Glover made a 59-yard run, overtaken finally by Pinckert. The Trojans retaliated with a march that produced the game's first touchdown, scored by end Ray Sparling, who had dropped back into halfback position. Baker kicked the extra point and USC jumped ahead, 7–0.

The score remained 7–0 until both teams erupted in the third quarter. On runs of 30 and 23 yards, Pinckert scored two touchdowns through the great Jerry Dalrymple's territory at right end. Not a Tulane player touched Pinckert on either run as USC combined masterful trickery and blocking. In Dalrymple's defense, it should be remembered he had suffered a kidney injury in an earlier game and was handicapped by protective padding that required frequent readjustments. When he used more than

his allotted time out, USC captain Stan Williamson demonstrated fine sportsmanship by telling referee Herb Dana, "Let him have all the time he needs."

Glover got a bee in his pants, however, and executed some runs for Tulane that set up a touchdown pass from Don Zimmerman to Haynes. Zimmerman's extra-point try was blocked. A Zimmerman pass to Dalrymple set up a scoring change; Dalrymple batted the ball in the air and caught it as it started downward. Glover then skirted end for the touchdown. Pinckert knocked down a Tulane pass in the attempt for an extra point. Final score: USC 21, Tulane 12.

Bierman said, "USC has more power than any team I have ever seen." The Trojan performance perhaps whetted Bierman's appetite for power, because when he became coach of his alma mater, Minnesota, the following season, he developed some of the most bruising power teams in college football history.

Howard Jones's great powerhouse team lost only one game during the 1931 season. The loss came at the hands of tiny St. Mary's College—the very same institution which had lost to California, 127–0, back in 1920. That same 1931 season St. Mary's joined USC in handing Cal its only losses. In 1939 little St. Mary's was to win the Cotton Bowl classic.

Howard Jones

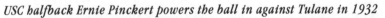

USC halfback Ernie Pinckert powers the ball in against Tulane in 1932

Bernie Bierman

Mary Pickford

USC's Cotton Warburton

1933
America's Sweetheart

The nation was in the throes of depression in 1933, and it required remarkable fortitude from Tournament leaders to plan a parade under such circumstances. The result was a significant achievement, summed up in the words of the *Los Angeles Times*: "Whatever economists may think of existing conditions will be belied by the great parade, for there is no depression in the world of flowers, nor in the spirit of Pasadenans and their neighbors in other Southern California cities who have contributed entries for the dazzling pageant."

No doubt, much of the joy which spectators felt derived from seeing "Amcrica's Sweetheart," Mary Pickford, riding in a coach drawn by four white horses with reins and harness of white satin. Dressed in white with floral decorations of the same hue, the famous motion picture star presented an unforgettable picture at the head of the parade as grand marshal. She was both the first female grand marshal and the first Hollywood figure to accept the parade's most honored role. Many people swarmed into Pasadena just to see her in person.

The queen of the 1933 Tournament

Grand Marshal William May Garland in 1932

was Dorothy Edwards of Covina, California. Edwards was one of the first queens selected through the system that exists today, in which students in Pasadena area schools compete for the honor.

Another Battle of the Undefeated: USC 35, Pittsburgh 0

Once again the Rose Bowl paired two powerhouse teams which matched almost perfectly on paper. Southern California finished the 1932 season with a perfect 9–0 record, and an aggregate point margin of 166–13. Pitt won eight games and tied two, while outscoring the opponents, 182–25. Ironically, both Pitt ties were 0–0 scores, against Ohio State and Nebraska.

Jock Sutherland's team came to Pasadena with high expectations, but USC's Cotton Warburton led the Trojans to a 35–0 runaway before eighty-four thousand spectators who came to see the struggle between the two undefeated elevens. Weighing only 145 pounds, Warburton scored two touchdowns as Howard Jones's team wore down Pitt.

A 50-yard pass from Homer Griffith to Ford Palmer put USC on the scoreboard in the first period. Bill Henry described the play in the *Times*:

"As the ball arched high in the air, Pitt's safety man Sebastian set himself to knock it down in the end zone. Palmer came charging in from his left at top speed, and he and the ball hit Sebastian at the same time. Both players were a couple of feet off the ground. There was a brief but decisive wrestling match in mid-air. Palmer, perhaps aided by the impetus of his run, wrenched the leather away from Sebastian and lit in the end zone for the game's first score. Mr. Sebastian and the 84,000 people were surprised, and they were still gasping when

Ernie Smith's suitcase-size shoe nudged the pill squarely between the posts for the first of four perfect placements for the day.''

Pitt stalwarts included Warren "Heza" Heller, Charles Hartwig, Joe Skladany and Ted Daily. Heller was a great runner, and Skladany, the Czech sensation at end, was constantly wreaking havoc in USC's backfield.

The cotton-topped Warburton made his presence felt first defensively, before breaking loose offensively. He stopped Pitt's Weisenbaugh in a last-man effort after the bruising runner had gained 32 yards. This play signaled the end of Pitt's chances. Fumbles were costly to Pitt after that. The Panthers tried to rip Warburton's shirt off in an attempt to stop him, but the little speedster was too much as he carried the ball twenty-two times for 87 yards.

1934
The Great Flood

After nearly fourteen of the driest years the country had ever seen, Prohibition officially ended in the United States on December 5, 1933. The end of the dry spell seems to have brought on a veritable flood for the 1934 Tournament whose theme was, appropriately, "Tales of the Seven Seas." With water evidently in mind, Tournament president George S. Parker invited top naval officer Admiral William Sims to be grand marshal.

During the forty-eight hours before the parade began, twelve inches of rain fell on Pasadena—nearly half a normal year's annual precipitation. Scores of houses floated away, and the Rose Bowl was so flooded that Pasadena's fire department brought pumps to get the water off the playing field. Only thirty-five thousand fans braved the elements to

Long Beach's award-winning swan float in 1934

watch Stanford take on Columbia.

Admiral Sims himself nearly missed the parade on account of the storm. He was guest of honor at dinner on the Navy flagship U.S.S. *Pennsylvania* on New Year's Eve, when the storm grew so violent that orders were given for him to remain on board. The admiral demanded to be transported ashore. "I'm going to lead the parade if I have to swim every inch of the way, and my fleet will be in good formation even if every ship is floating.''

In addition to Sims, sixteen other ranking naval officers attended the event. Former President Herbert Hoover and his wife also were there. Spurning an umbrella provided for him in the reviewing stand, the ex-president sat in a green slicker, rain dripping from his hat, as the floats sloshed down the parade route. Four bands failed to show. Some bands rode in buses. The popular song played was "It Ain't Gonna Rain No More.''

The 1934 Tournament was also memorable because of a parade ruling making

After Stanford teams had lost five consecutive games to USC up to 1932, freshmen team members vowed never to lose to USC again. They kept this promise and helped Stanford beat the Trojans three straight times. Immediately after the "Vow Boys" class graduated in 1936, Stanford lost its next USC game, 14–7.

Columbia's Al Barabas scores game-winning touchdown against Stanford in 1934

Lou Little

it compulsory for all horse entrants to have silver-mounted trappings. In addition, the riders were obligated to outfit themselves in Spanish costumes. These restrictions improved the general appearance of the equestrian divisions which are an annual parade feature.

Long Beach won the 1934 Sweepstakes award with its float "The White Swan," the giant swan constructed of white carnations. Treva Scott was queen. Appropriately, the Long Beach float represented that city as "Queen of the Beaches." Young women riding aboard were garbed as mermaids.

Renewed Vows:
Columbia 7, Stanford 0

The 1934 Rose Bowl game presented Stanford's "Vow Boys" coached by Claude E. "Tiny" Thornhill against Lou Little's Columbia eleven. The Stanford team got the name "Vow Boys" as freshmen when they vowed they would never lose to USC—a vow they kept even though it took them three years as a unit to win a Rose Bowl game. In those three years, they had three tries at it. This team had Bob "Horse" Reynolds, who played every minute of three Rose Bowl games, Bobby Grayson, who carried 152 yards against Columbia, ends Monk Mosecrip

and Keith Topping, and right guard Bill Corbus, quarterback Frank Alustiza, and blocking back Bones Hamilton.

In the late 1980s, as Columbia University compiled the all-time record losing streak in college football, it was hard to grasp the concept of a powerful Columbia football team. But such is exactly what it had in 1934. Damon Runyon, the accepted authority among eastern sports writers, ballyhooed Columbia, a team with a 7–1 record, over Stanford, 8–1–1. Stanford made him look good by fumbling eight times.

Columbia won the game in the second quarter on a skillfully executed hidden-ball play in which everybody but the Stanford waterboy made a dive for quarterback Cliff Montgomery while Al Barabas, like a sneak thief at night, slipped unseen around the Indians' right end for 17 yards and the game's only touchdown. It was a play that moved Jack James, a Los Angeles sports writer, to quote the Book of John, "Now Barabas was a robber."

The Columbia team lined up in single-wing formation strong to the right with an unbalanced line. Montgomery was directly back of center, with Barabas to his right. Cliff received the ball from center and midway in a spin handed it to Barabas. Then he completed his spin, pretended to hand the ball to Brominski, the Columbia right halfback, and then headed for the hole between the Stanford left tackle and left end. These two gentlemen, not daring to take a chance on Montgomery's having the ball (which he pretended to have tucked deep under his chest), stayed where they were to check Montgomery.

Meanwhile, Brominski, also pretending to have the ball, charged over the Stanford right tackle. The purpose of this

Grand Marshal Harold Lloyd, Queen Muriel Cowan and President C. Elmer Anderson meet each other before the 1935 festival

decoy was to pull Keith Topping in after Brominski, and the Stanford right end, a sophomore, fell for it. Bones Hamilton, the Stanford right half, also charged in after Brominski but was blocked out.

All this time, Barabas held his hands on his hips and gave an imitation of a man who did not have the football in his "pocket." He moved to his left far to the outside. Maxwell Stiles wrote, "When he reached the 15-yard line he stopped to chat with the little old lady who was selling red apples." Barabas had time to breeze laughingly over the goal line untouched and undetected. Newell Wilder converted, and Columbia won, 7–0. Stanford had its chances, but mishaps—such as fumbles or blown plays—always seemed to happen.

1935
Howell to Hutson

Movie comedian Harold Lloyd was grand marshal in 1935. Lloyd was no stranger to the parade, for years he pursued a hobby of photographing the various floats. This time the photographers of the world gathered to photograph him.

The 1935 president was C. Elmer Anderson, who served two years. The 1935 Sweepstakes winner was Santa Barbara's "The Jay and the Peacock," a floral depiction of seven peacocks which turned from side to side. Seven men inside the sixty-five-foot-long float manipulated the moving birds and were in continual communication via built-in telephones. The 1935 Tournament also saw the addition of commercial floats to the parade, but Tournament officials made certain there would be no advertising.

Taking the Vow (Apart):
Alabama 29, Stanford 13

Sports writer Mark Kelly told the story of the 1935 game, in which Alabama defeated Stanford's "Vow Boys," when he wrote: "Open that page once more in the Book of Football Revelation and add under the names of Dorais to Rockne, Wyman to Baston, and Friedman to Oosterbaan, those of Howell to Hutson. The latter should top the list of two-man combinations in football to make his-

The 1935 queen, Muriel Cowan, was perhaps the only woman in Tournament history chosen while wearing a baggy skirt, sweater, roll-over wool socks, and tennis shoes. She later recalled: "We were told to wear dressy clothes and high heels. I got the day of judging mixed up and appeared in my old clothes. I was a standout. Maybe that's why I won."

Stanford's "Vow Boys": Bones Hamilton, Bill Paulman, Bobby Grayson and Jimmy Coffis

Matty Bell

Stanford's Bob Reynolds

Pitt's Bobby LaRue picks up part of his 199 yards against Washington

Marshall Goldberg adds more yards for Pittsburgh

Don Hensley intercepts for Pitt

Alabama's Walter Merrill clears a path through Stanford

tory." Other sports writers concurred.

Grantland Rice wrote: "Dixie Howell, the human howitzer from Hartford, Alabama, blasted the Rose Bowl dreams of Stanford with one of the greatest all-around exhibitions that football has ever known. The slender, 161-pound stripling led a passing, kicking, and running attack that beat a big game Stanford team, 29–13, as 85,000 sat beneath a blue California sky and saw the sunny

Don Hutson, Phyllis Brooks and Dixie Howell strike a publicity pose after the 1935 game

atmosphere full of flying footballs thrown from Howell's rifle-shot hand into Don Hutson's waiting arms."

USC's coach Howard Jones described the passing as the best he had ever seen. Writer Kelly went further: "Then like arrows from Robin Hood's trusty bow, there shot from Howell's unerring hand a stream of passes the like of which have never been seen in football on the Coast. Zing, zing, zing! They whizzed through the air and found their mark in the massive paws of Hutson and Bryant, 'Bama ends.''

Alabama coach Frank Thomas

Howell completed nine of twelve passes and he punted six times for an average of 44.8 yards. Hutson caught six of six passes thrown to him for 164 yards and two touchdowns, little Joe Riley sharing some of the passing with Howell.

1936
Vow Boys Come Through

The Tournament of 1936 will go down in history as the beginning of the Rose Bowl sellout era. The credit for the greatest boom in ticket sales the Rose Bowl had experienced goes to the state of Texas. More than two hundred thousand requests for tickets to the Stanford–Southern Methodist game were turned back when the 84,784 seats in the bowl were gobbled up by an invasion of excited Texas folk who made the Pasadena trip a crusade. Pasadena hospitality was extended to the point that Texas Gover-

Governor James V. Allred

nor James V. Allred was invited to be grand marshal. Ex-president Herbert Hoover was among the dignitaries who came for the big game.

South Pasadena produced the Sweepstakes winner in the parade with its float "Louis XVI and Marie Antoinette." Barbara Nichols was the queen.

Vows Made Good:
Stanford 7, Southern Methodist 0

Stanford's Vow Boys, twice beaten in Pasadena, made another vow—never to lose another Rose Bowl game. In 1936 they made good, finally, winning, 7–0, over the Mustangs from Texas who came in with a 12–0 season record only to fizzle out. SMU had been a Southland favorite ever since coach Matty Bell's team, led by All-American halfback Bobby Wilson and his cheerleading sweetheart Betty Bailey, put on a show in a midseason 21–0 triumph over UCLA. Then the Mustangs defeated TCU in Fort Worth, 20–14, to qualify for the Rose Bowl trip—the big play that beat Sammy Baugh and his teammates being a sensa-

tional catch by Wilson of a Bob Finley pass. Stanford was forced by public demand to invite Southern Methodist to be its Rose Bowl opponent.

Keith Topping played a tremendous defensive game at end for Stanford. Backfield men Bill Paulman—who scored the game's only touchdown on a short blast—Bobby Grayson and Bones Hamilton were more than a match for SMU.

1937
Equestrians Hailed

A rainstorm struck the night before the 1937 Tournament, the downpour tearing open the roof of a huge tent where the floats were decorated and housed. The faithful workers refused to stop their decorating, however, and the parade, whose theme was "Romance in Flowers," went off on schedule. The parade was shortened that year, with the accent on making the presentations more beautiful than ever. Santa Barbara responded with a stunning creation called "Omar Khayyam," presenting a Persian garden in violent colors. The

Eugene Biscailuz

Andy Castle, a parade judge in 1936, had a heart attack as the parade started and was rushed to Hollywood Presbyterian Hospital. "My wife had heard over the radio that I passed away," he said afterwards, "I believe I am the only person truly to come back from the dead during a Tournament of Roses parade."

South Pasadena's 1936 "Louis XVI and Marie Antoinette" float

Cyril Bennett

George S. Campbell

Leo Carrillo

huge throngs along the parade route gasped at this spectacular Sweepstakes winner. Nancy Bumpus was queen.

Equestrians returned as grand marshals during the 1937 regime of Tournament president Cyril Bennett and the 1938 regime of president George S. Campbell. California's beloved native son and noted law officer, Sheriff Eugene Biscailuz, was the grand marshal in 1937. The year following, Leo Carrillo, familiar movie figure, descendant of one of the early Spanish California families, and expert horseman, consented to serve. He had ridden in the parade for some time and his appearance was to be a parade feature for years to come.

The San Gabriel Mountains had been snow-sprinkled the day before the 1937 parade to provide a most striking setting for the festivities.

Sweet Revenge:
Pittsburgh 21, Washington 0

Pittsburgh and Washington had identical 7–1–1 records going into the 1937 game, but Pittsburgh was unpopular because of its previous defeats in Pasadena. Stung by criticism, the Panthers of Dr. Sutherland, who had worked hard in San Bernardino for two weeks to get ready, walloped Jimmy Phelan's Huskies, 21–0. Straight power, featuring Bobby LaRue, Frank Patrick, and Marshal Goldberg as runners, and blockers Michelosen, Daddio, Matisi, Glassford, Hensley, Daniell, Hoffman, and Chickerneo, proved too much for the Huskies. LaRue wound up with 199 yards on fifteen carries, as Patrick scored twice and Bill Daddio once.

1938
'Bama Finally Loses

The 1938 Tournament opened the door

of movie fame to Queen Cheryl Walker, who signed a contract with Paramount the day after the parade and starred in the popular film *Stage Door Canteen* three years later.

"I was impressed with the reaction of PCC students the day after the newspapers announced my selection as Rose queen." recalled Cheryl. "They would stare or look over their shoulders while passing in the corridors. When entering a classroom all would stand and applaud. I thought, 'This for me?' I was just a modest kid and quite overwhelmed with the attention."

The Burbank city schools won the Sweepstakes float award in the parade with a "Playland Fantasies" theme.

Bears Blank 'Bama:
California 13, Alabama 0

The 1938 Tournament will also go down in history for producing Alabama's first Rose Bowl defeat after four previous conquering invasions. Once again, both teams came to Pasadena undefeated. Alabama had a perfect 9–0 record, while California had racked up nine wins and a tie—a scoreless affair against the previous year's western representative, Washington. Coach Leonard B. "Stub" Allison's California team blanked Frank Thomas's Crimson Tide, 13–0. The victory gave California some measure of compensation for its past bad luck in the Rose Bowl, but it has not won a Rose Bowl game in the fifty years since.

Vic Botari scored both of California's touchdowns in the second and third quarters of the football game. Sam Chapman, who became a major league baseball star, kicked one extra point.

1939
Little Girl with a Badge

When Lathrop K. Leishman lost out in a bid for presidency of the United States Junior Chamber of Commerce, he responded by thinking, "I figured I wasn't a big-time boy. So I decided to stick with being a home-town boy."

"Lay," as he was to his friends in Pasadena and throughout the United States, had been destined to become an active Tournament man from the day he peeked through the keyhole and listened to his father, William L. Leishman, and companions plan a "Yale Bowl" for Pasadena. He became president for the 1939 festival—the fiftieth year of the world's premiere New Year's Day classic.

"I decided there was no name in America as big as Shirley Temple, the child movie star," said Leishman, who was president at the young age of thirty-five, "So I decided she should be our grand marshal—if we could get her."

Leishman visited the Temple family at the film studio to ask them to accept the invitation. "It was a big moment when her parents said 'Yes,'" Leishman recalled. "Their main concern was her security. They wanted to be certain that she would be safe." To that end, Sheriff Eugene Biscailuz promised to provide a posse that would surround Shirley's

float. A large plastic bubble to protect against inclement weather was constructed over the spot on the float where Shirley was to ride, but it wasn't needed.

When Shirley first heard from her parents that she could be the grand marshal, she beamed with complete Shirley Temple charm.

"Oh goodie!" she said. "Will I get to wear a badge?

"You bet you will," replied Leishman. Bill Dunkerley, manager of the Tournament, had a badge more than a foot long specially made for the young film star.

"Shirley liked it when she heard the siren when we took her to the Tournament luncheon," said Leishman. "After the parade, she asked me to have the policemen blow the siren."

When Lathrop Leishman was made grand marshal in 1979, the court from 1939—his year as Tournament president—was reassembled: Queen Barbara Dougall Ward recalled her memories from forty years earlier: "Happiness, excitement, responsibility, meeting Shirley Temple, praying it wouldn't rain, hoping I wouldn't slide off my seat on the float, and not wanting to smile again for a week."

Tournament president Lathrop Leishman pins a badge on Grand Marshal Shirley Temple

*USC's Doyle Nave (above)
and Al Krueger (below)*

She was loudly cheered during the parade, and she smiled back with typical sweetness. When Culver City's "Wizard of Oz" float passed, Shirley said, "Look Mother, it seems like fairyland." After the parade was over, Shirley commented, "I liked everything and everybody. Riding in the parade was the greatest thing I've ever done."

Leishman remained active in Tournament affairs as chairman of the Football Committee, which conducts the Tournament's duties in administration of the Rose Bowl game and maintains all relationships with the collegiate world. He has been a dominant force in preserving harmonious relationship between the colleges and the Tournament. He also has planned and negotiated improvements in the Rose Bowl. Despite the importance of all of his many solid achievements, he looks back with special satisfaction at Shirley Temple's role during his term as president.

Harlan Loud, a lifetime associate of Leishman's in community activities, served as chairman of the Football Committee in 1939. Loud became Tournament president the next year.

"Golden Memories" was the theme of the fiftieth Tournament. When Leishman announced the theme, he said, "It was chosen because the development of Southern California, the progress of the West, the advances in science, music, art, and literature, as well as many other achievements of man, have been so closely linked with the Tournament of Roses throughout the past half-century."

On December 31 the first telecast of a special event from the Tournament of Roses took place when station W6XAO of Los Angeles, with commentator Don Lee, described the New Year's Eve preparations of the royal court.

Laguna Beach artists entered one of the most impressive floats in Tournament history—a portrayal of *The Last Supper* in an exquisite blending of natural flowers. Of the sixty-three floats in the parade, Burbank had the Sweepstakes winner. Union Oil Company stunned the audience with a float depicting Will Rogers. A riderless horse, head bowed, with a flag below, told a story of the great American who had met an untimely death in Alaska.

Last-second Heroics: USC 7, Duke 3

Maxwell Stiles was the first to tell the complete true story of how Southern California defeated Duke 7–3 before ninety-two thousand in the 1939 Rose Bowl game. It is one of the most amusing of football's many legends.

"The man who told me the inside story of the strange events that made it possible for Doyle Nave of USC to come off the bench, throw four passes to 'Antelope Al' Krueger that won the game, is Ensign Joe Wilensky of the U.S. Navy, former Trojan running guard and tackle and an assistant coach at USC in the 1938 season," wrote Stiles. But Wilensky did not dare tell the story until six years after the game.

Duke went ahead on a 23-yard field goal by Tony Ruffs at the start of the final quarter. The climax was set up when fullback Bobby Peoples took a short pass from quarterback Grenville Lansdell and put the ball on Duke's 34-yard line with less than two minutes left to play.

Braven Dyer, the popular *Times* writer, was among those who had started for the exits to get a jump on the homeward rush when the big story unfolded. Ironically, it had been Dyer who had editorially urged Coach Howard Jones to "give

The program for the 1939 Tournament

USC's chancellor Dr. Norman Topping could never forget the 1939 Rose Bowl game against Duke: "I was dying. . . . I had Rocky Mountain Spotted Fever, running a temperature of 105°. I wasn't aware of much else, but I asked for a radio to listen to the Rose Bowl . . . They said it was impossible. I insisted, demanding that they grant my last request. They brought me a radio. And then when Doyle Nave threw those passes to Al Krueger to beat Duke in the final minute . . . my temperature immediately started going down. I recovered. I also won $50 on the game."

my boy Doyle Nave a chance.'' Nave had played only twenty-eight minutes during the season, while Grenville Lansdell, Mickey Anderson and Ollie Day alternated at quarterback. Dyer had argued that Nave deserved a chance to earn a letter as long as the quarterback job was such a community project.

Jones had admitted Nave could pass, but the coach insisted that young Doyle lacked the all-around skills he demanded of his quarterback.

While Nave's champion Dyer was gaining a motor escort to get to his office to write his story, Wilensky was manning the telephone on the bench, relaying the messages of assistant coaches Sam Barry, Bob McNeish and Julie Bescos, who had been observing the action high above in the press box.

Suddenly Wilensky got an idea. He decided to take a chance to do something to pull out victory. He knew that the coaches above already had left the press box and were on their way to join the team. Nobody had scored a point all season against the great Duke line. "Our only chance is to get Nave in there to pass,'' thought Wilensky. "He has the arm to hit Krueger and dent this great Duke defense."

Wilensky snatched the phone. "Yes,''

he shouted so everybody on the bench could hear. "Yes, yes—I get it. I'll tell him right away." He slammed the receiver on the hook and excitedly nudged assistant coach Bill Hunter.

"The word is to send in Nave and have him throw to Krueger," said Wilensky to Hunter, who in turn passed it on to Jones. Nave didn't wait for Jones to respond. He leaped off the bench and rushed into the game. Jones did not stop him. Nick Pappas, also from the Navy, who helped Jones with the coaching and later became a member of the USC athletic administration staff, verifies that this is the true story of how Nave got into the game.

Duke played a "prevent" defense in which all but one man drifted back to cover the receivers. Nave was thus rushed by only one man.

"Just fade back with the ball and throw it to me when I give you the sign by waving my arms, no matter where I go," Krueger, also a substitute, said to Nave.

Nave followed instructions perfectly. He faded deep on each of his four passes to Krueger. He eluded the rusher, Duke's E.L. Bailey, and waited for Krueger to jockey the great Eric "the Red" Tipton.

The first pass gained 13 yards to put the ball on the 26 (USC had been penalized 5 yards for an extra timeout when Nave went in). When Krueger was open, the throw was like a second baseman firing to first. Another strike put the ball on the 17. The next pass lost 2 yards. On the payoff pass, Krueger shook off Tipton with a sudden stop, then raced to the corner of the end zone where he danced up and down with his arms high in the air. Nave was back on the 31 by then, but he let fly. Krueger caught it easily for a touchdown. Phil Gaspar kicked the point with a minute remaining, and a perfect Duke season was ruined.

THE 1940s

THE   ERA   OF   NEGOTIATION

Charlie flirts with Queen Margaret while Edgar Bergen listens in

The 1940 Rose queen Margaret Huntley remembered French soldiers who sent her a long letter and a photo of about forty of them holding her newspaper picture. "They asked me to be their 'Marianne.' We wrote several times back and forth. I sent each of them a small picture of their American 'sister.' . . . Then Hitler crossed the Maginot Line and I never heard from my French pals again."

1940
Charlie McCarthy

Leaders of the Tournament of Roses have never assumed that colleges *must* play in Pasadena's nationally famous game. There were days when many colleges shunned post-season football games to avoid commercialization and over-emphasis of athletics. The sixth decade of the Tournament of Roses was the time when the place of the Rose Bowl game in college football was defined.

Much of the current success of the Tournament is owed to the leadership of the Tournament leaders during the war years. Harlan Loud, the Tournament president, may have forgotten his lines when he helped crown Margaret Huntley as the 1940 Rose queen; however, he never forgot how to cooperate and negotiate with university administrative and athletic authorities. Neither did Lathrop Leishman, C. Hal Reynolds, John Biggar, Louis R. Vincenti and others in the Tournament family.

It was this "Tournament Plan" for understanding collegiate problems and collegiate people, while at the same time helping the academic community to see the festival's point of view, that

finally sealed the marriage between campus and community.

At meetings of the National Collegiate Athletic Association (NCAA), the national governing body for college athletics, and at various conference meetings of Pacific Coast schools, Pasadena people laid the groundwork for the present amicable relations. Understanding and respect grew during those days of mutual faith-building between Pasadenans Leishman, Loud, Reynolds, Vincenti, Biggar, Nicholas, Hahn, Dorn and college leaders like Hugh Willett, Wilbur Johns, Bill Hunter, Al Masters, Bill Ackerman, Vic O. Schmidt, L.W. St. John and Kenneth L. "Tug" Wilson, as well as the modern groups which include collegiate leaders like Bill Reed, Tom Hamilton, Wayne Duke, Walter Byers, J.D. Morgan, Wiles Hallock, Tom Hansen and Jess Hill, as well as many others.

The theme of the 1940 Tournament, "The Twentieth Century in Flowers," connoted peace, progress and love of nature. However, by New Year's Day, half the world was at war—a war which was eventually to take the life of one of the stars of that year's Rose Bowl game.

Outside our nation, the world was thinking about anything but peace, progress and love of nature, but Pasadena remained serene and its parade emphasized such upbeat themes as Boulder Dam; progress in transportation and in the air; art and literature as represented by the Huntington Library; and astronomy, represented by the Mt. Wilson Observatory. Santa Barbara's float won the Sweepstakes with a scene in flowers of three modern racing sloops rounding a weather marker.

Charlie McCarthy was in his heyday as a headliner of the airwaves, so Loud invited Edgar Bergen and his famed dummy to serve as grand marshals. Charlie snapped back many a "Hi" to his thousands of admirers along the parade route; he never had a bigger smile. Charlie was so tired when the day was over, Bergen reported, that he was placed in a trunk and didn't move for days.

Malicious, one of the most popular horses ever to run at nearby Santa Anita race track, walked the length of the parade with special shoes protecting his tender racing hoofs.

All Good Things Must Come to an End: USC 14, Tennessee 0

The 212 points that Tennessee scored during the 1939 season may not seem exceptional for a ten-game season; when put up against the *zero* points scored by opponents, however, 212 points look very impressive indeed. Then, when you note that Tennessee had won twenty-one

Harlan Loud

straight games, back to the end of the 1937 season—a streak in which they outscored opponents 520–20—the story gets better. Add one more impressive statistic: the ten straight games they were to win during the 1940 regular season (in which they piled up a 319–26 scoring advantage), and you have the makings of another true "wonder team."

It is easy to see, then, why Tennessee might have been a bit upset about being skunked, 14–0, by USC in the 1940 Rose Bowl.

Tennessee, with its sensational record, was an obvious eastern representative in the 1940 game. On the western side, USC and UCLA were also undefeated, and they played to a scoreless tie in their final game with each other. USC won the vote of the Pacific Conference, which by then had contracted with the Tournament to have one of its teams ap-

Float animation, 1940s style

GAY'S LION FARM
EL MONTE

Biff Jones

pear annually in the Rose Bowl.

USC's triumph over Tennessee was Howard Jones's fifth victory in the Rose Bowl—and his last. Before he could produce another great team, he passed on.

"With his passing, there ended an era of football in the West," wrote Maxwell Stiles. "No man ever brought so much gridiron glory to the southern section of California. No man ever gave more of himself to the game he loved. To him, football was the first bright rays of dawn, the noonday sky, and the stars that shine by night."

Major Bob Neyland's Tennessee team brought to Pasadena proven greats—All-American guards El Molinsky and Bob Suffridge, All-American quarterback George Cafego and All-American halfback Bobby Foxx.

Jones's squad more than matched Tennessee, with guards Harry Smith and Ben Sohn, who outplayed the Tennessee pair; tailback Granny Lansdell and Ambrose Schindler, who outplayed the injured Cafego; blocking backs Joe Shell and Bob Hoffman, who outplayed Foxx; best ends of the day Bill Fisk and Bob

President J.W. McCall, Queen Sally Stanton and 1941 grand marshal, Mayor E.O. Nay

Winslow, top tackles Stoecker and Gaspar and center Ed Dempsey.

By playing almost perfect football, the Trojans scored the first points Tennessee had yielded in more than a year and ended a Volunteer winning streak that went back to 1937. Major Neyland told Bob Hunter of the *Examiner*, "We were badly beaten by a superior team."

UPI's whimsical Henry McLemore summed up Tennessee's plight:

"They raise them rugged out here. Perhaps nature sees that they do so in order that they will be able to withstand earthquakes, unusual weather and the taste of the water that comes out of the taps. There is a lesson to be learned from this Rose Bowl game. There is no sense in betting on a team that buys its clothes in the boys' department to beat a team that has to shave twice a day and is fitted for suits in the grown-up section."

Ned Cronin of the *News* wrote that Schindler ran with his knees clear up around his chin. Dick Hyland of the *Times* called the Vol line a sieve. Shell's blocking for USC drew heavy praise. On that day the Trojans did no wrong.

After getting to the 22 of Tennessee early, only to be denied when Lansdell slipped on fourth down, Schindler started ripping and carrying tacklers in a manner that brought him the tag of "Desperate Amby." Schindler bowled over Suffridge for the touchdown and Jimmy Jones—who was later killed in the war—kicked the point for the Trojans, to make the score 7–0 in favor of USC.

Tennessee rallied in the fourth quarter, but Sam Bartholomew fumbled on USC's 15, where Roy Engle recovered for the Trojans. Engle caught a key pass, and Schindler passed to Al Krueger for the second and final touchdown to send Tennessee home a loser for once.

1941
Chrysanthemums and "T"

As the Second World War grew uglier, the Tournament's "America in Flowers" theme allowed the nation to express its patriotism in float designs in the parade headed by Tournament president J.W. McCall Jr., with Pasadena Mayor E.O. Nay serving as grand marshal.

Just eleven months before Japan attacked Pearl Harbor, the Central Japan Association's entry of "Cherry Blossom Time in Washington" proved a popular parade feature and won the Theme prize. The Japanese float depicted the U.S. Capitol with thousands of white chrysanthemums and a flag of red and white carnations. Five young American women of Japanese ancestry rode the float under a grove of cherry trees.

A New Style of Football:
Stanford 21, Nebraska 13

The year 1941 will go down in history as the year that Clark Shaughnessy of Stanford "sold" the T-formation to the football followers of the country during the stunning 21–13 victory his Stanford magicians scored over Nebraska.

Shaughnessy, before his death in 1970, rated his backfield of quarterback Frankie Albert, halfbacks Pete Kmetovic and Hugh Gallarneau, and fullback Norm Standlee one of the greatest of all time. He also rated the 1941 Rose Bowl clash as among the greatest games.

Biff Jones's Nebraska team came in with an 8–1 record, but Stanford's 9–0 team served up too much "T." The skillful execution of Shaughnessy's T-formation combination of pitchouts sold this type of football to the college world.

Nebraska jumped ahead, 7–0, when fullback Vike Francis galloped through like a wild horse. While Stanford con-

centrated on stopping the reverses of Butch Luther, the Husker running star in previous games, Jones took advantage with the Francis spinner play that featured a fake to Luther and a Francis shot into the line.

Stanford revised its defense and quickly struck with a touchdown gained through a combination of T-formation tricks that stunned the crowd. Gallarneau scored and Albert kicked the point.

A Nebraska quick kick was lost by Kmetovic in the sun. He touched the ball and it was recovered by a substitute Nebraska halfback named Allen Zikmund on Stanford's 33. Herman Rohrig passed over Gallarneau's head to Zikmund for the touchdown, although Stanford center Lindskog blocked the extra point to leave the score 13–7, Nebraska.

The passing and running of Albert, the speed of Kmetovic and finally a pass from Albert to Gallarneau, who eluded Zikmund and Rohrig, eventually produced a Stanford touchdown. Albert's

What do float drivers do to occupy their minds while creeping along in the parade? While young Chuck Rubsamen drove his float in 1941, he gazed through a tiny peephole at Queen Sally Stanton on the float ahead. After the parade, he wasted no time in getting acquainted. They had their first date fourteen days later and eventually married.

Stanford's pioneering T-formation team

Nebraska's Vike Francis

Band leader Kay Kyser was grand marshal of the 1942 parade that never was. His memories of the aborted event understandably were less than vivid. "I stand out from all other grand marshals because I never got to lead the parade," he wrote in 1969. "That's my story. There is nothing more to tell." Dolores Brubach, the queen without a parade that year, had the satisfaction of riding aboard a float in 1956.

successful placement put Stanford ahead for good, 14–13.

There was only one touchdown in the entire second half, but that single score was the coup de grâce and the greatest single play of the game. Nebraska had made a magnificent goal-line stand in the third quarter and had taken the ball on downs on the 2-inch line.

"Hippity" Hopp, standing deep in the end zone, punted. The ball was caught by Kmetovic on the Nebraska 39 near the side line. Kmetovic took four or five steps to his left and, just as he succeeded in drawing most of the Husker team over after him, turned and cut sharply back to his right. He began to pick up blockers. Dick Palmer cut down George Knight and Francis. Francis was hit so hard he did a pinwheel somersault high into the air and was knocked cold when his head hit the turf. Chuck Taylor, later athletic director at Stanford, put a block on one of the last Huskers remaining on his feet. Kmetovic, meanwhile, swivel-hipped his way behind the crushing blocking and finally beat Luther, who made a futile dive as he zipped into the end zone. Shaughnessy called the team's total punt return effort the greatest he had ever seen.

1942
Parade Cancelled: Game Moved
On December 7, 1941, Japan bombed Pearl Harbor. The next day the United States was at war. In the interest of public security, as the West Coast braced for possible Japanese attacks, the Rose Parade was cancelled. It would be four years before the Tournament of Roses was back to normal. Lee Merriman, a Pasadena newspaper editor, suggested that the country create a parade in bonds instead of flowers.

It was a cold, lonely and sad day in Pasadena that January 1. Dolores Brubach, the 1942 Tournament queen, formed a "Victory Court" in which Helen Creahan was princess of the armed services; Patricia Lee, princess of agriculture for defense; Clare Blackwell, princess of health and welfare; Doris Burns, princess of defense stamps and bonds; Patricia Wiseman, princess of industry for defense and Barbara Forbush; princess of civilian defense.

Brubach and her court drove quietly down Colorado Boulevard unnoticed by the few pedestrians on the deserted street. Sixteen members of the Tournament of Roses band gathered at a war memorial flagpole where Orange Grove and Colorado intersect. Led by Jack

Radio personality Kay Kyser

McLeod, they formed a "V for Victory" and marched down Colorado Boulevard playing military songs and singing "Stout-Hearted Men." In the dining room of the Huntington Hotel that afternoon, Queen Dolores and her court were guests of honor at a display of thirty-three miniatures of the floats that were intended for the parade before Pearl Harbor. She also spent a few moments in an otherwise empty Rose Bowl with Don Wilson and numerous sportscasters broadcasting on a coast-to-coast hookup at half time in which they all ended up singing "Auld Lang Syne."

The next day, Japan occupied Manila, forcing the American army to withdraw to Bataan in what became one of the worst American setbacks in the war.

In contrast to the royal court, Tournament president Robert M. McCurdy had waited several years to ride down Colorado Boulevard. He still was able to look back upon his tenure with satisfaction: "I installed the first electric scoreboard in the Rose Bowl. Otherwise, my big satisfaction remains in the fact that I am one of the lifetime directors of our fine organization."

It appeared that the Tournament's 1942 football game between Oregon State and Duke was doomed along with the parade, but then one of the most cooperative ventures in the history of any festival took place and the game was switched to the Duke campus in Durham, North Carolina. While the United States government "blacked out" the West Coast for security reasons, it was generally believed that continuing the Rose Bowl would boost public morale.

Bill Login, who published the *Tournament of Roses Pictorial* for forty-three years, recalled how the gamesite was transferred to Duke. "President

Duke Stadium, site of the 1942 "Rose Bowl" game

Lon Stiner

McCurdy had called a meeting at the then Vista del Arroyo Hotel when the Oregon State–Duke matchup was made," he told Margaret Stovall of the *Pasadena Star-News*. "We were checking the lineup for the game when the Army's West Coast headquarters announced on the radio there would be no Rose Bowl game while this war was on.

"Hal Reynolds, who was at the meeting, called the general in San Francisco, and then Percy Lacey, the Oregon State manager, got on the phone. They wanted to know if they couldn't have the game for just five thousand people. The general said no. They wanted to know if they could have it just for the press. The general said no—no game; period.

"The meeting broke up with a decision to send a delegation to San Francisco. When they came back with no satisfaction, McCurdy suggested they have the game at Duke. We had eighty thousand tickets that had to be cut up and burned to keep them from scalpers. Meanwhile, they decided we could use the programs, of which we had about one-third printed. My aide Tommy Kyser and I lived at the shop for three days fin-

President Robert H. McCurdy, who electrified Rose Bowl scoring

Since the Tournament started selecting grand marshals from outside the organization, only three people have been grand marshal twice: Earl Warren, in 1943, when he was California's governor, and 1955, when he was chief justice of the U.S. Supreme Court; Richard Nixon, in 1953 and 1960; and Bob Hope, in 1947 and 1969.

ishing the programs and cutting up the tickets. Union Pacific helped us get the programs across the country. We got them to the stadium just before the gate opened.''

In slightly more than two weeks, Duke authorities increased the seating capacity of their stadium from thirty-five thousand to fifty-six thousand.

Bob Hunter, a *Los Angeles Herald-Examiner* sports writer who had been on an eastern football assignment for his newspaper, served as Pasadena's unofficial representative in Durham for two weeks before the transplanted Rose Bowl game. ''My paper told me to rush to Durham,'' said Hunter. ''I attended luncheons and civic affairs, and found myself in the position of a Pasadena ambassador. They even had me at the depot with the official welcoming committee when the real Tournament of Roses representatives arrived in Durham.''

No Home-Field Advantage Here: Oregon State 20, Duke 16

Oregon State won the game 20–16, the winning touchdown coming when Bob Dethman threw a 40-yard pass to Gene Gray who caught the ball on Duke's 28 and eluded Duke's Moffat Storer to dance over the goal line. It didn't matter that Oregon State star Don Durdan later was tackled for a safety. Durdan gained only 54 yards compared to 129 for Duke's Steve Lach, but he held the crowd spellbound with his left-handed passing and left-footed punting. Duke fans mobbed Durdan after the game and it took him half an hour just to get to the dressing room. He averaged 44.4 yards on eight kicks, Lach a 47.1-yard average for the same, both outstanding records, particularly in the rain.

1943
War Bonds Time

Although the wartime blackout of parade activities continued, the Tournament continued to elect officers and maintain its organizational format. James K. Ingham was the 1943 president, California's Governor Earl Warren was named grand marshal, and Mildred Miller was made the queen.

While the parade was banned, the game was permitted in the Rose Bowl in order to focus national attention on war bonds, which communities sold while competing for prizes. A total of $65,887,857 was raised, with Honolulu winning the competition by selling $4,350,000 worth of bonds.

In It to Win: Georgia 9, UCLA 0

The theme of the restricted festival was ''We're in It to Win''—and this was precisely the attitude that the University of

Georgia players brought with them to Pasadena. Maxwell Stiles recalled the story of three special Georgia players who got back together two-and-a-half years after the game, in August,1945:

"The three men were 'Fireball' Frankie Sinkwich, Charley Trippi and George Poschner. On New Year's Day, 1943, these three men, with considerable help from Van and Lamarr Davis, right end and right halfback, respectively, and from Willard 'Red' Boyd, a sub tackle who blocked a punt for a safety, contributed the most to Georgia's 9–0 victory over UCLA in the first Pasadena game won by a southern team in eight years. Georgia, coached by Wallace Butts, had a 10–1 record compared to the 7–3 mark of Edwin 'Babe' Horrell's UCLA team.

"Sinkwich, in and out of the game six times while nursing two sprained ankles, scored the game's only touchdown. Trippi, the sensational sophomore, was a bright Rose Bowl star. Poschner, at left end, had been a power offensively and defensively.

"On this humid night of August 30, 1945, the three 'met' again. The scene was a bed at the Lawson General Hospital in Atlanta. One young man smiled as he listened to a radio broadcast of a game being played at Soldier Field in Chicago, Green Bay vs. the College All-Stars. It was a game in which Sgt. Charley Trippi played so well that 200 of the 206 newspapermen voted for him as the outstanding player of the all-star squad. It was a game when Pvt. Frankie Sinkwich received from Commissioner Elmer Layden the most valuable player trophy of the National Football League for 1944.

"As he listened, the young man on the bed fumbled for a medal that had been lying on a little table beside his radio.

Attached to the medal was a ribbon with a broad blue band down its middle, edged on either side by a pin-stripe of white and a slightly wider one of red.

"This was the Distinguished Service Cross, the nation's second highest military decoration. It, too, was a newly won trophy. It had been presented on this day by Brig. Gen. William Sheep, commander of the hospital, to the man on the bed. It was presented for gallantry in action in the Battle of the Bulge. There at Kohlhutte, France, on January 8, 1945, at the end of a one-man charge, Lt. George W. Poschner lay unattended on a frozen battlefield for two days.

"Now he was in the hospital with both legs and part of his right hand gone, but with memories that were rich. With a grim grin of irony, he recalled by himself how two sprained and swollen ankles had kept Fireball Frankie Sinkwich from tearing the UCLA line apart but did not prevent him from completing three passes or from scoring the game's only touchdown. He recalled how it was the Sinkwich ankle injuries that had given Trippi the chance to make his mark.

"The young man on the bed resolved that what Sinkwich did that New Year's Day on two bad ankles, he George Poschner, would do in the future on those mechanical legs the docs had promised soon would be his."

James K. Ingham

Georgia's Frankie Sinkwich

1944
West vs. West

The 1944 "parade" was a token affair—three decorated autos, one carrying Tournament president Frank M. Brooks, one carrying Queen Naomi Riordan, and a third carrying Grand Marshal Amos Alonzo Stagg, the grand old man of American football. Even the football was scaled down in 1944.

Amos Alonzo Stagg

Frank Brooks

All in the Family:
USC 29, Washington 0

Wartime travel restrictions forced the Rose Bowl game to be an all–West Coast affair in which Jeff Cravath's 7–2 Southern California squad crushed Washington, coached by Ralph "Pest" Welch, 29–0. While USC came into the game after completing an almost normal schedule against mostly college opponents, the Huskies arrived after playing just four games against hopelessly overmatched service teams.

One of those service teams—March Field, which Washington had beaten by 20 points—had smashed USC, 35–0, late in the season. After that embarrassment, nobody believed Cravath had a chance against Welch. Cravath had, however, a young quarterback named Jim Hardy and a guard named Norm Verry. Both were "verry" good.

Against Washington in 1944, Hardy contributed part one of a remarkable two-game exhibition of passing, punting and signal-calling that stands out in all-time Rose Bowl annals. In that game, Hardy equaled the Russ Saunders record of passing for three touchdowns. Against Tennessee a year later, he was to pass for two more and score another one himself.

Verry, out for the regular season with leg injuries, dragged his injuries with him into the Rose Bowl and played what Cravath described as "the greatest defensive game of guard the Bowl ever saw." Helping Verry murder the Washington offense were Bill Gray, center, and John Ferraro, All-American tackle.

"You'll have to put that boy Norman Verry on the all-time Rose Bowl team some place, somehow," wrote Rube Samuelsen, known by many as "Mr. Rose Bowl," in the *Star-News*.

Bob Hebert in the *Los Angeles Daily News* wrote, "Jeff Cravath's magnificent coaching job was reflected in every move of the Trojans."

Cravath revealed the following inside story to George Davis, *Herald-Express*:

"The Washington coaches kept talking so much about Sam Robinson's and Al Akins's passing that I thought they were overplaying their hands to conceal the weakness that none of them was effective in that department. So, acting on this hunch, I changed our pass defense on Thursday while working out in the gymnasium from a man-to-man to a zone, and I'm certainly happy that I did."

Washington completed only five of nineteen passes and had it three intercepted.

1945
A Grateful President

The 1945 Tournament marked the fourth and last paradeless year. Tournament president Max H. Turner gave a pregame luncheon at the Huntington Hotel to honor dignitaries like former president Herbert Hoover, who was grand marshal, and Queen Mary Rutte.

It happened that Pasadena had given Hoover the biggest majority that he had received from any city in the United States in the 1932 election. He was thus able to express deep and sincere gratitude to the citizens of Pasadena.

Volunteer Nightmare Revisited:
USC 25, Tennessee 0

USC's Rose Bowl theme was "Hold a Victory So Hardy Won." Little did the selectors of that theme realize that Jim Hardy himself was again to provide the passing impetus for a 25–0 USC triumph over another powerhouse Tennessee team.

Coach Jim Barnhill's young Tennessee team came in with a 7–0–1 record com-

USC's Blake Headley bucks for extra yards against Tennessee's Wildman

USC halfback Don Burnside

pared to the 7–0–2 mark of Cravath's Trojans. Wartime-depleted rosters produced unprecedented situations during the game. At one point, for example, Tennessee had seven starting freshmen and three sophomores on the field against USC, while Cravath was using two halfbacks—Blake Headley and Ben Schlegel—who had not played a single minute of varsity football in their lives.

The game was also unusual in producing both the quickest touchdown in Rose Bowl history and the latest. The Trojans scored their first touchdown one minute and fifty seconds after the opening kickoff, when Jim Callanan scooted in with a punt blocked by John Ferraro. The Trojans scored in the last seconds of the game on a touchdown pass from Hardy to Doug MacLachlan, who had to fight off scores of youngsters already storming the field to rip down the goal posts. No other Rose Bowl receiver has ever caught a pass among so many bodies.

Hardy may also have been the only player ever to run directly to the dressing room *while* making a play. On the extra-point try, he called a running play so he could keep the football as a personal memento. Once downed, he got up and ran through the tunnel before the mob caught him.

Rube Samuelsen wrote in the *Star-News* that Hardy's quarterbacking, in the opinion of Chick Meehan, former Syracuse mentor, was on a par with the best of Sid Luckman of the Chicago Bears.

Coach Jeff Cravath confided to Al Santoro, *Examiner* sports editor: "Hardy was the greatest T-formation quarterback I have ever seen in action."

1946
Troy Finally Falls

Football is not what Californians like to remember from the 1946 Tournament—and with good reason. At the time, however, there was a much more significant development on people's minds. Throughout the nation, the important news was that the war had ended. V-J Day had been proclaimed in August 1945. President Charles A. Strutt's parade theme was "Victory, Unity and Peace." Admiral William F. Halsey was grand

1945 marked the beginning of Stella Morrill's thirty-year career as secretary to the Tournament manager. When she retired in 1975, she was honored for having contributed the most years of service to the Tournament. "Through all these years, one thing has never changed," she said. "The volunteer Tournament workers today function with the same devotion and spirit of cooperation that the volunteers had when I started."

President Herbert Hoover

USC's Ted Tannehill

Adm. William F. Halsey

marshal and Patricia Auman was queen.

With five stately "task forces" moving behind him, the admiral set the pattern for a parade which symbolized what he and other American fighting men and women had fought for and won. When asked what he thought while leading the parade, Halsey answered, "I thought about all those other New Year's Days— the tough ones—that led up to this." The admiral had declined to ride a white horse offered him, claiming his equestrian prowess had been greatly overrated.

Long Beach won the Sweepstakes float award in the parade with a floral replica of the aircraft carrier *Shangri-La*. The raising of the flag by Marines at Iwo Jima also was presented on a float.

Post-War Disaster for the West:
Alabama 34, USC 14

As Tennessee discovered in the 1940 Rose Bowl game, USC in 1946 learned that all good things must end. It suffered its first defeat in nine Rose Bowl appearances, succumbing to Frank Thomas's 9–0 Alabama team, 34–14. USC didn't merely lose: it gave up more points to Alabama in this one game than it had allowed its eight previous Rose Bowl foes *combined*.

"USC was the sorriest looking eleven that ever stumbled, fumbled, and groped its way through a game in the Rose Bowl," recalled Maxwell Stiles, who regarded Alabama's victory as less a surprise than the thoroughness with which they trounced USC, which had come into the game 7–3. Alabama's great quarterback Harry Gilmer had been expected to carry Alabama to victory on the strength of his great throwing arm, but he threw only a dozen passes and completed just four. Alabama simply tore the Trojans apart on the ground. Gilmer ran

for 116 yards himself.

Troy did have some standouts, however. Ted Tannehill was a defensive demon with six tackles in the first half and more to come. Punters Jerry Bowman and Verl Lillywhite averaged 47.8 yards on six punts, three each. Ironically, Alabama averaged only 19.8 yards on four punts. USC had only 6 yards net rushing. Its 41 yards of total offense also was an all-time low for one team.

Ned Cronin of the *Daily News* perhaps best described the trend of the game when he wrote: "The ushers were having trouble finding places in the stands, for guys wearing white jerseys and red helmets who were constantly being thrown up there by the Alabamans."

The Trojans had one undeniable distinction. They had the biggest player on the field: 320-pound linesman Jay Perrin—one of the few Trojans to play well enough to get some praise in the papers the next day.

1947
The Pact Begins

The 1921 Tournament of Roses football game between California and Ohio State provided the first stimulus for the pact between the modern Pac-10 Conference and the Big Ten. It is today the most logical, the most financially sound and the most popular agreement between two conferences that exists in the post-season collegiate gridiron world.

Big Ten interest in the Tournament of Roses football game goes back to 1920, when Howard Lucas, president of the Ohio State Alumni Association of Los Angeles responded to the clamor from Big Ten alumni clubs to put a Big Ten team in the Rose Bowl by wiring an invitation from the Tournament of Roses to L.W. St. John, Ohio State's athletic director, asking him to send his championship 1920 football team to Pasadena.

St. John secured the permission of Ohio State's President William Oxley Thompson and faculty to place the question before the Big Ten Conference. At the urging of an Ohio State faculty representative, the Big Ten permitted Ohio State to accept the Rose Bowl invitation.

After Ohio State lost that 1921 game, the Big Ten took official action against post-season games. Rose Bowl spokesmen later invited many Big Ten teams to play, but no team from the conference was permitted to return to Pasadena for twenty-six years. Big Ten faculties argued that the football season was long enough already. Nevertheless, the matter was brought up each year at Big Ten meetings. Major John L. Griffith, commissioner of the Big Ten, was a strong advocate of a rule change that would permit Big Ten participation in the Pasadena game—and the item was on the agenda when Kenneth L. "Tug" Wilson became Big Ten commissioner in 1945.

Meanwhile, as the wrangling over prospective Rose Bowl opponents increased in Pasadena, with almost everybody having his favorite nomination, the wise decision of Tournament of Roses officials to put the negotiations and administration of the Rose Bowl game into the hands of the Pacific Coast Conference and the competing schools had been made preceding the 1924 game.

Wilson recalled, "When I succeeded Griffith in 1945, I sincerely felt the question of Rose Bowl participation should be settled once and for all. The directors of the conference at that time were Doug Mills of Illinois, Zora Clevenger of Indiana, E.G. Schroeder of Iowa, Fritz Crisler of Michigan, Frank G. McCormick of Minnesota, Ted Payseur of

President William Welsh, Queen Norma Christopher and Grand Marshal Bob Hope consult before the 1947 festival

Northwestern, L.W. St. John of Ohio State, Guy J. Mackey of Purdue and Harry Stuhldreher of Wisconsin."

Wilson negotiated an agreement which assured the faculties there would be no time lost from classes, no team could go two years in a row, and each school and the conference office would receive a share of the receipts.

Wilson also recalled that the uniting of the two great conferences was not received with much enthusiasm on the West Coast, which wanted the agreement to be postponed a year so that Army, which then had one of its greatest teams, could appear in the Rose Bowl. But Illinois was selected, while the Pacific Coast named UCLA.

"As commissioner," Wilson said, "I sensed the feeling that had been created against the start of the Rose Bowl pact when I spoke briefly at the *Los Angeles Times* sports awards dinner. It was my bad luck to follow a young football player named Glenn Davis. A California boy, he was the star of the grand team from West Point that year, and he was receiving an award as the best college football

National radio shows originated at Tournament events in the 1940s. Kay Kyser described the 1947 queen-selection festivities on NBC-KFI. Bob Hope broadcast his Pepsodent Show from the Pasadena Playhouse. "This will be my first game from a 50-yard line seat," said Hope. "Last year I had a dollar ticket." "Dollar ticket? Where did you sit?" Queen Norma Christopher asked Hope. "I didn't. . . . I was eighty-sixth in line for the telescope at Griffith Observatory."

Paul Patterson scores for Illinois against UCLA in 1947

Bert LaBrucherie

Ray Eliot

UCLA's Al Hoisch returns Illinois kickoff 102 yards for an all-time record

player in the country. When he spoke, he said it had always been his hope to play in the Rose Bowl.

"I was actually booed when I was introduced as the next speaker. I told them Illinois was not a second-class team and

that the conference had worked hard on this pact with the Pacific Coast for many years. I even stuck my neck out by saying I thought Illinois would take care of that situation."

The pact leading to the game between Illinois and UCLA was not the only significant development happening in the 1947 Tournament.

The parade was telecast locally for the first time and viewed in Los Angeles on the seven-inch screens then available. Bob Hope made the first of his two appearances as grand marshal. Norma Christopher served as queen, and a "queen mother" was named for the parade. The woman selected, Maudie Prickett, paid tribute to Queen Norma and her court with the remark, "What a pleasant way to get a family of seven lovely daughters."

The Long Beach Mounted Police started a tradition in 1947's "Holiday of Flowers" parade which they have since maintained annually. They rode at the head of the procession on matched palominos, with all thirty riders carrying American flags.

Bob Roberts roller-skated the entire five miles of the parade at the head of the Los Angeles Rams band.

Grand Prize winner among the floats was Van de Kamp's "Tulip Day in Holland." The entire deck of the float was made up of more than five thousand multicolored tulips placed in rows to give the appearance of a tulip field. Each tulip was placed in an individual vase, similar to a test tube.

The Pact Is Back: Illinois 45, UCLA 14

No team ever played more inspired football in the Rose Bowl than Coach Ray Eliot's Illini. Illinois rushed for 326 yards and had twenty-three first downs on the way to trouncing UCLA, 45–14. Illinois had Claude "Buddy" Young, Julius Rykovich, Paul Patterson, Russ Steger and Perry Moss. Records, like Bruins, fell all over the place. Little Al Hoisch of UCLA was Coach Bert LaBrucherie's star. Weighing only 139 pounds, second only to Oregon's 128-pound Skeet Manerud among the mighty midgets of the Arroyo Seco, Hoisch returned an Illinois kickoff 102 yards to become the first Rose Bowl player ever to return a kickoff for a touchdown. He just missed returning another for a touchdown, needing one more block after going 51 yards. He averaged 44.5 yards for four kickoff returns.

"The boys from Westwood went too far. They should have stopped off at Forest Lawn," declared Ned Cronin in the *Daily News*.

"What running by Julius Rykovich," said Al Santoro in the *Examiner*. "Call him Orange Julius."

1948
Michigan the Great

Louis Vincenti, the man who had so much to do with negotiations between the Pacific Coast Conference and the Big Ten, was Tournament president in 1948. General Omar Bradley was grand marshal. The queen was Virginia Goodhue, who became a professional model after her reign.

The floats in the 1948 parade utilized more animated figures and puppets than ever before. Yes, the age of Walt Disney had come. San Francisco won the Sweepstakes award, now that ingenuity was vying with beauty in the big spectacle. Its float featured a cable car which, of course, personified San Francisco. The car, about three-quarters the size of an actual cable car, even turned around on a replica of the Powell Street turntable.

Pacific Coast Nightmare Revisited: Michigan 49, USC 0

The Tournament theme in 1948 was "The Golden West"—which was exactly what the Big Ten found, as it went about panning for gold in the Rose Bowl. The maize and blue of Fritz Crisler's 1948 Michigan team may well have been the greatest team ever to play in the Rose Bowl.

Led by a magnificent All-American halfback named Robert Chappuis and a whirling dervish fullback named Jack Weisenburger, Michigan swirled and twisted its giddy way down the arroyo like a midwestern cyclone and blew down the University of Southern California Trojans, 49–0.

Chappuis and Weisenburger, the latter handling the ball one way or another on almost every play, got plenty of help. The charge of Crisler's unstoppable line, the pursuit of the entire defensive platoon in gang-tackling the hapless and helpless Trojans, set standards of excellence not seen at Pasadena since that day in 1902 when Michigan beat Stanford, 49–0, in the first Tournament of Roses game played.

Dick Hyland wrote in the *Los Angeles Times* that Chappuis "looked every bit as good as Dixie Howell of Alabama did when he gave Stanford a passing lesson a dozen years ago. His receivers, all of them, were great, making almost unbelievable grabs." Chappuis and Weisenburger shared rushing honors with 91 yards each. Chappuis also had 188 by air.

Vincent X. Flaherty in the *Examiner*: "A terrible thing happened here this afternoon. They threw the Trojans to the Wolverines in full view of ninety-three

Michigan is the only team to play in two consecutive Tournament of Roses games with identical scores. And it won both games, 49–0—a score that is still a Tournament record, both for the largest margin of victory and for the most points scored by a single team. Michigan's two consecutive 49–0 wins may be another record as well, coming, as they did, forty-six years apart—in 1902 and 1948.

Gen. Omar Bradley

Louis Vincenti

Michigan stars Bob Chappuis (above) and Jack Weisenburger (below)

thousand horror-stricken onlookers. And it shall go down in history as the most macabre spectacle ever beheld since they fed the Christians to the lions rare. And by golly, it was awful!''

Ned Cronin in the *Daily News*: "University of Southern California's football club needs one of two things, and possibly both. Reading from left to right, they are: (1) a couple of barrels of plasma, and/or (2) a new matchmaker.''

1949
The Phantom Touchdown

Nobody has ever stated the spirit of the Tournament of Roses better than what California's governor Earl Warren wrote in the official program for 1949:

"Here in this day's events you will find much that reflects the spirit of California—much that embodies the will to grow and develop that has brought our state such progress in less than a hundred years. California is proud of the tradition fostered by this great annual event. Here on New Year's Day we strive to give emphasis to the American spirit of teamwork, good will and fair play with the hope that it will become dominant in our approach to all our problems during the year to come.''

"The Tournament of Roses is made possible only through the cooperation of all people of Southern California," added Tournament president Harold C. Schaffer in an official statement marking Pasadena's extension of its community hand to its neighbors in making the Tournament "as much American as the soda in our corner drug stores.''

Perry Brown, national commander of the American Legion, was the 1949 grand marshal.

The theme, "Childhood Memories,'' lent itself to many novel and beautiful

President Harold Schaffer crowns Queen Virginia Bower

floats, with Long Beach's entry "Fairy Queen" capturing the Sweepstakes. Other outstanding floats were "Circus Days," a series of small floats hitched together, depicting animal cages with floral occupants, a large giraffe and a calliope, all drawn by a floral elephant, and "The Barnyard," a typical barnyard scene with animated floral animals.

The football game that year was one of the most bitterly fought and controversial games in Rose Bowl history.

Last-second Heroics:
Northwestern 20, California 14

By dusk, the day was dying, and so was Northwestern. With the score 14–13 in favor of California, the Wildcats from Evanston had between them and resuscitation a long 88 yards on embattled ground, a short six minutes on the clock, and a fired-up California team looking to cap an undefeated season with a win in the Rose Bowl. If Northwestern was to cross those barriers, it had to do it on the ground; it clearly had no aerial attack that day.

Somehow Northwestern made those 88 yards, and did it in just three minutes and two seconds, leaving two minutes and fifty-eight seconds on the clock and a 20–14 lead posted on the scoreboard.

The 165-pound Ed Tunnicliff at right half opposite the brilliant Player of the Game, Frank Aschenbrenner, haunted California's "Pappy" Waldorf.

For Pappy, who had previously coached twelve years at Northwestern, the nightmare began on the Wildcats' 12-yard line. California had apparently recovered a Northwestern fumble there with six minutes to go. But what many believed was a fast whistle by referee Jimmy Cain of Washington nullified the recovery, leaving Northwestern with the ball. Tunnicliff didn't have the ball when he landed head first, but the whistle had been blown.

It was at this moment that Northwestern completed its only successful pass of the game, 17 yards from Aschenbrenner to Don Stonesifer, to put the ball on its own 29. Then reserve fullback Gasper Perricone raced to the 44.

When Waldorf sent Norm Presley in to replace his starting left end, Frank Van Deren, California was penalized 5 yards for having twelve men on the field. The penalty advanced the ball to the Bear 46, second down, with only a yard to go. It took Perricone three plays to make that vital first down, by inches, on the 45.

Aschenbrenner tried left end but made only 2 yards, to the 43.

And so here it came—the only direct pass the Wildcats used all afternoon.

Perry Brown

California coach Lynn "Pappy" Waldorf with halfback Jackie Jensen

Queen Virginia Bower described how she felt during the 1949 parade: "As we rode on our float down Colorado Boulevard . . . I smiled for so long (I truly felt like smiling) that when we arrived at the end of the parade route, I could not stop smiling. The muscles in my face wouldn't relax . . . a strange sensation, indeed."

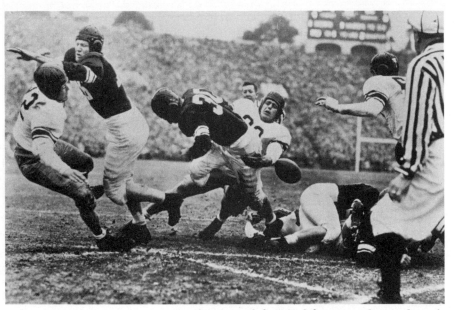

Northwestern defeats California on disputed touchdown—did Art Murakowski cross the goal line before he fumbled?

Tunnicliff received the direct pass in Coach Bob Voights's surprise strategy and started around his own right end as the California left wing Presley came charging in too fast. The Kewanee Kid needed no blockers to swing around Presley. But soon an escort picked him up as he raced down the sideline 43 yards to the winning touchdown.

Northwestern's first two scores had come on a brilliant 73-yard run by Aschenbrenner and fullback Art Murakowski's 1-yard plunge—the legality of which has never been established to anyone's satisfaction.

On his touchdown play, Murakowski fumbled the ball—every photograph taken of the play shows the ball falling off his left hip while both his feet are still on the field of play. Referee Cain raised his arms to signal a touchdown after field judge Jay Berwanger (Chicago's all-time great) had signaled to him that Murakowski had poked the nose of the ball beyond the goal line before the fumble. This decision is disputed by every photographic evidence there is, but camera angles are deceiving and Waldorf said if it was a score in the eyes of Berwanger that was good enough for him. The only thing certain about this play is that when Murakowski himself crossed the goal line, the ball was falling to the ground like a hot pumpkin. It is also certain that Jim Farrar missed the extra point, so Northwestern's lead was only 13–7.

There was even an argument over who recovered the ball in the end zone after Murakowski's fumble. Both Will Lotter of California and George Maddock of Northwestern claimed to have done so.

Jackie Jensen, who was destined for major league baseball fame, earlier ran 67 yards for a touchdown.

TOURNAMENT OF ROSES
Pasadena, California
New Year's Day
1935
THE STAR-NEWS
THE POST

GOLDEN LEGENDS

THE PARADE

The Equestrians

The horse has always been a major Tournament parade attraction—first pulling the original floral buggies and later appearing in the equestrian sections of the parade displaying trappings and costumes worth thousands of dollars.

Approximately 225 equestrians are invited to appear in every parade. All must pay their own expenses. Through the years, most famous movie cowboys have marched: Hopalong Cassidy (Bill Boyd), Gene Autry, Roy Rogers, Montie Montana and others. Sheriff Eugene Biscailuz and Leo Carrillo are famous equestrians who also have served as grand marshals. Another early equestrian of note was M. S. Pashgian.

Among the stars, a particular parade favorite is George Putnam, the veteran Los Angeles television commentator who annually has ridden astride his famed palomino, Diamond. After working in a closed television studio, Putnam has liked riding in the parade and seeing the faces of his audience. "Few people realize the involved procedure in preparing horses for a parade as important as this one," he said. "We keep our horses in the pasture until two days before the parade. Then the horse is clipped, bathed repeatedly, the tail and mane are bleached, the horse is blanketed and kept in a stall.

"There is worry connected with riding in a parade. First, there is the fear that someone will shove a baby carriage, a go-cart or a toddler in the path of a skittish horse. The average person doesn't realize that a horse, unlike a dog, explodes under certain circumstances such as a sudden noise or movement or unfamiliar object. A horse bolts easily. Pavement is unnatural footing. We shod our horses in barium, a substance that lessens the danger of slipping or skidding on pavement."

The equestrians do not ride in the

parade for prizes. There isn't any judging. They do it because they love horses and want to show them to the world in their finest. Westerns, palominos, Morgans, Arabians, Andalusians and pintos all draw cheers. So do the giant Clydesdales along with the world's smallest horses, even donkeys and mules. The Bashkir curly registry is popular.

The roll call of prominent equestrians through the years would require several pages. The 1988 parade presented such novelties as the Galloping Gossips, a square-dancing unit led by Kelly Hannon, and the American Miniatures, just thirty-four inches tall, led by George Shutt. Rose parade participation often is a family affair—the Fettermans, the Hamblens and the Martinezes. Among the popular mounted groups have been the Al Malaikah Temple Silver Patrol and the Long Beach Police.

A rope artist performs during the parade

George Putnam

Everybody loves a marching band . . .

. . and flag twirlers, too

The Bands

The first band ever to appear in a Rose Bowl parade was the Monrovia town band in 1891. In the beginning, Rose parade bands were groups quickly organized to march on January 1.

Six specialty bands appear every year. They are the U.S. Marine Band, the Pasadena City College Band, the Big Ten Band, the Pac-10 Band, the Salvation Army Band and the Los Angeles Unified School District Band.

In addition to the specialty bands, five California high school bands are chosen each year, along with ten bands from other parts of the country. Nearly three hundred bands annually apply to be selected for the 5-1/2 mile, two-hour parade. The Tournament's band committee considers their qualifications and invites the bands considered most colorful and talented.

When viewers of the Rose parade watch all these bands march in Pasadena on New Year's Day, many of them one hundred to two hundred fifty members strong, the question arises, "Where do they get the money to travel thousands of miles for this brief appearance?"

The answer is, they earn it. They pay their own way with money raised in projects back home. A single band's expenses can be as high as $100,000.

In the 1988 parade, the Oak Grove band from Bessemer, Alabama, staged a pig raffle and sold fifteen thousand dozen doughnuts, three tons of onions and several thousand cases of soft drinks.

The band from O'Fallon, Illinois, township sold pizzas, hawked themselves in an adopt a bandsman program, and presented a craft show.

A car-wash program and solicitation of support from several Atlanta corporations made

Pasadena population: a million at parade time

possible the Lassiter Trojans' trip from Marietta, Georgia.

The Choctawhatchee marchers from Ft. Walton Beach, Florida, hired out as part-time workers throughout the area and sold Indian headdresses.

Raffles and bingo paid off for the Blackstone-Millville band from Blackstone, Massachusetts. The Toms River marching Indian band from New Jersey enlisted sponsors to pay for each hour they spent in rocking chairs in the school gym.

A car dealer contributed to the Jefferson City, Missouri, band based on every new car sold.

The Northrop band from Ft. Wayne, Indiana, held an auction of more than three hundred donated items.

Voluntary contributions financed the Pella, Iowa, Dutch band.

Two popular bands of the past in the parade were the McDonald All-American Band, made up of two high school musicians from each state selected in local competition, and the Top Hatters, a collection of union musicians originally brought in during a labor dispute who disbanded after several annual appearances. Paul Lavalle, former director of the New York City Radio City Music Hall orchestra, headed the McDonald Band.

Tournament of Roses
Pasadena, California
1927

New Year's Number
Pasadena Evening Post

Rose Tournament Weather: Not a Myth

Each year the vice president of the Tournament is given an assignment in jest. He is "chairman in charge of weather" for the coming festival.

Nine times out of ten he has performed this duty with honors. The weather, almost always, is grand on New Year's Day. It is so beautiful that thousands of visitors want to stay and live in sunny southern California.

Only nine times in the one-hundred-year history of the Tournament has rain marred the festivities: 1895, 1899, 1906, 1910, 1916, 1922, 1934, 1937 and 1955. Since the last rain, the vice president has been on a thirty-four-year "winning streak," although several times it has rained considerably prior to the big day only to clear up in time for the parade and game. Often it has been cool, downright chilly, at parade time, but seldom has the temperature caused much discomfort.

The average Pasadena temperature for January is 69.2 degrees Fahrenheit maximum and 45.3 degrees minimum with a mean of 57.3 degrees. The average rainfall for the first three months of the year is 8.86 inches.

Rotary's owls talk to parade crowds in 1988

THE 1950s

BIG TEN DOMINANCE

1950
The Pact Under Attack

The Big Ten–Pacific Coast Conference pact did not survive without difficulty. After the 1949 game, Dr. J. Louis Morrill of Minnesota, an athletic faculty representative at Ohio State before he accepted the Minnesota presidency, spoke out against the pact. He said he wanted it discontinued.

"I will vote against renewal and I will use every possible means to influence other schools to ballot against the agreement," he said. He didn't like the pressure the pact put on coach or school.

Despite opposition like this, the pact survived until the Pacific Coast Conference dissolved it in the process of dissolving itself. Then a new five-school conference, called the Athletic Association of Western Universities, was formed. The Tournament made an agreement with the AAWU to supply the western team. The Big Ten, meanwhile, left it up to its individual membership whether to accept an AAWU bid to be the eastern team each year. Ironically, Minnesota voted for the pact in 1953, voted to accept the bid for the 1961 game, and independently agreed to compete when Ohio State's faculty rejected the bid in 1962. This switch by the school that previously had opposed the pact led to a new signed agreement, which still stands.

Meanwhile, it was hardly a surprise that Long Beach won the Sweepstakes prize in the 1950 parade with a float titled "Freedom." Patriotism ruled the Tournament that year—a year whose theme was "Our American Heritage." The parade included such features as "The Story of American Flags," a presentation of the banners that had flown over the country during great moments in his-

tory. This and other displays helped earn the Freedom Award from the Freedom Foundation at Valley Forge. The award was something of which Drummond J. McCunn, the Tournament's president that year, was most proud.

A colorful float was "Show Boat," the Edison Company's two-story re-creation of a Mississippi river boat, with fifty real passengers. There was a floral waterwheel, and smoke came from the stacks. The float had to be operated with the assistance of an intercom system because the man who handled the gears and the man who steered were thirty feet apart. Between them were four other operators, two for the smoke effects and two to play the music. The paddle wheel revolved, churning up a wave of light and dark blue flowers.

Springfield, Illinois, entered a float which depicted Abraham Lincoln's birthplace and emphasized his ideals.

Under McCunn's administration a telephone system was installed along the parade route to control the movement of floats. Another innovation that year was the filming of the parade in color for showing at functions throughout the United States.

Hollywood celebrities had a particularly active part in the 1950 Tournament activities. James Stewart appeared at the queen's breakfast. Bob Hope again broadcast his network radio show from Pasadena, and Edward Arnold did the narration at the coronation of Queen Marion Brown.

Grand Marshal Paul G. Hoffman, the administrator of the Marshall Plan, recalled his experiences in Pasadena:

"I was most impressed by the vast amount of work that went into the preparation of floats for the parade. I remember in particular one float on which

Drummond McCunn

During his navy days, future U.S. president Jimmy Carter and his wife briefly lost their son Jack at the 1950 Rose Parade. "In the huge crowd, we didn't know where he had gone," Carter recalled. "Then someone said they had seen a little blond-headed kid walking in the parade. So we ran ahead and finally found him about a mile down in the parade walking right behind a group of clowns."

there were 10,000 little glass tubes for 10,000 roses. My most interesting experience was riding down the street before a million-and-a-half Americans. There was an element of excitement in it for me because several anonymous postcards had been received which stated that I would be bombed somewhere along the line of march. I rather assumed that if a serious effort was going to be made to bomb me, I wouldn't have been warned, but I couldn't fully erase from my mind the possibility.''

Time Runs out Again:
Ohio State 17, California 14

Until slightly more than two minutes before the final gun in the 1950 Rose Bowl game, some 100,936 football fans seated in the huge stadium believed that ''The Hague'' was a municipality devoted to peace located somewhere in the Netherlands. Suddenly all these people learned that *The* Hague was actually a fellow named James Hague from the town of Rocky River, Ohio, who had come equipped, not for peace, but for war—with a gridiron battlefield.

For it was this James Hague who booted a 17-yard field goal that gave Wes Fesler's Buckeyes a hard-won 17–14 victory over California before the largest crowd yet to see a Rose Bowl game.

Breaking the 14–14 deadlock, Hague decided a game in which the Ohioans had been much the superior team through most of the contest. A freak incident gave Ohio possession deep in Golden Bear territory. Freak, that is, if you will agree that it is a bit unorthodox for a right-footed kicker being forced to punt, while on the run, with his left. The play put Pappy Waldorf's team in something of a pickle, since time was beginning to run out.

With two minutes remaining on the clock and the score tied at 14–14, California forced Ohio State to punt from the California 38. Fred ''Curley'' Morrison—the game's outstanding player—booted the ball into the end zone, giving California possession on its own 20 on the ensuing touchback.

Quarterback Bob Celeri, who had previously had a punt blocked to set up an Ohio touchdown, called on fullback Pete Schabarum, who lost 5 yards. With fourth down and 15 to go, Cal kicked.

Cal's first-string center, George Stathakis, was out of the game with an injury. His replacement, George ''Ozzie'' Harris, had no experience at all in passing the ball 10 yards deep to a punter. All he'd ever done was hand it back to the quarterback in the usual T-formation.

This was the time, the place and the perfect cast for disaster. Given California's history of bad breaks in the Rose Bowl, disaster wasn't long in coming.

Harris rolled the ball back along the ground to Celeri, who had no chance to kick from where he finally retrieved the rolling, tumbling ball. Buckeyes were swarming like bees upon the hapless Celeri. All he could do was run, scampering out of the way as best he could.

At last, in desperation, Celeri applied his left foot to the ball, which promptly went out of bounds on the 13-yard line.

California stopped the Ohio charge, but the ball was close enough to enable Hague to make the rather easy field goal that cost California the game.

Years later Fesler told this story about Hague's winning field goal:

''On fourth and 2, I sent in Hague to kick the winning points. I closed my eyes, said a prayer as I waited (I never mentioned Pappy Waldorf in it either) and I stood in total nervous anticipation.

Wesley Fesler

Peggy, the first Hollywood movie using the Tournament of Roses as a theme, appeared in 1951 with Diana Lynn, Charles Coburn and Rock Hudson. The story of the tribulations of a Pasadena City College coed who was secretly wed premiered at the Pasadena Civic Auditorium.

Suddenly there was silence. I opened my eyes and here were my holder and my kicker running off the field toward me.

"Bewildered, I asked them, 'How come you didn't kick?' They replied, 'The fellows held a meeting and decided to go for it.' I sent the two men back in and said the field goal was my command. However, we were assessed a 5-yard penalty for taking too much time, so Hague had to kick from farther out.

"The announcer on the world-wide radio broadcast credited me with genius. He said, 'That brilliant Wes Fesler, under the most severe tension pressure, had the sense of mind to take an automatic penalty in order to give his kicker a more favorable angle.'"

1951
A Private's Progress

The parade of 1951 marked the first network telecast of that colorful event. It was transmitted by station KTTV of Los Angeles through microwave to KPIX, San Francisco, with Prudential the sponsor.

More than one hundred thousand or-

President Clifford Kenworthy and his wife wave to the crowd

chids were flown in from Honolulu for the "Hawaiian Holiday" float. Monterey Park won the parade Sweepstakes with an *Arabian Nights* creation. The state of North Dakota entered an unusual float, depicting a table with a potato on each plate and steam rising from hot turkey. To many spectators it must have been the perfect embodiment of that year's theme, "Joyful Living."

Significantly embodying the theme of the 1951 parade was Union Oil's float, "Joyful Living." It featured a frozen pond of real ice covering three hundred square feet on which Canadian skating champion Helen Legge performed.

General Dwight D. Eisenhower, then president of Columbia University, had been selected by President L. Clifford Kenworthy to serve as grand marshal. However, because of his sudden return to military duty, he had to cancel his Pasadena visit. On his suggestion, Robert Stewart Gray, a Marine private back from Korea, substituted for him.

Eisenhower had accepted Kenworthy's invitation to be grand marshal, and he and his wife Mamie came as far west as Denver, where they spent Christmas with Mamie's relatives. Eisenhower then telephoned Kenworthy to tell him he had been ordered back into active military service by President Truman and was leaving immediately for Paris to set up the new SHAEF organization.

Eisenhower and Kenworthy eventually decided that Ike would pick a "buck private" from the rear ranks—someone wounded in combat—to represent him and all the armed forces in Korea. Consequently, Bob Gray came to Camp Pendleton, where he was greeted by Tournament officers, Pasadena city officials and Queen Eleanor Payne. The queen and her court later visited many of the wounded in the Camp Pendleton hospital, where they left television sets and boxes of oranges.

Mary Baker, who with her late husband coordinated the first Rose Parade network telecast, had many memories of Rose Parade televising since starting in 1951. Baker was in the thick of the frenetic activity on Orange Grove and Colorado boulevards each New Year's Day.

Baker's first problem, back in 1951, was squeezing a two-and-a-half-hour parade into a one-hour telecast. She later recalled:

"Our prime advertisers in the early years were Woolworths the first four years and Quaker Oats for nine years. The director of the show has a tougher job than the director of the telecast from the football game. He can't leave out a band or a float, and coordinating everything with the time slots isn't easy. We have had many tense moments in the telecasts.

"I will never forget Jeanette MacDonald's year as a parade commentator. It must have been her first appearance as a live television commentator because she was very nervous and was having much difficulty with her contact glasses. We felt sorry for her because she was really in distress, but Gene Raymond picked up for the show beautifully.

"Of all our commentators through the years, Bess Myerson gets my vote as the most adept and most beautifully prepared for the role. She always had tremendous interest in the parade and had so much feeling for the role of bringing the story to the public. Vin Scully, the baseball broadcaster, did a marvelous job one year, too. He prepared himself so completely."

Nowadays, two-and-a-half hour Rose Parades fit even longer telecasts.

The Third Time's Not the Charm: Michigan 14, California 6

Late in the afternoon of New Year's Day, Lynn "Pappy" Waldorf, a large, friendly bear of a man who could tell you about all the victories and defeats in the Civil War, sat in the Rose Bowl catacombs trying to explain another defeat of his own on January 1, 1951.

Waldorf had just become low man on the Rose Bowl totem pole by becoming the first coach ever to lose three consecutive Pasadena contests—a feat not matched until thirty years later. The game he had just lost, by a 14–6 margin, was one that his critics believed he should have won.

Once again, California, though tied, 7–7, by Stanford, came to Pasadena undefeated and it was rather generally agreed—especially among men from the Big Ten—that Cal's opponent was not one of Michigan's better teams. It had lost games that season to Michigan State, Army and Illinois, and had been tied by Minnesota. In the game program, Les Etter, Michigan's athletic publicity director, described the team he publicized as follows: "A tale of courage, of fortitude, and the ability to rise above handicaps that would have daunted lesser men—that's the story of the 1951 Michigan Rose Bowl team."

Definitely, it was not one of Waldorf's better days. His team had left the field leading at half time, 6–0. It could have been 9–0 but for Pappy's failure to call for a field goal on fourth down on the Wolverine 4-yard line.

"If that situation doesn't call for a field goal then all I have ever learned about how to win football games is worthless," Braven Dyer wrote in the *Los Angeles Times*. "Particularly since Cal had missed the conversion. Six

Pvt. Robert S. Gray

Ben Oosterbaan

One year when Ronald Reagan was the TV commentator for the Rose Parade, somebody had neglected to arrange for his transportation to the television booth on the corner of Orange Grove and Colorado. They couldn't get a cab anywhere, so they sent an ambulance after him and it got through the traffic beautifully.

and short, Ortmann completed six of eight strikes (one perfect shot dropped).

He was flicking screens. Dufek took one on the left wing and roared for 14 big yards to Cal's 37 before he was nailed by Solari. Dufek bagged another first down and Ortmann hit Lowell Perry on the 15. Cal's line stopped Dufek at center, so Ortmann went upstairs again to hit Harry Allis on the 4. The Bears dug in and it took Dufek four plays to go over into the end zone. Allis converted and it was 7–6 with 5:37 to play.

Michigan's second touchdown was a gift. The Wolverines took over on the Cal 13. It was Dufek 3 and 6, then Dufek around end from the 1-yard line and people started tearing down the goal posts.

Dufek moved into all-time Rose Bowl contention at fullback with 113 yards in twenty-three tries. Ortmann passed for a record of fifteen for nineteen for 146 yards.

1952
Seven Years of Famine

Max Colwell, a former Pasadena newspaper reporter, became manager of the Tournament in 1952, the year that Leon Kingsley was president.

Colwell was not a big man physically, and his frame was made even smaller after he was slugged by some Manhattan ruffians while walking to his hotel on a New York business trip. He had been a vigorous, yet quietly efficient, guardian of Tournament affairs.

"We have the greatest organization in the world," Colwell, who started as a working member, declared:

"The Tournament workers are dedicated people. Political influence means nothing in this organization; capacity to work and produce does. When we send out our notices of annual dues, ninety

points in this day and age are nothing. Nine points at half could have won the game. Instead, Cal tried another line smash and lost the ball."

In the second half, California stayed in its seven-diamond defense, which was picked apart by quarterback Charles Ortmann's passes, particularly a series of screen passes, and the rugged rushing of fullback Donald Dufek.

At half time, California had led in total yards, 192–65, and in first downs, 10–2. It was Michigan, 226–52, and 15–2, in the second half of the game.

The third quarter was scoreless and there were only about twelve minutes to play when Michigan began its winning drive from its own 20. Throwing long

Seven Medal of Honor recipients share grand marshal duties in 1952 festival

per cent of the checks are back in four days. The volunteer workers are the kings in our organization. I try to remain in the background. If I have been successful, it is because I have been able to give out the idea and let them run with it. Nobody can say we sift off the community's leadership. Our leaders are the leaders in other community operations. My biggest reward is working with volunteers and seeing the eagerness of these volunteers to do a job.''

Colwell completed his term as president of the International Festivals Association in 1969, proof of the esteem in which he is held by his fellow festival managers around the world.

Max started his Tournament interest in 1922 when he was a correspondent for the *Pasadena Post* while he attended Pasadena High School. He reported float descriptions during the Christmas holidays. He got to know the Tournament people well and soon became a member.

After Colwell's years of various committee jobs in the Tournament while he was full-time city hall reporter for the

Pasadena newspapers, William Nicholas, Tournament president-to-be for the 1953 festival, said, ''Max, you would make a good manager.'' To that point, the Tournament manager had been the Chamber of Commerce executive also. Colwell was the Tournament's first full-time manager with no other duties.

Colwell told an interesting story of how the Top Hat Band became a fixture in the parade. During the WPA days, the musicians' union insisted upon a union band playing to match the amateur high school musicians in the parade. One union band was paid four times to equal four high school bands. The union band, the Top Hatters, became so popular it remained an annual feature.

In a sharp break from past tradition, Tournament president Leon Kingsley named seven different men grand marshals for the 1952 parade—all Congressional Medal of Honor winners: Maj. Carl L. Sitter, Capt. Lewis L. Millet, Lt. Stanley T. Adams, Lt. Thomas J. Hudner, Lt. Raymond Harvey, Sgt. Ernest R. Kouma and Sgt. Joseph Rodriquez. The seven war he-

Tournament manager Max Colwell recalled even bigger crises than the six straight Pacific Conference defeats at the hands of the Big Ten—like the time Dinah Shore's golden dress was scorched by exhaust from the motor in her float, and when Steve Allen got lost trying to get to the parade starting point. He said Roy Riegels's wrong way run also was costly because the Tournament had a clipping service to see how it was doing in publicity. After Riegels's run, the mailman brought in so many newspaper clippings, it almost went broke paying for them.

roes were cheered wildly by the spectators viewing the parade.

Queen Nancy Thorne reigned over the parade, two of whose floats carried twenty thousand roses each. The theme, "Dreams of the Future," gave an opportunity to the Southern California Floral Association to capture the Sweepstakes prize with "Every Girl's Dream Comes True." There were rare fresh blooms depicting a Japanese garden on which floral butterflies alighted. It was a particularly calm and friendly parade, but all was not so serene on the football field.

Max Colwell

The Carnage Continues:
Illinois 40, Stanford 7

The 1952 game is known for the convincing manner in which Illinois dished out a 40–7 whipping to Stanford in the Big Ten's sixth straight triumph over the West. It also was the occasion for the first nationwide telecast of the Rose Bowl, with Mel Allen doing the play-by-play.

Stanford, 9–1 in the regular season, led 7–6 at half time over Illinois, 8–0–1. In the second half the Illini opened with a 76-yard touchdown drive in six running plays by Pete Bachorous and Don Tate, including a 41-yard blast by Tate to the 5, from which Bachorous scored. Don Sanders blocked Sam Rebecca's extra-point try. Gary Kerkorian's passing sparked a retaliatory score by Stanford that put the Indians ahead. Kerkorian connected to Pasadena's own Harry Hugasian, Bill McColl and Ron Cook before Hugasian scored from the 4. Kerkorian's extra point gave Stanford its lead.

Then came the Stanford collapse that jolted the West and exasperated the Indians' Coach Chuck Taylor.

"A defensive halfback, a kid who seldom gets his name in the papers, lit the fire at a time when Stanford was heading for another touchdown in the third quarter and, in all probability, a lead which the Illini would not have overcome," wrote Braven Dyer in the *Times*. The young man Dyer pointed to was Stan Wallace, sophomore, who intercepted a pass from Kerkorian aimed from midfield at Bill Storum, Stanford end. Wallace raced back to Stanford's 12-yard line. Soon Tate took a pitchout and scored. Stanford wilted badly after that; Illinois crossed the goal line virtually every time it got the ball. Tate scored again, and touchdowns were added by John Karras, Don Stevens and John Ryan. Illinois gained 371 yards running and 73 passing in burying Stanford. Tate himself gained 150 yards in twenty carries.

Stanford's Sam Morley said, "Illinois kept grabbing our shirts. They did some slugging and they used their elbows in the clinches. But they did it all very cleverly and got away with it."

Mel Durslag reported in the *Los Angeles Examiner* how Illinois turned the tide with a switch in strategy at intermission. Illinois coach Ray Eliot told Durslag, "We changed our pass defense. We had to cover their hook passes near the side lines. So we moved our line-backers out and back about 2 yards. Of course, it helped that they lost Kerkorian in the third quarter."

With the Big Ten–West Coast Rose Bowl pact having one more year to run, West Coast sports writers started to clamor for an end to the carnage. Bill Leiser of the *San Francisco Chronicle* urged patience. "You don't call a halt because you lose six in a row," he wrote. "You just go out and try to win the next one."

L. H. Gregory, *Portland Oregonian,* added, "The only hope for the future is that, having fulfilled the Biblical prophecy of a seven-year famine, the Pacific Coast should have seven good years to come.''

Al Santoro of the *Examiner* was less lenient. He said, ''The Pacific Coast Conference men, who made the pact with the Big Ten, like the men who built the race tracks, certainly did not do it for our benefit. After six defeats in a row, it appears the West is a sucker who has not yet learned the old frontier adage, 'Never play a man at his own game.'''

1953
Nixon Remembers

''Rose Bowl games are kind of special to us. Pat and I had our first date at the Duke-USC game in 1939,'' said Richard Nixon, newly elected vice president of the United States, when he accepted Tournament president William Nicholas's invitation to be grand marshal of the 1953 festival.

Nixon, who was raised in nearby Whittier, added, ''I saw my first parade as a kid nine years old. We came real early that morning and sat along the curb.''

Originally, Nicholas had invited President-elect Dwight Eisenhower to be grand marshal.

''Actually, knowing that my term was coming in an election year, I decided to contact the heads of both the Democrat and Republican parties asking them to deliver as grand marshal the president-elect. I had a firm agreement from both parties,'' recalled Nicholas. ''When Mr. Eisenhower was elected president, he agreed to fulfill the commitment. However, in late November he phoned me to say that he hadn't realized how much work was involved in getting ready to set up legislation and get ready for the new Congress which was meeting in early January. He suggested Vice President

Nixon come in his place.''

Even the vice president was not easy to get. Nicholas had to route Nixon's invitation to Mexico City, where Nixon was making a ceremonial appearance as the representative of the United States.

Nicholas's tribute to the Tournament of Roses, after years of committee work, the Tournament presidency and later a Football Committee post, sums up the feelings of many men who have devoted their time and energy to making the Pasadena festival worthy of the respect it holds around the world. Nicholas expressed it this way:

''Ringling Brothers does not have the greatest show on earth. The Tournament of Roses has to be the greatest show of them all. I don't think there has been any president in the history of the Tournament who ever went into the organization and its various chairs with any thought of personal gain. It is the most remarkable organization when so many people on a volunteer basis will perform so many duties—the dollar value of this talent is so much more than any organization could afford to buy. There is satisfaction in knowing that each year of the Tournament is greater than the previous year.''

Mr. and Mrs. Nicholas were guests of the Mexican government in Mexico City, along with Tournament queen Leah Feland and her court. ''Dean of Women Calkins of Muir High School was busy handling the seven lovely girls, who were being swept off their feet by the Latin lovers,'' said Nicholas.

''Melody in Flowers'' was the theme for the 1953 parade. The Anheuser-Busch Clydesdale horses, a popular feature each year thereafter, drew the St. Louis float which was entitled ''Waiting for Robert E. Lee.'' Glendale won the

Vice President Richard Nixon

William H. Nicholas

Sweepstakes award. San Gabriel presented a float which needed a mermaid—a job which attracted 163 applicants.

The "Song of India" float, a neighborhood entry, carried $10,000 worth of electronic equipment to operate the organ played by organist Korla Pandid, wearing an Indian turban.

A Drought Ends:
USC 7, Wisconsin 0

The 101,500 spectators at the football game between USC and Wisconsin received an extra thrill in addition to the ending of the West's losing streak, which had reached six straight games.

USC defeated Wisconsin, 7–0, on substitute quarterback Rudy Bukich's 22-yard touchdown pass to Al "Hoagy" Carmichael in the third quarter. Bukich had taken the place of USC's All-American Jimmy Sears, whose leg was broken on the ninth play of the game. Sam Tsagalakis kicked the extra point. "I guess we should have passed more," said Jess Hill, USC coach, after the victory.

A fullback on the USC team that defeated Pitt in the 1930 Rose Bowl, Hill became the first man both to play on and coach winning Rose Bowl teams. He also was the athletic director during several later USC Rose Bowl triumphs.

Wisconsin put a great deal of pressure on USC after Alan Ameche, the bruising Badger fullback who gained 133 yards in twenty-eight carries, ran around end for 54 yards in the third quarter. He was caught by Frank Clayton, who was described by the *Mirror*'s Sid Ziff as an "unknown hero."

Marv Goux, who became a USC assistant coach, was one of the stars of USC's victory over Wisconsin, according to Dick Hyland in the *Times*. Goux, a linebacker, and his teammates like Charlie

Ane and George Timberlake were the key men in stopping Wisconsin, whose game featured the running of Ameche and the passing of Jim Haluska.

Trojan guard Elmer Willhoite chose New Year's Day for his wedding to Mary McCallag of Pasadena. Ironically, he was put out of the game by referee Jack Sprenger for using his fist on defense. "The official said I was using my fist but I wasn't," explained Elmer. "I was using my shoulder."

1954
Biggie Finishes Big

The president of the Tournament in 1954 was Harry W. Hurry. He selected for his grand marshal General William F. Dean, a hero of the war that had just ended in Korea. Barbara Schmidt was that year's queen.

The theme of the parade was "Famous Books in Flowers," and Long Beach won the Sweepstakes with a float on which rode Miss France handing Miss America a deed to the Statue of Liberty. Myrna Lanson was Miss America and Christine Martel Miss France.

That year the good feelings from the festival seemed to carry over onto the football field, where a hard-fought game was brought to a mutually satisfying resolution.

Best of Enemies:
Michigan State 28, UCLA 20

Biggie Munn, coach at Michigan State, later to become athletic director, had built up Spartan football from relative obscurity. His seven teams from 1947 through 1953 won fifty-three games, lost nine and tied two. He brought a team with an 8–1 record to the Rose Bowl in 1954, an opportunity that arose when the Big Ten renewed the pact with the

Jess Hill

During the 1953 Rose Bowl game, Richard Nixon got so excited, according to Tournament president William Nicholas, who sat next to the vice president, "He started bopping the people in front of him with his program. He really enjoyed the game. Afterward, he visited both dressing rooms before we returned to the Huntington Hotel."

Pacific Coast Conference for three more years, thanks to the deciding vote by Minnesota, Munn's alma mater.

"You never tried to steal our players in our recruiting territory," Bernie Bierman once told Munn. Until his death in 1974, Munn was grateful to Minnesota for making his Rose Bowl trip possible.

Munn used the strategy of chalking an "Off the Floor in '54" message on the cement of the dressing room to inspire his Spartans between halves. It seems to have worked. After falling behind, 14–7, in the first half, the Spartans scored two touchdowns in the third quarter and another in the fourth in what the *Mirror's* Sid Ziff called "the greatest second-half explosion in Rose Bowl history." They went on to defeat Henry "Red" Sanders's UCLA Bruins, 28–20.

Max Stiles in the *Mirror* praised Munn and Sanders for playing the game under "the most cordial relations." According to Stiles, "No two coaches ever did more, never went further out of their way to make friends than did Red and Biggie. They were constantly going overboard doing things for everybody. Nor did they glare coldly at one another, as rival mentors so often do. At the Pasadena Kickoff Luncheon yesterday they sat side by side, had their arms around one another much of the time, and patted each other on the back. There were no sour grapes of any kind, no beefs or bellows after the game."

Sanders himself burst into the Michigan State dressing room and said to Munn, "Congratulations, Biggie. This was one of the cleanest and finest games I ever saw a team play. I still think we had a great team. You were just greater."

Ziff's story in the *Mirror* excellently summarized what happened:

"A Bruin lineman missed his block in the second quarter, and Ellis Duckett, Spartan left end, slashed through to hit the football as it was leaving the foot of Paul Cameron. Duckett scooped up the bouncing ball and carried it 6 yards into the end zone. The Bruins had led, 14–0, at the time on a 12-yard pass from Cameron to Bill Stits and a plunge by Cameron plus two conversions by John Hermann.

"Michigan State went ahead, 21–14, on touchdowns by the great LeRoy Bolden and equally great Bill Wells plus conversions by Evan Slonac in the third period. UCLA cut it to 21–20 early in the last quarter when Rommie Loudd took a 28-yard scoring pass from Cameron, although Hermann's conversion failed.

"Cameron punted the ball low and on the line to Wells in the fourth period. The kick was made to order for Wells. Cameron had kicked away from the mass of players on the right side. Wells had a running start down a clear alley along the west sidelines. He didn't stop running until he had reached the end zone 62 yards away. That made it 28–20 with the conversion.

"UCLA went into the game with a record of seven blocked punts against opponents. UCLA hadn't had a punt blocked. Yet, in the final analysis, it was the punting game that beat UCLA in the Rose Bowl."

Biggie Munn

1955
Justice Is Served

Elmer Wilson, a Pasadena music promoter, held a most unusual distinction. He personally had witnessed every Rose Bowl game played since 1916. In 1955, when he was Tournament president, enough rain fell throughout New Year's Day to challenge anyone's dedication. One reporter called the muddy condi-

Red Sanders

When Walter O'Malley, who had moved his Dodgers from Brooklyn to Los Angeles in 1957, saw the Tournament of Roses game, he said, "The Rose Bowl looks like a good place for my club." However, subsequent negotiations led to the Dodgers' remaining in the Los Angeles Coliseum until O'Malley built his own stadium in Chavez Ravine.

tions in the Rose Bowl the worst-ever in the history of the game.

A *Miami Herald* reporter covering the Orange Bowl festivities before watching the Rose Parade wrote:

"We had no fog, no smog, no predawn frost, and no long underwear here in Miami to hide the loveliness of the parade beauties. In Pasadena, the parade and game spectators shivered in the rain and near-freezing temperature, while spectators huddled around fires, young women on floats compared colors of their long underwear, a far cry from the beauty that was Miami's."

Tournament manager Max Colwell, always good for a quick retort, replied, "Okay, bud, we did have some rain on New Year's Day. But you are wrong about the long red flannels. Our young women just *wished* they had some."

The weather didn't deter Elmer Wilson. Years later he told an interesting story of his experiences in the rain:

"My grand marshal, Chief Justice Earl Warren, and I got soaked riding down the parade route. A luncheon annually is held for the president and grand marshal at Brookside Park near the Rose Bowl. En

Grand marshals Roy Rogers and Dale Evans, Elmer Wilson and Chief Justice Earl Warren

route to that affair, we thought we would stop off at the home of C. Lewis Edwards, one of our Tournament executives. Lewis had a warm fire and a bracer for us, and it was so comfortable there that we remained longer than we anticipated.

"The Secret Service people, here to protect the Chief Justice, had received some false reports that efforts would be made against Warren's life during the parade, so all concerned with his safety were alarmed when he could not be located. Somehow nobody knew that we had gone to Edwards's home. When we showed up a bit late at Brookside for the luncheon, a search of the town already was in full force. Warren turned out to be quite a football fan. We sat through the entire game in the rain, and he loved every minute of it."

Warren himself, who had long been an avid fan of the Tournament, said:

"I have attended thirty consecutive Tournaments over a period of years and perhaps ten others somewhere along the line prior to that time. The Tournament is a great public enterprise carried out with much dignity. For me it is always a happy occasion, particularly when the team from the West wins."

Rain was one of many unexpected things that went wrong that day. Wilson and Warren, for example, were not the only ones to get lost. The West Point band got so confused during the parade that it did not finish the route.

When the Monterey Park float lost a wheel in the formation area, a parade committeeman climbed the fence of an auto-wrecking lot and returned with a wheel, which was put on the float.

Tournament Manager Colwell had to solve a sudden crisis when the Shah of Iran, a guest of the Tournament, arrived with fourteen extra people in his party and accommodations at the parade and game had to be obtained.

Automobiles parked at the 1955 game did some $20,000 damage to the Brookside Golf Course adjacent to the bowl.

Despite the poor weather, the crowd was over a million along the parade route, and newspaper headlines described the spectacle presided over by Queen Marilyn Smuin, as "glittering." The theme was "Familiar Sayings in Flowers." Again Long Beach won the Sweepstakes with a float entitled "A Thing of Beauty Is a Joy Forever."

Woody Comes to Town: Ohio State 20, USC 7

Never known for making the statement his opponents most wanted to hear, Ohio State's coach Woody Hayes let loose with a string of outrageous statements after his number-one ranked team ran over the USC Trojans, 20–7. He told Sid Ziff of the *Mirror,* "My coaches who sat in the press box said we would have beaten USC by a higher score on a dry field. They thought our men would have gone a little farther on every play."

Hayes also said, "There are about four, possibly five, teams in the Big Ten that could beat USC . . . Big Ten teams are better in the Rose Bowl because they are raised on tougher competition. . . . "

This was the beginning of a stormy Hayes career in the Rose Bowl. He was destined to become one of the most controversial figures in Rose Bowl history.

When USC coach Jess Hill heard that Hayes believed at least four other Big Ten teams could have handled the Trojans, he retorted, "Is that so? Well, that's mighty generous of him. Just say for me I'd like to play Ohio State again on a dry field. The rain hurt us a lot. We planned to throw and rely on our speed. We were

handcuffed both ways by the rain."

The Ohio State victory increased the howling in the West for an end to annual beatings in Pasadena. The Pacific Coast Conference was indulging in the luxury of not permitting its champion to compete two years in a row, and scribes like Ziff shouted, "We should play our champion each year or get out. If we can't beat them with our best, we shouldn't try to do it with our second best."

Dave Legget, Ohio State quarterback, was loudly praised by most writers. He did not fumble the ball once in slipping it to Hopalong Cassady, Bob Watkins and Dick Harkrader on quick opening shots which called for split-second timing. Marvelous Marv Goux was given most of the praise for what stop-work Jess Hill's Trojans managed during the mudfest.

Paul Zimmerman of the *Times* wrote:

"Drives of 77, 68 and 35 yards resulted in Ohio State's three touchdowns with Legget playing the feature role. He scored the first touchdown on a 3-yard plunge on the second play of the second quarter, threw a 21-yard pass to Watkins for the second score only a half-dozen plays later, and then flipped a pitchout to Harkrader for a 9-yard scoring run in the final period."

Zimmerman described an Aramis Dandoy 88-yard touchdown punt return for USC's only score as follows:

"There was little more than five minutes of the second quarter remaining when Dandoy cut loose with the most brilliant run of the afternoon to put the Trojans temporarily in striking distance.

"Hubert Bobo, back to kick, had to duck away from two charging Trojans and barely got the ball away. The punt was a line-drive affair that went 55 yards before Dandoy fielded the dribbling ball on his 14. The Trojan eluded the onrush-

Earl Warren

Dinah Shore decorates the 1955 parade

Woody Hayes

After winning the 1955 Rose Bowl, the always-outspoken Woody Hayes said that the bands should have stayed on the sidelines instead of performing on the football field. "Bands are a fine thing," he said, "but they owe their popularity to football, not the other way around. If you don't believe that, invite the bands out to the Rose Bowl some year without the football teams and see how much of a crowd they would draw."

ing Buckeyes and fought his way to midfield where George Belotti, 231-pound tackle, served up the key block. The fleet Trojan did a neat job of eluding Bobo after that as he sped toward the end zone."

1956
A Man Named Duffy

Back in the days when William Howard Taft was president of the United States and the Tournament's chariot races were the biggest thing going in the festival, a young boy named Alfred Gerrie earned ten cents an hour for tying flowers on a float. Then he ran home to don an angel's costume so he could ride on it.

Things were different in 1956. That same boy, now Dr. Alfred L. Gerrie, was working a great deal harder on Tournament preparations, but he was getting less than ten cents an hour, and he didn't get to wear an angel costume in the parade. He rode in a car—he was the *president* of the Tournament of Roses.

Dr. Gerrie's grand marshal was Secretary of Defense Charles E. Wilson, and he had a queen in the June Allyson mold, Joan Culver.

The theme of the parade during Dr. Gerrie's year as president was "Pages from the Ages." Burbank won the Sweepstakes prize with a float depicting the planets, sun, moon and stars made of many thousands of orchids, sweet peas and rose petals.

David Llewellyn of Los Angeles, who rode in the first Pasadena parade in 1890 and in every parade thereafter through 1956, appeared with his world champion palomino, One in a Million, whose saddle and trimmings were worth an estimated $75,000.

The Post Cereals float, "I Love a Western," created the illusion of a stagecoach

emerging from a television set as a family watched the show. Television western stars Roy Rogers and Dale Evans added a realistic touch.

Occidental Life Insurance Company brought back memories to parade goers with its "Tournament First Ladies" float, a tribute to Rose queens of other years. Riding on the float were Hallie Woods McConnell, first Rose queen (1905); Dolores Brubach Chase (1942), who had not been able to ride in a parade that first month of World War II, and four other queens.

More Last-second Heroics: Michigan State 17, UCLA 14

The big story in 1956 was the continuing Big Ten domination in the Rose Bowl. Duffy Daugherty's Michigan State team defeated UCLA, 17–14, on a 41-yard field goal by Dave Kaiser with seven seconds left to play. This may have been the most dramatic field goal kicked in the Southland until the 1969 season, when USC's Ron Ayala defeated Stanford with a field goal as the final gun cracked.

A series of penalties against UCLA had forced Ronnie Knox to punt from behind his goal line, thus setting the stage for Kaiser's clutch field goal when Michigan State, too, got bitten by the penalty bug.

Daugherty, a popular storyteller as well as a winning coach, revealed how a lost contact lens may have been the deciding factor in his 1956 triumph.

At the crucial moment, the score was 14–14. "We had time for just one more play with the ball on UCLA's 24-yard line and the clock stopped," said Daugherty. "Two of our kickers had previously missed field goal attempts. Our best kicker, Kaiser, had not been doing his chore for us during the latter part of the season due to a leg injury. He had not

David Llewellyn

Duffy Daugherty

"Immediately after the kick, Kaiser turned around and waited for the referee to make the signal. He did not follow the course of the ball through the air. It wasn't until he saw the referee's arms go up that he knew the kick had been true. His kick is one that every Spartan will long remember. Dave will go down in Michigan State football history as Golden Toe Kaiser."

Harvey Knox, stormy stepfather of UCLA tailback Ronnie Knox, blamed Coach Red Sanders for the defeat.

"Kaiser's kick didn't beat UCLA. Sanders blew the game in the second quarter," Harvey Knox told Melvin Durslag of the *Examiner*. He said Sanders overdid the running stuff when, with the score 7–0 in UCLA's favor, he let Ronnie sit on the bench when Ronnie could have offered some run-pass variety to the Bruin attack, which had gained field position for a possible touchdown.

Vincent X. Flaherty of the *Examiner* said, "It was a good thing Kaiser made his kick when he did because if it had been a second later, the goal posts wouldn't have been there. Happy Michigan State rooters toppled them over as soon as the ball cleared the bar."

Daugherty added, "Tell the folks back home it won't be so cold now." The next Spartan win was thirty-two years away.

practiced kicking field goals for two months. I knew Kaiser had the ability to kick the ball 41 yards, but the gamble was whether he could be accurate after so long a layoff.

"In addition, Kaiser normally wore contact lenses but did not have them available the day of the Rose Bowl game. He had lost one and didn't have the set. This meant he could not see the goal posts with any degree of clarity.

"I decided to let Dave make the kick. The lost contact lens was probably the reason he kept his head down and met the ball squarely. If he had had these lenses in his eyes, he might have let curiosity get the better of him. He might have looked up to see whether the kick was good.

1957
Famous Firsts

World War I flying ace Capt. Eddie Rickenbacker was the grand marshal, John S. Davidson the Tournament president, and Ann Mosberg the queen in 1957.

The theme for the festival was "Famous Firsts in Flowers." Among the "firsts" depicted in the parade were "Baby's First Tooth" and the "First Satellite." Indio, California, copped the

When John Biggar was Tournament treasurer in 1955, he went to Alaska to sign up float entrants for the parade. He returned very optimistic about one particular entry he had been promised and gave the name of his key Alaska contact to the parade committee chairman. Letter after letter went to this party in Alaska to firm up the details of the entry. Finally, after an inquiry in Alaska, Biggar's "Alaska big shot" turned out to be a second assistant cook in a lumber camp.

Dr. Alfred L. Gerrie

Charles E. Wilson

Forest Evashevski

Sweepstakes trophy with a float entitled "First Date Festival." Despite its title, it had nothing to do with first dates, as in dating; it was about "date festivals." The float depicted an Arabian setting in delicate pastel-shaded petals. Real dates in clusters were suspended from floral trees for which twenty thousand orchids were used.

More "Firsts":
Iowa 35, Oregon State 19

One "first" missing from the 1957 Tournament was the West's first win over the Big Ten since 1953. The omens were all bad for the West going into the 1957 Rose Bowl. The West's football pact with the Big Ten received a jolt well before the 1957 Tournament of Roses when the Pacific Coast Conference barred Washington, USC, UCLA and California from playing in the Bowl because of infractions of conference rules. It also restricted many players in those universities to just five games on the season—an action that greatly weakened the teams.

The result was that Oregon State was able to fit right into the 1957 Tournament theme with its first PCC title and first Rose Bowl berth. Meanwhile, Big Ten champion Iowa earned its own first Rose Bowl bid and became the Beavers' opponent. The teams had met early in the season, when Iowa won, 14–13.

"It Gets Easier All the Time for Big Ten," was the *Mirror* headline in after Forest Evashevski's Iowans defeated Tommy Prothro's Beavers, 35–19.

"If this keeps up (10–1 for the Big Ten to date), the Humane Society will have to step in," moaned Sid Ziff in the *Mirror*. Ziff didn't spare any feelings in summing up the West's latest defeat: "Pitiful line, miserable tackling, poor strategy. It all fits the weakest team we have ever

sent into the Rose Bowl." Ziff accused Oregon State players of just grabbing Iowa tacklers instead of tackling them.

Evashevski told reporters that Iowa had won the game for Cal Jones, the Iowa All-American tackle from the year before who had been killed in a Canadian air crash. "His spirit was in the back of our minds all day," said Ken Ploen, the Iowa quarterback who led the Hawkeye triumph. Braven Dyer of the *Times* called it a "Ploen beating." Ploen completed nine of ten passes and rushed for 59 net yards. He opened the scoring with a 49-yard run. Collins Hagler scored twice, once on a 66-yard run.

Oregon State fumbled the ball away three times. Prothro said, "Our first fumble and their first long run were very significant." He was referring to Beaver fullback Tom Berry's fumble to Iowa end Frank Gilliam on Iowa's 40 in the opening minute and Ploen's touchdown run five plays later.

"It beats me why the team that is rougher, tougher and more aggressive always has to come from the Big Ten," said Maxwell Stiles in the *Mirror*. "Why can't our own men hit harder, run harder, just once in a while?"

Oregon State's best were Joe Francis, who ran 73 yards and completed ten of twelve passes; Sterling Hammack who caught four passes, one for a touchdown; and touchdown scorers Nub Beamer and Tom Berry.

1958
Oregon Inspired

John Biggar, father of the Tournament's centennial year president, and the president of the 1958 festival, summed up much of the spirit and success of the Tournament of Roses when he said, "Participation in this great civic event is

Beautiful Wrigley Mansion, the Tournament House

the motivating force and success is the reward for taking part." True to his word, after his presidency, Biggar served for many years on the Tournament's Football Committee.

Biggar later rated as his biggest thrill inviting Dr. Robert G. Sproul, president of the University of California, to be his grand marshal. His queen was Gertrude Wood, one of the many women who had to survive a rain squall that broke up a judging session.

"Daydreams in Flowers" was the 1958 theme. "Recycling" might have been a more apt theme, as Burbank won the Sweepstakes award with a replica of the gold cup it had received two years before as the Sweepstakes winner.

All Guts and Heart:
Ohio State 10, Oregon 7

Woody Hayes again became a winner when his Ohio State team defeated un-derdog Oregon, 10–7, on a 34-yard field goal by Don Sutherin in the fourth quarter. Oregon, however, was the team that won the hearts of the 98,202 spectators with a tremendous effort, after being given little credit before the battle started.

Oregon led in first downs, 21–19, and made more yardage—351–304. It did not even have to punt once during the game. There were no runbacks of the two Ohio State punts, since both went out of bounds. Nevertheless, Mr. Hayes came off a winner again.

"Sutherin was our star," said Hayes. "He had a bad back and a bad leg, and he hadn't kicked for a long time until a week before the game because of his injuries."

"I was sure I would make it good," said Sutherin of his game-winning field goal. "I didn't look up. It felt good. I didn't know it was good, though, until my holder, Frank Kremblas, jumped up

127

Len Casanova

Robert Gordon Sproul

John H. Biggar

Cy Burick, *Dayton News:* "You have to give Len Casanova a lot of credit for defensing Ohio State after seeing those pictures. Ohio State didn't give the ball away. That's why it won."

Oliver Kuechle, *Milwaukee Journal:* "I had written before coming to California that this would turn out to be the weakest defensive team the Big Ten had ever sent to the Rose Bowl. Oregon deserved to win and I'm sorry they lost. Oregon was well coached and took full advantage of Ohio State's defensive weaknesses."

George Pasero, *Portland Journal:* "It was no surprise to me that Oregon played so well. The Ducks have played some good games because they have real desire and have reacted to humiliation."

and said, 'Thank God.'" Indeed.

Oregon's Jack Crabtree was the real star of the game, as he quarterbacked the surprising Ducks' attack, completing ten of seventeen passes and contributing some effective running. Oregon's Ron Stover caught ten passes.

Afterwards, even Big Ten writers said that Oregon had deserved to win. Bert McGrane of the *Des Moines Register,* for example, wrote, "Oregon tore a gaping hole in Big Ten prestige. They were all guts and all heart. They were another version of the Gas House Gang."

Charles Johnson, sports editor of the *Minneapolis Star and Tribune,* added:

"Ohio State had to fight for its football life and only one bad break kept Oregon from the upset of the season. Crabtree was a sensation. Oregon should have won. We hate to pull against our own territory, but we wish Oregon had won today."

There were others in the Midwest.

1959
In-Evy-table!

In addition to Iowa's football team saluting itself on the first day of 1959 with a super performance, the Tournament of Roses saluted Alaska—the forty-ninth and newest state. The parade theme was "Adventures in Flowers," and one of the most interesting adventures was South Pasadena's elephant, animated by eleven operators riding unseen inside. Glendale won the Sweepstakes award, and Quaker Oats won the Grand Prize in the business division.

The fact that the space age was just around the corner showed up in many floats. Long Beach's "Adventures in Universe," for example, featured a rocket blast of white pompons. The city of Gardena presented "The First Moon Shot," and San Gabriel came up with a portrayal of "A Visit to the Planet Earth."

E.L. Bob Bartlett, the newly elected senior Alaska senator, was the choice of

Tournament president Stanley K. Brown for grand marshal and Pamela Prather was the queen.

Nearing the End of an Era:
Iowa 38, California 12

After Iowa drubbed California in 1959—the twelfth Big Ten win in thirteen Rose Bowl games during the pact, the West won twenty-one of the next twenty-nine Rose Bowls to take the overall lead in the inter-conference series.

The Pacific Coast Conference was crumbling by the time the 1959 game rolled around. The wounds of the purge by the northern members hadn't healed,

President Stanley K. Brown and Queen Pamela Prather

but schools like California were now permitted to play in the Rose Bowl. The feeling in the West among some PCC members was that the conference ought to disband and abandon the Rose Bowl pact with the Big Ten. Meanwhile, the Big Ten got caught in a 5–5 vote for renewal of the pact; hence, it was left up to the individual Big Ten schools to negoti-

ate with the West if they wished to compete in Pasadena on January 1.

Iowa, with its second Big Ten champion in three seasons under Forest Evashevski, was only too happy to invade Pasadena to meet Pete Elliott's California Golden Bear Team.

Evashevski and Elliott, both outstanding athletes during great careers at the University of Michigan, will go down in football history as two of the Rose Bowl's most distinctive coaches. Evashevski came out with a winner twice. Elliott not only played in the Rose Bowl with Michigan in 1948, he also coached on both sides of the Rose Bowl pact. While he lost in 1959 as a coach of the western team, California, he returned as a Big Ten mentor in 1964 to lead Illinois over Washington.

The 1959 game was advertised as a battle of quarterbacks: Randy Duncan of Iowa against California's Joe Kapp, who was destined to become king of the NFL quarterbacks with the Minnesota Vikings in 1969. As things developed, however, Duncan didn't have to duel Kapp in any passing war. Iowa gained 441 of its total of 528 yards on the ground, with 298-pound Mac Lewis at guard opening holes for Bob Jeter and Willie Fleming, the star runners of the day.

Maxwell Stiles, in the *Mirror*, after the decisive Iowa victory, commented: "Maybe it is just as well the Pacific Coast Conference is dying. That's one way to end the pain. Until we signed the pact with the Big Ten, I always thought Vassar was located in the East. Now I'm not so sure." Further, Stiles wrote: "Evashevski knew where Cal was weakest, at the tackles. That's where Iowa hit. As long as it worked (and the speedy Iowa backs whistled by while they worked), why change it?"

The 1959 Tournament of Roses might be called the start of "The Pamela Period." Pamela Prather was queen in 1959. Over the next eleven years, two more young beauties named Pamela were to become queens—Pamela Anicich in 1969 and Pamela Dee Tedesco in 1970.

When California coach Pete Elliott said that before the 1959 Rose Bowl his men had worked hard on stopping Iowa's outside stuff, forcing Iowa to go inside, Maxwell Stiles commented, "That's like being happy if you don't lose all your money in the stock market. You lose it to the ponies instead."

"I'm probably the lousiest-feeling winning coach in Rose Bowl history," Evashevski said after the game. He had the flu with a temperature of 101 degrees the day before the game, and got up out of a sickbed to handle his team.

Jeter wound up with 194 yards for the day, to beat by 43 yards Bobby Grayson's total for Stanford in 1934.

Queen Pamela with Alaska's Senator E.L. Bartlett, the 1959 grand marshal

Robert Harold Sinclair of Fairbanks, Alaska, an amateur photographer, bailed out of a plane over the Rose Bowl into the waiting arms of the police. He was trying for unique aerial shots of the game, he said, but he missed the stadium—and his pictures. He landed twenty feet outside Gate 9 at half time. Police arrested him, but then released him because there was then no ordinance prohibiting what he had done.

THE 1960s

WEST COAST RECOVERY

Ray Dorn

Grand Marshal Nixon's appearance at the 1960 Tournament was delayed by strike negotiations. Just five minutes before he was due to speak at the Kickoff Luncheon on New Year's Eve, he arrived near the Rose Bowl by helicopter and at the Civic Auditorium. When his daughters, Tricia and Julie, were invited to ride in the official grand marshal's car in the parade, they replied, "How can we see the parade if we ride in it?" So they sat in the stands.

1960
How the West Was Won

Much happened in 1960 that changed the the way we see the world: The sudden independence of many African nations, the launching of the first communications satellite, the formation of OPEC, and John F. Kennedy's election to the presidency. It was also a big year for the Rose Bowl.

On the first day of 1960, something happened in Pasadena which forever changed the way we look at the Rose Bowl. After six consecutive losses, and twelve losses in thirteen games, the West defeated a Big Ten team. And it not only defeated that team, but smashed it by the third-greatest point margin in Tournament history.

While the 1960 Tournament is best remembered by sports fans as the year that Washington stopped the Big Ten's winning streak with a 44–8 triumph over Wisconsin, there were other developments which have had an important impact on the Tournament. Tournament president Raymond A. Dorn looks back with particular pride on several accomplishments. In addition to having Vice President Richard Nixon make his sec-

ond appearance as grand marshal, Dorn negotiated the gift of the William Wrigley mansion and gardens on South Orange Grove Boulevard to the city and the Tournament for use as a public park and Tournament headquarters. Today it is one of Pasadena's beauty spots, visited by thousands each year.

The theme of the 1960 parade was "Tall Tales and True," and Long Beach again took the Sweepstakes Trophy. Occidental Life—another long-term active Tournament participant—won the Grand Prize. A Minneapolis-born beauty, Margarethe Bertelson, was queen.

UW Thrashes UW:
Washington 44, Wisconsin 8

Milt Bruhn's Wisconsin team waltzed into Pasadena with every expectation of dealing the University of Washington a knockout blow, but it quickly discovered it was in trouble. Washington, led by quarterback Bob Schloredt, who had only one eye, and halfback George Fleming, had a 17–0 lead before Wisconsin even made a first down.

Coach Jim Owens had worked his Huskies hard for this game to remove the West's defeatist complex. His men came

Wisconsin's Hobbs and Washington's Wooten scramble for loose ball

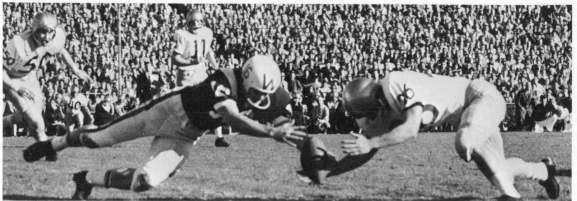

Queen Margarethe Bertelson and her 1960 court

in fired up. They believed they could win and knew they had both the weapons and the battle plan. That battle plan included the run-or-pass option work of quick-hitting Schloredt.

Wisconsin's own star, Dale Hackbart, was completely bottled up by the Washington defense. Schloredt, meanwhile, rushed twenty-one times for 81 yards and completed four of seven passes for 102 more yards.

Said Owens, "Our agility offset their weight edge. We made a lot over their strong side."

After the game, Tom Hamilton, the executive director of the newly formed Athletic Association of Western Universities—which was to replace the Coast Conference in Rose Bowl matters— said, "The belief existing here, call it Big Tenitis, that the Big Ten is always superior, has been disproved. This Washington team is good. From now on, the Big Ten had better be ready when New Year's Day comes around."

1961
One-eyed Backs

What does the governor of Hawaii have to say after coming to California to serve as grand marshal of the Tournament of Roses parade?

Governor William F. Quinn, later president of the Dole Company in Honolulu, summed it up after leading the

Washington players carry winning coach Jim Owens off the field

1961 parade through Pasadena:

"All of my experiences were interesting. I nearly froze when I got up early in the morning to be interviewed on television. Naturally I could not wear a top coat, but I had borrowed some longies which I did wear. They were fine until the warmth of the hot sun started to beat down about eleven in the morning. I shall always be grateful to the unknown spectator at the parade who saw me squinting in the brightness and ran out to

In a dubious show of West Coast solidarity, Caltech students sabotaged Washington's half time card tricks in 1961 by juggling the instruction sheets. Washington fans got their first surprise when the cards spelled "Washington" backwards. The second surprise came when "Caltech" appeared in place of "Washington."

William F. Quinn

Arthur W. Althouse

At the Kickoff Luncheon honoring the coaches and teams, the 1961 grand marshal, Hawaii's Governor Quinn had an experience which later gave him chills. He was extremely myopic and had to leave his glasses off for repair. The luncheon at which he spoke was a stag affair in those days, and he came perilously close to telling a dirty joke. Luckily, he decided not to. Just before he finished speaking, a messenger delivered his glasses. The moment he put them on, he realized, for the first time, that he had been speaking on television.

the car and handed me sun glasses to relieve the glare.

"I was motivated to accept the role of grand marshal by the very pleasant personal call from Art Althouse, the president of the Tournament. His invitation was so cordial and the honor was so great that I felt I should accept."

In the Tournament Football Committee plan of always striving to make the Rose Bowl a finer place for this greatest of all bowl games, the new $350,000 press box, financed again through the cooperation of competing schools in a plan of selling advance tickets, was put into operation for the 1961 game. "Ballads in Blossoms" was the theme for the parade. Burbank won the Sweepstakes award with its entry "Orchids in the Moonlight." Queen Carole Washburn reigned over the festival.

Doormats No More:
Washington 17, Minnesota 7

The Big Ten was unable to agree on a contract with the AAWU after the 1960 game, but the Tournament of Roses allied itself with the AAWU, which was given authority to select its Rose Bowl foe until a pact could be negotiated. It was here that Minnesota again proved to be the saving factor in Big Ten–AAWU relations by agreeing to come for the 1961 game against Washington while it was still riding high as the top-ranked team in the nation.

Gate receipts for the game surpassed one million dollars when 99,281 spectators saw Bob Schloredt of Washington continue his Rose Bowl mastery by leading Jim Owens's Huskies to a 17–0 first-half lead over Minnesota. Washington held on in the second half to win, 17–7.

Mannie Pineda wrote in the *Pasadena Star-News*, "No gophers ever dug them-

selves a deeper hole than did the Golden Gophers from Minnesota."

The game featured a battle of rooting sections. "We're Number One," said Minnesota rooters. "Not for long!" answered the Washington side.

Coach Owens said, "I felt we would win from the time we started workouts for the game. We were determined to whip the national champions. We had to slug it out toe to toe this time. Last year against Wisconsin we gained early momentum and rode with it."

Bob Hivner, a Washington star, added, "We had a feeling when we took the field that we had everything under control."

Murray Warmath, Minnesota coach, said, "We lost because of a couple of punts we didn't field and a couple of end sweeps we didn't turn. We were not tense. Washington was well prepared. We had evaluated Washington as a running team and didn't expect them to pass so much. We know what we did wrong but we don't know why."

Washington got the jump by gaining field goal position through better punt play and scoring early on George Fleming's 44-yard kick. Washington drove in for a touchdown with 62 impressive yards of Schloredt's play-choosing. The big gainers were a 12-yard pass from Schloredt to Ray Jackson, a 19-yard Jackson run through Minnesota's line and giants Tom Brown and Frank Brixuis, an 11-yard dash by Charlie Mitchell after a pitch, and a pass to Brent Wooten.

Minnesota tried to retaliate but Washington repeated another long march with Schloredt the big gainer, once for 31 yards on a sneak. Schloredt scored to make it 17–0 at half time, Fleming adding the extra points.

Minnesota came back fighting after intermission and moved from the 26 to Washington's 35, where Roger Hagberg, strong-legged fullback, was stopped inches short of a first down by Jim Skaggs. Hivner fumbled and Bob Deagan recovered for Minnesota on the Washington 32. Soon Sandy Stephens climaxed some steady Gopher gaining by pitching out to Bill Munsey, who scored.

1962
Sandy's Revenge

The growing importance of the state of Washington in the Tournament was evident in 1962, when Governor Albert D. Rosellini was named grand marshal. The parade theme was "Around the World with Flowers," and the state of Washington entry was decorated with roses from fifty countries.

Pasadena Superior Court Judge H. Burton Noble served as Tournament president, and Martha Sissell was queen of the 1962 Tournament. The Girl Scouts of America celebrated their fiftieth anniversary with the float, "The Girl Scout Rose." Santa Monica paid tribute to the late Leo Carrillo, who had ridden in the parade for many years, with a floral likeness of the popular movie star entitled "Mr. California." San Diego won the Sweepstakes.

Gophers Go for Glory:
Minnesota 21, UCLA 3

The 1962 Rose Bowl game was the first to be televised nationally in color.

By 1962 the Big Ten–Pacific Conference pact with the Tournament of Roses had lapsed and the future of the Rose Bowl was in doubt. Ohio State qualified for the game when it won the Big Ten's 1961 championship. The Buckeye football team wanted to come, but the faculty said no. Riots erupted on the Buckeye

campus and on High Street in Columbus.

Second-place Minnesota—which had originally opposed the East-West pact—came to the game's rescue by accepting the bid to meet UCLA after the Tournament president visited the campus. Coach Warmath, Athletic Director Ike Armstrong, and the Gopher administration wanted to avenge the 1961 defeat. And the Gophers made good by trouncing the Bruins of Bill Barnes, 21–3.

Representatives of the AAWU—made up of California, Washington, Stanford, UCLA and USC—met with Big Ten authorities after the game to stimulate good feeling for a renewal of the pact that had previously existed between the Big Ten and the Pacific Coast Conference. It was agreed the Big Ten would maintain a no-repeat rule, while the AAWU would send its champion each year. During the following year, both conferences approved the renewed pact, which became effective at the 1963 Rose Bowl game.

The 1962 game was a convincingly methodical victory for Minnesota. It was the kind of game in which, if you were watching in Paducah, Kentucky, you could safely go into the kitchen and mix a New Year's tranquilizer without having to ask what happened upon your return. It was monotonous fun only for the Minnesota rooter.

The *Star-News* account caught the flavor of the game:

"The quick and brutal Minnesota defense stopped the opening UCLA single wing lightning in time. Tenacious Minnesota then forced UCLA to make the mistakes. Sandy Stephens brilliantly called an inside-the-tackle grinding Minnesota T-offense sandwiched with key passes on opportune switches to pro spreads. The Gophers punched and

Governor Albert D. Rosellini

Murray Warmath

H. Burton Noble

Bill Barnes

Paul Zimmerman of the *Los Angeles Times* accused the officials of over-officiating the 1963 USC-Wisconsin game, suggesting, in fact, they were hamming it up before the television cameras. "Who were the boobs in striped shirts?" he asked. As far as he was concerned, only the remarkable play of the two teams kept the officials from spoiling the contest.

punched inside the tackles against a UCLA defense well prepared to watch the outside rollouts of Sandy Stephens. The big gaps were sugar plums for Sandy. His use of the reverse by his halfback and the middle socking of his fullback monopolized the clock and ground out yardage. There have been few better demonstrations in which a team followed its own game plan more closely."

Minnesota coach Murray Warmath later said, "This was the most gratifying victory of my career and for the team. I am especially glad we won for the team's sake. Most of the men played in the Rose Bowl last year, and all they've heard for a year is how bad they were."

Was UCLA's heavy dependence on the single wing the cause of its downfall? Minnesota's Bobby Bell, later a star linesman for the Kansas City Chiefs, said, "UCLA has a good line, but they better get rid of that single wing. You've got to run 4 yards to travel 1. They've given up on it in the Big Ten."

On the other hand, UCLA's coach Barnes said, "We didn't throw enough single wing at them. We used too much garbage and made too many mistakes."

1963
Memorable Moments

The Tournament of Roses acknowledged the space age in more ways than one in 1963. Tournament president Stanley L. Hahn selected as grand marshal Dr. William H. Pickering of Pasadena's Jet Propulsion Laboratory, where many of this nation's space achievements originated. In addition, a floral replica of *Mariner,* an early deep-space satellite that went to Venus, appeared in the parade. The city of Torrance entered a float depicting the soon-to-be-launched space shot to the moon, and Minute Maid told the Telstar

satellite story with spectacular flowers.

In the midst of all this space-age symbolism, President Hahn and his family rode in a gaily decorated carriage, thereby reminding parade viewers that mankind had not always zipped about through space. And, of course, there were many themes other than space featured in the 1963 parade. Santa Monica won the Sweepstakes with a depiction of "First Love," and the Quaker Oats float presented "The Birth of the Republic." Nancy Davis was queen.

Hahn, a pleasant, quiet, diplomatic individual, made a major contribution to Tournament of Roses football negotiations through the years, Lay Leishman often insisted. Hahn knew how to think with the educators, to deal with them and retain their good will.

When Spectacular Wasn't Good Enough: USC 42, Wisconsin 37

The 1963 parade theme, "Memorable Moments," aptly described the Rose Bowl game that year. USC and Wisconsin came into the game number one and number two in the nation. Both quarterbacks set records that still stand. USC's Pete Beathard threw four passes for touchdowns, and Wisconsin's Ron VanderKelen had thirty-three completions in forty-eight attempts. Even the place kickers were great that day. USC's Tom Lupo was six-for-six in conversions, and the Badgers' Kroner went five-for-five.

Beathard's and VanderKelen's incredible aerial game lasted into near darkness as Wisconsin staged one of the most amazing comebacks in football history. So impressive was the Wisconsin effort, when the game was over, it wasn't crystal clear which team had won. Wisconsin outgained USC, 486 yards to 367, beat them in first downs, 32–15, and generally left the Trojans reeling. Nevertheless, USC held on to win, 42–37, thereby preserving their number-one status in the polls and giving coach John McKay his first national championship.

Rube Samuelsen of the *Star-News* called VanderKelen's performance the finest one-man effort in Rose Bowl history. "Ernie Nevers and George Wilson have no choice but to move over," Rube said.

A combination of many pass plays and frequent penalties—USC was penalized 93 yards, Wisconsin 77—slowed the game. It required three hours and five minutes to reach the finish of game in hazy darkness. "Only slightly less long than the War of 1812," in the words of Jim Murray of the *Times*. "If the game had lasted one more quarter, they would have run into next year's Rose Bowl traffic." The late finish revealed the inadequacy of the Rose Bowl's lights, and the Tournament's committee started a campaign for better ones, which were finally installed in 1969.

The scoring duel started when USC fullback Ben Wilson opened with a softening of the Badgers, who sent their linebackers keying on the Trojan man in motion. Beathard then threw a touchdown pass to Hal Bedsole, only to have it called back because the officials said Pete had run past the line of scrimmage. The Trojans then lined up quickly with tackle Ron Butcher at end. Butcher broke straight ahead in the hole left clear by the roaming linebackers and took a snappy 13-yard toss from Beathard for the first touchdown of the day.

A Wisconsin passing show led to the Badgers tying the score on a plunge by Ralph Kurek, who teamed with Lou Holland in catching the ball as end Pat Richter—who caught eleven passes for the Badgers on the day—opened as a decoy.

A pass interception by USC's Damon Bame launched the next USC score, which was set up by a Willie Brown run and finally some Wilson smashes. Bill Nelsen's pass to Willie Brown—who hauled it in over his shoulder with Jim Nettles on his back—was good for 45 yards and set up a 25-yard cutback by Ron Heller to make the score 21–7.

Just before the half, VanderKelen dropped a bomb into the hands of Holland for an apparent touchdown, but the officials whistled the Badgers guilty of clipping and called the play back. This call so angered Badger coach Milt Bruhn that he protested to the officials as the teams left the field at intermission. Bruhn also accused the men in stripes of blowing a quick whistle which prevented a Badger recovery of a Nelsen fumble.

In the third quarter Bedsole made it 28–7 on a look-in pass from Beathard in the vacated linebacker zone which he carried 57 yards for a touchdown. VanderKelen retaliated with a 17-yard Badger touchdown on a rollout, but then Bedsole got the points right back by leaping over Nettles in the corner of the end zone for a 23-yard touchdown—one of the finest catches of his career.

With less than a quarter to play, USC took a 42–14 lead after Lupo intercepted a pass and ran it to the Badger 14, from where Beathard tossed a touchdown strike to Fred Hill. Things looked hopeless for Wisconsin. However, what happened in the next fourteen minutes made the finest quarter of football in Badger history and one of the most exciting periods in Rose Bowl history.

On his next drive, VanderKelen completed eight of ten passes to set up a 13-yard Holland touchdown three minutes

Dr. William H. Pickering

Stanley L. Hahn

USC's Pete Beathard

Wisconsin's Ron VanderKelen

President Dwight D. Eisenhower

Hilles Bedell

and nineteen seconds into the quarter. After the Trojans' Wilson fumbled the ball to the Badgers on USC's 29, Vander-Kelen hit Kroner with a touchdown pass.

VanderKelen drilled completion after completion to Richter and others. On a pass from the 4, Brown made a big save by intercepting in the end zone. USC couldn't move, and a bad pass from center produced a safety. With the score now 42–30, VanderKelen completed a touchdown pass to Richter to close to 42–37. Over two minutes remained to play, but USC froze the ball until it had to punt on the last play of the game.

Most USC fans were glad just to see the game end. However, John McKay summed it up thusly: "We came in number one. They came in number two and lost. That makes us still number one."

1964
Diamonds and Gold

In 1964 the Tournament had two major occasions to celebrate. The Tournament as a whole observed its seventy-fifth anniversary with the parade theme, "Symbols of Freedom." Meanwhile, the 1964 Rose Bowl game was the golden fiftieth in Tournament history.

Long Beach took the Sweepstakes with a float honoring the Tournament's diamond jubilee. Occidental Life depicted Betsy Ross and the making of the American flag with an impressive float, "First Symbol of Freedom." Nancy Kneeland was the Rose queen.

The big event of the Tournament was former president Dwight Eisenhower's finally making it to Pasadena to serve as grand marshal of the parade after two failed attempts. Tournament president Hilles M. Bedell pulled off the feat and was rewarded with a friendship between his family and the Eisenhowers that last-

ed throughout Ike's remaining years.

Bedell later recalled Eisenhower: "He fit right in. He got into the spirit of the Tournament. He was impressed by the lack of politics in our operation. He spoke in short sentences and simple words. He seldom carried money with him. In his military and political life, he hadn't needed ready cash. He was warm to our children." Ike was particularly impressed by the Tournament directors' dinner, where each man introduced himself to the audience. "Everybody is equal here," he remarked.

In Palm Springs, Bedell played golf with Ike, who, he said, "drove a golf cart like a maniac. We came up to a green where I thought a man putting looked familiar. I said, 'Let's stop and watch if he sinks his putt.' Ike obliged. That man turned out to be Stanley Hahn, former president of the Tournament."

After the Tournament, Bedell and Ike corresponded and exchanged visits often. When Bedell later faced open-heart surgery, Eisenhower wrote, "Welcome to the club. If you submit to the rules set down by your doctors, you can live a long and useful life." The last letter Bedell received from Ike was written by his chief aide, who reported that the former president was too weak to write but had sent along his good wishes. Bedell outlived Eisenhower by one year.

During the New Year's Day parade, Eisenhower followed the Marine band. Despite his unquestioned patriotism, mile after mile of the Marine Corps hymn left him feeling like he had personally been from the halls of Montezuma to the shores of Tripoli and back again. He needed a rest before the Rose Bowl game. He stopped at the Pasadena armory, where a cot awaited him. Who should show up for a brief rehearsal? The

Marine band, of course, and what did they practice? The Marine Corps hymn.

While the former president got no rest before the Rose Bowl game, Washington's Huskies were to get no rest during it.

Systematic Liquidation:
Illinois 17, Washington 7

Illinois rolled over Washington in the fiftieth Tournament of Roses football game. "Illinois won the game the same way that Castro won Cuba—by a systematic liquidation," wrote Jim Murray in the *Times*. "Illinois was like Sonny Liston—not very smart—but they didn't have to be. I think they hurt Washington just shaking hands with them before the kickoff."

Paul Zimmerman of the *Times* called the game a "rugged, hard-hitting contest that was utterly devoid of the spectacular. A crowd of 96,957 shirt-sleeved spectators basked in 85-degree weather to watch Pete Elliott's Illinois crash to a pair of touchdowns over the outclassed but determined Huskies in the second half after trailing 7–3 at intermission. Whatever chances coach Jim Owens's smaller, slower squad had were dissipated in the first five minutes when its star quarterback, Bill Douglas, was carried from the field with a knee dislocation. Bill's replacement, Bill Siler, who had been out all season with hepatitis, threw three interceptions, fumbled the ball twice, and generally had a discouraging afternoon."

Owens kept the press away for thirty-five minutes after the game. Then he said: "It hurt us to lose Douglas, but that was not the difference. We made too many mistakes and gave up the ball too often."

Washington actually started fast, as Douglas picked the Illinois defense apart with pitchouts, short passes and

keepers to advance 53 yards to Illinois's 15. On a 12-yard scamper around right end, Douglas was felled by Bill Pasko, who hit him from behind. He was carried off the field. Little Siler came in and moved the ball to the 10, but his short look-in pass was bobbled by Al Libke with Wylie Fox recovering for Illinois.

After keeping Illinois bottled the rest of the first period, Washington got back to the Illinois 18, where Siler fumbled and Fox recovered again for the Illini. Then quarterback Fred Custardo of Illinois fumbled and John Stupey of Washington recovered on the Illinois 27. Siler passed to Joe Mancusco to the 6. On a pitchout, Dave Kopay ran wide, got a good block from Ron Medved, and scored. Medved kicked the point.

Just before the half, after Siler fumbled yet again, Bruce Capel recovering, Illinois's Jim Plankenhorn kicked a 32-yard field goal that made the score 7–3.

An interception by George Donnelly gave Illinois the ball on Washington's 32 in the third quarter. Jim Warren soon scored on a pitchout from Mike Taliaferro, and Plankenhorn's conversion gave Illinois a 10–7 lead. Some fine plunging by Junior Coffey gave Washington a chance on the 9-yard line, but a Donnelly interception saved the day for the Big Ten team. An 85-yard march by Illinois in the fourth quarter led to Jim Grabowski's scoring the insurance touchdown. Grabowski was named player of the game after he netted 125 yards on twenty-two carries.

1965
An Army Invades

After years of watching top government officials, politicians and war heroes serve as the Tournament's grand marshals, President Walter R. Hoefflin Jr. did

Pete Elliott

Prior to an engagement at the Tournament House, Grand Marshal Eisenhower went to the restroom for a few moments of privacy away from the crowds. When an old sliding door to the washroom that he closed too abruptly locked, the former supreme commander of allied forces in Europe was trapped inside. Tournament president Bedell's son, serving as a guard, thinking Ike wanted to be left alone, turned away everyone who might have come to his rescue.

Frank Hardcastle, who was one of Eisenhower's security men in 1964, pleaded continually with a float builder to correct a poor welding job, but was ignored. On the day the floats were tested for maneuverability, Hardcastle jumped up and down on the welding point to test it. The float broke in half. At that moment Hardcastle became known as "Float Destruction chairman."

Fritz Crisler

Arnold Palmer

Walter R. Hoefflin

something new: He named a leading sports figure, Arnold Palmer, grand marshal of the 1965 Tournament. It was a popular choice. Arnie's Army came to the parade, whose theme was "Headlines in Flowers." Dawn Baker was the Tournament queen.

The sports theme was carried further by the St. Louis float, which featured World Series stars Bob Gibson and Tim McCarver. Chrysler, on the other hand, depicted one of the era's great news events with a float entitled "Britain Crowns Queen Elizabeth the Second." "It was a personal highlight for me to have Arnold Palmer as grand marshal," said Hoefflin, executive vice president of Arcadia's Methodist Hospital of Southern California. "It meant much to me to get acquainted with him, his adorable wife and their two fine daughters. As far as I am concerned, Arnold made my year. Our close friendship continues. During each of his public appearances, he said just the right thing at the right time with absolutely no coaching."

Anthony and Cleopatra:
Michigan 34, Oregon State 7

Oregon State's Paul Brothers directed the Beavers to an early 84-yard touchdown drive and a deceiving 7–0 lead. Afterwards, however, it was no contest, as Michigan scored 34 unanswered points to win, 34–7, for Coach Bump Elliott, brother of Pete Elliott.

Michigan did it with two break-away runners and a break-away pig. Mel Anthony sprinted a record 84 yards and Carl Ward picked up another 43 on runs which broke the game open. Michigan fans got so excited they released a speedy pig named Cleopatra. It was a fitting name because Anthony, with three touchdowns, was the leading man of the

day. He fell on a blocked punt and his run was the longest in history—3 yards more than that of Iowa's Bob Jeter in 1959. Cleopatra ran the wrong way on her scoring dash, executing the most notable wrong-way effort since Roy Riegels. But she tried to amend by coming back the right way. A fan made a diving tackle to halt the critter. If the fan came from Oregon State, he made the best Oregon State tackle of the day.

Oregon State coach Tommy Prothro summed up the game as he saw it: "Our offense did as well as we expected to do. But our defense didn't. We thought our best hope was to punt for field position and try to hold it."

The defeat, Prothro's second in the Rose Bowl as a head coach, didn't ruin his career beyond some immediate criticism in the press for punting on second and third down and presenting an unexciting offense. Charlie Park of the *Times,* for example, said Prothro's "Mad Dogs" on defense were actually "Pooped Pooches." Prothro was hired as UCLA's new football coach as soon as J.D. Morgan, athletic director, could pry him loose from the Beaver campus. And Prothro came back to the Rose Bowl the very next year to stage one of the biggest upsets in Rose Bowl history.

1966
It's a Small World

A dozen years before Randy Newman scored a satiric hit with the song "Short People," the 1966 Tournament of Roses made the word "small" mighty big. Mickey Mouse, not a big guy in anything but public acceptance, led the parade, and his creator, Walt Disney, served as grand marshal. The theme of the parade, of course, was "It's a Small World." There was even a team of Sicilian ponies,

Michigan coach Bump Elliott

Mel Anthony begins his record 84-yard run

Before the 1965 Tournament, Walter Hoefflin sent some publicity films to a nurse in Norway for showing in hospitals. Afterward, Hoefflin invited the nurse, Kari, to come to Pasadena to see the festival she had helped to publicize. In a dinner in her honor at his home, the Tournament president introduced Kari to his manager, Max Colwell. It was love at first sight. The couple were soon married at Tournament House.

twenty-seven inches tall, pulling a pumpkin carriage. And to top things off, the hero of the Rose Bowl game was himself an unusually small player.

J. Randolph Richards, owner of the Pasadena Athletic Club, served as president for the 1966 Tournament. He later recalled that his "most interesting experience had to do with getting Mr. Disney to serve as grand marshal. After he had given due consideration to my invitation, he stated that he couldn't think of anything more undesirable from his standpoint than to ride for two hours in parade doing nothing but trying to smile and wave to the crowd. However, he stat-

ed that if we would allow him to have 20 or 30 of his characters, such as Mickey Mouse, Donald Duck and others, surround his car so that he could play with them, he would accept."

The million-and-a-half spectators along the parade route loved every minute of Disney's appearance. Disney later said he could "think of no time in my life when I have been treated to nicer or more sincere hospitality."

As an extension of the "Small World" theme, Richards traveled around the world to recruit parade participants. Lebanon entered a float depicting its "Cedars of Lebanon" heritage, and a Jap-

Randy Richards

Tommy Prothro

The 1966 queen, Carole Cota, said: "This may sound crazy—but one of the things that impressed me most was that the selecting of the queen wasn't 'fixed.' I guess there is always going to be someone who can't believe that a really good thing can be honest—but it won't ever be me. Every detail about the tryouts was so fair and so much fun. Even those who didn't become a member of the court weren't really crushed. They just chalked it up to a 'groovy experience.' "

The Rose Bowl's player of the game annually is selected by the board of the Helms Athletic Foundation, founded by Paul Helms and directed by W. R. "Bill" Schroeder. The winner is awarded a trophy and his picture is placed in the Rose Bowl Hall of Fame. The Hall of Fame, once housed inside the Rose Bowl and visited by thousands of visitors to Pasadena each year, was moved to the Tournament House.

anese high school entered a marching band. Richards said that throughout his travels he did not find one person who didn't know of Walt Disney.

The national flowers of twenty-one countries were flown to Pasadena for the parade. Canada was well represented with the Vancouver Beefeater Band, the Canadian Mounted Police and floats from Alberta and British Columbia. The state of Montana won the Sweepstakes award.

Sumtin's Bruin:
UCLA 14, Michigan State 12

The late Duffy Daugherty's Michigan State team came into the 1966 Rose Bowl undefeated in a ten-game season that had opened with a 13–3 victory over UCLA. The 7–2–1 Bruins weren't given much of a chance against the Spartans; however, the mightiest of mighty mites, UCLA's Bob Stiles, was the hero of a football game that will be remembered as long as football is played. A defensive left halfback, Stiles intercepted passes and finally made the big save that enabled UCLA to win.

UCLA shocked Michigan State by jumping off to a 14–0 lead, and then

held on to preserve its lead after two Michigan State touchdowns later in the game. After each Michigan State score, Tommy Prothro's determined defense faced a 2-point conversion attempt which threatened the Bruin lead.

UCLA scored twice in the second quarter on 1-yard dives by the future Heisman Trophy winner, sophomore Gary Beban. The first UCLA touchdown was set up when UCLA recovered a fumbled punt by Michigan's cocaptain, Don Japinga, on the Spartan 6-yard line. John Erquiaga fell on the ball to give UCLA possession. Beban skirted left to the 1 and then bucked in.

The second shocker was set up by Kurt Zimmerman's brilliant on-side kickoff, recovered by Dallas Grider, and the bomb that UCLA had learned to love when it had rallied over archrival USC to gain the Rose Bowl bid. Beban fired a 27-yard strike to end Kurt Altenberg to State's 1, from which Beban dove over. Zimmerman kicked both extra points.

UCLA's defense then asserted itself and bullied Spartan quarterback Steve Juday into trouble. Three times it took the ball away from Michigan State on fourth down stops. Three times it intercepted Juday passes when he was forced to throw hurriedly under pressure. And twice it recovered Spartan fumbles.

The UCLA stalwarts up front were Jim Colletto, John Richardson, Steve Butler, Alan Cleman, Erwin Dutcher, Dallas Grider, Jim Miller, Jerry Klein and future Bruin coach Terry Donahue.

Michigan's game-ending comeback attempt was as rapid as it was dramatic. With only six minutes and thirty-eight seconds remaining in the game, substitute Spartan quarterback Jim Raye lateraled to Apisa, catching UCLA by surprise. *Continued on page 151*

TOURNAMENT OF ROSES

Pasadena California

New Years 1915 Day

MIDWINTER FLORAL PAGEANT

ROMAN CHARIOT RACES

The aspiration of many a young lady in high school in the Pasadena area is not to become a movie star. The typical teenage girl in the land of the Tournament of Roses dreams of becoming Rose Queen.

Each year approximately six hundred girls between seventeen and twenty-one compete for the honor of being queen or a princess in the festival's court.

The queen and her court are selected by a panel of judges, members of the Tournament selection committee, in a series of eliminations. Candidates must be unmarried and must be high school seniors or full-time students with at least a "C" average in any accredited school or college in the Pasadena Area Community College District.

The bases for selection are natural personality, poise, projection, capacity to captivate and glitter. "We do not run a beauty or talent contest," affirm Tournament officials. "We are looking for the typical American young lady, the nice girl on the block."

The Tournament's centennial queen in 1989 will be the seventy-first to reign. Hallie Woods was the first queen named in 1905, and for several years the queens were randomly chosen. They were asked to serve only for the day of the festival. Some years there was no queen, and, on at least two occasions, there were both a king and a queen. There has been an unbroken chain of queens since Holly Halsted in 1930.

Holly Halsted, now Mrs. Balthis, the oldest living queen as the 1989 centennial year began, said being a queen "is like belonging to one large family." She added that her role "has given me the opportunity and the impetus to make friends, do diverse things and stay mentally active and curious about people and current issues."

Mrs. Balthis annually attends Rose Queen functions at Tournament time. She declared she is impressed with the present-day young ladies' personality, skills, firm direction about their lives and their maturity.

In early Tournament years, the queen would help place decorations on floats, quickly arrange for a gown and return to her regular work the next day. In modern times, the queen and princesses work in their capacity—making personal and media appearances, traveling and greeting thousands of Tournament followers. "I am constantly amazed how so many former queens are handling marriage, motherhood and a career. I admire them," concluded Holly.

The 1988 queen, Julie Myers of Arcadia, plans to go to UCLA to study "so I can become another Barbara Walters." While many queens become career women for a while, most have settled down to raise families.

1905 Hallie Woods	1906 Elsie Armitage	1907 Joan Woodbury	1908 May Sutton
1911 Ruth Palmer	1913 Jean French	1914 Mable Seibert	1923 May McAvoy
1925 Margaret Scoville	1926 Fay Lanphier	1928 Harriet Sterling	1930 Holly Halsted
1931 Mary Lou Waddell	1932 Myrta Olmsted	1933 Dorothy Edwards	1934 Treva Scott
1935 Muriel Cowan	1936 Barbara Nichols	1937 Nancy Bumpus	1938 Cheryl Walker
1939 Barbara Dougall	1940 Margaret Huntley	1941 Sally Stanton	1942 Dolores Brubach

1943 Mildred Miller	1944 Naomi Riordan	1945 Mary Rutte	1946 Patricia Auman
1947 Norma Christopher	1948 Virginia Goodhue	1949 Virginia Bower	1950 Marion Brown
1951 Eleanor Payne	1952 Nancy True Thorne	1953 Leah Feland	1954 Barbara Schmidt
1955 Marilyn Smuin	1956 Joan Culver	1957 Ann Mossberg	1958 Gertrude Wood
1959 Pamela Prather	1960 Margarethe Bertelson	1961 Carole Washburn	1962 Martha Sissell
1963 Nancy Davis	1964 Nancy Kneeland	1965 Dawn Baker	1966 Carole Cota

1967 Barbara Hewitt

1968 Linda Strother

1969 Pamela Anicich

1970 Pamela Tedesco

1971 Kathy Arnett

1972 Margo Lynn Johnson

1973 Salli Noren

1974 Miranda Barone

1975 Robin Carr

1976 Anne Martin

1977 Diane Ramaker

1978 Maria Caron

1979 Catherine Gilmour

1980 Julie Raatz

1981 Leslie Kawai

1982 Katy Potthast

1983 Suzanne Gillaspie

1984 Ann Colburn

1985 Kristina Smith

1986 Aimee Richelieu

1987 Kristin Harris

1988 Julie Myers

The 1987 Court with President Fred Soldwedel, left, and emcee Kevin O'Connell

The Tournament's grand marshal, a distinguished person who serves as an image of lifetime achievement and goodwill, is selected for each Tournament parade and game by the Tournament president.

Four presidents of the United States have been grand marshals—Herbert Hoover in 1945, Dwight D. Eisenhower in 1964, Richard Nixon in 1953 and 1960, and Gerald Ford in 1978.

Three grand marshals have been chosen twice—Nixon, Earl Warren in 1943 and 1955, and Bob Hope in 1947 and 1969.

Prominent entertainers and actors have been named seventeen times. They are Hope, Gregory Peck, Danny Kaye, Jimmy Stewart, Lorne Greene, Frank Sinatra, Roy Rogers and Dale Evans, Kate Smith, John Wayne, Lawrence Welk, Walt Disney, Kay Kyser, Edgar Bergen and Charlie McCarthy, Shirley Temple, Harold Lloyd and Mary Pickford.

The heroes of the moon launching—astronauts Charles Conrad, Richard Gordon and Alan Bean—were grand marshals in 1970.

The world of sports has contributed five grand marshals—football coach Alonzo Stagg in 1944, golfer Arnold Palmer in 1965, major league baseball star Hank Aaron in 1975, professional football player Merlin Olsen in 1983 and the all-time top soccer player, Pelé, in 1987.

Although he was not a grand marshal, scientist Albert Einstein was honored in 1931 as a special Tournament guest. Dr. William Pickering, a leader in early space development, is the only scientist to be selected. Another educator who served as grand marshal, in 1958, was Robert Sproul, the president of the University of California.

Many military men have been picked—Col. George S. Parker in 1924, Col. L. J. Mygatt in 1926, Gen. C. S. Farnsworth in 1931, Adm. William Sims in 1934, Adm. William Halsey in 1946, Gen. Omar Bradley in 1948, seven Medal of Honor recipients in 1952, Pvt. Robert Gray in 1951, Gen. William F. Dean in 1954 and war pilot Eddie Rickenbacker in 1957.

Statesmen and government leaders have included Warren, Everett Dirksen in 1968, Thanat Khoman of Thailand in 1967, Albert D. Rosellini in 1962, William F. Quinn in 1961, E. L. Bob Bartlett in 1959, Paul G. Hoffman in 1950, Perry Brown in 1949, E. O. Nay in 1941, James Allred in 1936, William Garland in 1932 and James Rolph in 1930.

The media world produced columnist Erma Bombeck in 1986 and cartoonist Charles Schulz in 1974. In the world of religion, evangelist Dr. Billy Graham was the 1971 grand marshal. The business world presented Lee Iacocca in 1985.

In the early years of the Tournament, prominent Pasadena citizens were picked to be the grand marshal. The last Pasadena citizen to be so honored was Lathrop Leishman in 1979.

Dr. Francis F. Rowland, one of the Tournament founders, was grand marshal the most times—seven.

1890	Dr. Francis F. Rowland
1892	Dr. Francis F. Rowland
1894	Dr. Francis F. Rowland
1895	Dr. H.H. Sherk
1896	Edwin Stearns
1897	Edwin Stearns
1898	Martin H. Weight
1899	Martin H. Weight
1900	Charles Daggett
1901	Charles Daggett
1902	C.C. Reynolds
1903	C.C. Reynolds
1904	Dr. Francis F. Rowland

1905	Dr. Francis F. Rowland
1906	John B. Miller
1907	Dr. H. P. Skillen
1908	Dr. H. P. Skillen
1909	Walter S. Wright
1910	Dr. Francis F. Rowland
1911	Dr. Ralph Skillen
1912	E. H. Groenendyke
1913	Leigh Guyer
1914	Charles Daggett
1915	M. S. Pashigian
1916	Dr. Francis F. Rowland
1917	Dr. C.D. Lockwood
1918	Dr. Z.T. Malaby
1919	Frank Hunter
1920	Frank G. Hogan
1921	W.A. Boucher
1922	Harold Landreth
1923	H.L. Gianetti
1924	Col. George S. Parker
1925	Lewis H. Turner
1926	Col. L.J. Mygatt
1927	Dr. C.D. Lockwood
1928	John MacDonald
1929	Marco Hellman
1930	James Rolph
1931	Gen. C.S. Farnsworth
1932	William May Garland
1933	Mary Pickford
1934	Adm. William S. Sims
1935	Harold Lloyd
1936	James V. Allred
1937	Eugene Biscailuz
1938	Leo Carrillo
1939	Shirley Temple
1940	Edgar Bergen & Charlie McCarthy
1941	E.O. Nay
1942	Kay Kyser
1943	Earl Warren
1944	Alonzo Stagg
1945	Herbert Hoover
1946	Adm. William Halsey
1947	Bob Hope
1948	Gen. Omar Bradley
1949	Perry Brown
1950	Paul C. Hoffman
1951	Pvt. Robert S. Gray
1952	Medal of Honor Men
1953	Richard Nixon
1954	Gen. William F. Dean
1955	Earl Warren
1956	Charles E. Wilson
1957	Eddie Rickenbacker
1958	Robert Sproul
1959	E.L. (Bob) Bartlett
1960	Richard Nixon
1961	William F. Quinn
1962	Albert D. Rosellini
1963	Dr. William H. Pickering
1964	Dwight D. Eisenhower

Gregory Peck rides in $8.5 million Bugatti

Pelé brings friendship

Walt Disney and friend

UCLA's Bob Stiles

1967
Pros and Cons

When the rival professional football leagues—the NFL and AFL—agreed to merge in 1966, they needed a place to stage their first championship game in January of 1967. It was natural that they looked toward Pasadena's magnificent Rose Bowl as the venue of what was later known as the Super Bowl. Although there was considerable popular support within Pasadena for the pro championship, the city of Pasadena made an early determination that it would remain a college town and resist efforts to put the professionals in the Rose Bowl.

The first interleague championship would have been played a week after the Rose Bowl game. The college conferences associated with the Tournament of Roses objected to this invasion, believing it would take away from the significance of the Rose Bowl game. Pasadena's *Star-News* editorially supported the collegiate stand.

Admiral Tom Hamilton, the commissioner of the Athletic Association of Western Universities (AAWU), said:

"The Rose Bowl game already is number one in the national sports picture. You can't have two number-one games. One or the other has to become number two. An event as solid as the Rose Bowl game should not be subjected to that. . . . We have also participated in the construction and improvement program of the stadium. Strong loyalty has existed on both sides. It would be unwise to create a situation in which our faculties and school administrators would be tempted to take a new look at our pact because of a change in the commercial environment."

William Reed, Big Ten commissioner, expressed a similar attitude and pointed

Bob Apisa lumbered 38 yards to score. Juday tried to pass for two points on a fake, but reserve defensive end Klein broke it up with a rush.

Minutes later, Steve Juday dove eight inches to score the touchdown that cut UCLA's lead to 14–12. In came reserve Raye, an expert at the pitchout, to get the big two points. Raye started to his right, then flipped a pitchout to strong 212-pound Apisa, who tried to skirt right end. Colletto came up to him, but Apisa's strength still had to be reckoned with. Stiles stormed in, leaped on Apisa's shoulders, and spun him back just as he was about to cross the line. The play was stopped inches short.

Stiles was knocked cold from the blow he took. He could not hear the cheers, but triumph was reserved for Stiles and his mates. It would be another twenty-two years before Michigan State could avenge itself against a West Coast team.

When George Catavolos saved the day for Purdue, he made good the promise of his mother that he would someday be a hero. She had uttered that statement when friends wanted her to name her baby "Victor Edward" in honor of V-E Day—the day on which he was born. She nixed the suggestion, however, saying she would sell bonds to honor the end of the war but she was going to stick to the Greek name of George.

President Henry Kearns and Grand Marshal Thanat Khoman

Purdue's Bob Griese

out that Big Ten participation in Pasadena had passed by only a 6–4 vote the last time it had come up.

The Super Bowl was thus awarded to the Los Angeles Coliseum in 1967, and NFL commissioner Pete Rozelle, too, let it be known that professional football did not want to antagonize the collegiate world, which provides the NFL with talent in the collegiate player draft. All viewpoints were to change later, of course, when the 1977 Super Bowl game was accepted by Pasadena.

Meanwhile, the Tournament carried on with business as usual.

Henry Kearns, later president and chairman of the Export-Import Bank of the United States, was president for 1967. Kearns said he began his Tournament career as a float driver in the rainy parade "when," as he put it, "it was a little damp." His next assignment came in 1937 as a member of the traffic committee, "when it was my responsibility

to precede the parade and at certain intervals stop it to prevent gaps when the Santa Fe train went through east of Raymond Avenue."

For grand marshal of the 1967 parade, Kearns chose Thanat Khoman, the minister of foreign affairs of Thailand. This marked the first time the grand marshal's office was filled by someone from outside the country. Barbara Hewitt was the 1967 queen.

The parade theme was "Travel Tales in Flowers" as the Tournament again emphasized world-wide friendship. A float entitled "Around the World in Eighty Days" carried a baby pink elephant. South Pasadena won the Sweepstakes award with "A Voyage to Atlantis."

Al Stewart's all-male Purdue glee club won the hearts of Southland folks before the Purdue football team coached by Jack Mollenkopf stood off the bid of John McKay's Southern California Trojans.

Purdue also brought out an impressive band. It even moved the *Herald Examiner*'s Mel Durslag to write:

"As a West Coaster, I'm getting good and bloody sick of the Big Ten Rose Bowl pact. Wait a minute! It's not the football team. We can handle them. It's show business where they are clobbering us. In football, we're five for 21. In bands, they've shut us out. Purdue came out with a band that John Philip Sousa never dreamed of—plus they had four girls in sequins, balloons, smoke bombs, and more tubas than a hock shop on New Year's morning. The band had more people in it than the Washington Senators drew last season. I don't mean to take anything away from the poor kids at USC, but they looked like an Indian club act by comparison. 'What's the name of that combo?' asked the press box's Bud Tucker of the *San Gabriel Valley Tribune*, as

USC's thin red line trickled out onto the field. Our colleges should start recruiting Swiss bell ringers, not scatbacks, fiddlers, nor fullbacks."

Another Cliff-hanger:
Purdue 14, USC 13

The 1967 Rose Bowl game was another cliff-hanging thriller, but when it was all over, a clear victory in statistics was all that USC could claim; it won the total yardage contest, 323 yards to 244.

With just two-and-a-half minutes to play, USC's Rod Sherman—who had played high school football for Muir on the Rose Bowl field—almost became the all-time Rose Bowl game hero when he got behind Purdue's George Catavolos to pull down a 19-yard Troy Winslow pass to reduce Purdue's lead to 14–13. Catavolos was the goat only briefly, however. When McKay gallantly refused to settle for a tie and ordered Winslow to "go for it," the Purdue defender stepped in front of Jim Lawrence to intercept the pass which would have given USC the victory. It was that kind of game.

After two Purdue drives, Perry Williams had scored the first Boilermaker touchdown to make it 7–0. In the second period, USC's offense took charge, working up to two good scoring chances. Jim Lawrence ran 39 yards with a pass and would have gone all the way if he hadn't stumbled at the start. In the second drive, good catches by Sherman and Lawrence plus blasts by Homer Williams, playing for the injured Mike Hull, set up a touchdown by Don McCall.

USC mounted a third drive before half time with the big runs being 16 yards by McCall and 35 yards by Hull—both down the middle. Hull, too, stumbled, or he would have gone all the way. Tim Rossovich's 42-yard field goal attempt

was straight, but several feet short.

Each team blew scoring chances in the third quarter before quarterback Bob Griese connected on two passes to Bob Hurst to set up a second short Williams touchdown run.

USC wanted a touchdown so badly in the fourth quarter it controlled the ball twenty-six plays to Purdue's eight. A 34-yard pass from Winslow to Sherman, who got beyond the stumbling Leroy Keyes, seemed to set up the scoring chance USC wanted, but then Winslow was thrown for a big loss. After Purdue punted, USC got the break it needed when Purdue roughed the USC punter.

Catavolos gave Bill Miller of the *Star-News* this version of his save:

"They had to go for two points in a game like this. And they had to throw because they couldn't run on us down there. John Charles, our other defensive halfback, broke up Sherman on his pass pattern. This enabled me to step in front of Lawrence to intercept. I was playing between Winslow and Sherman. When Charles took care of Sherman, I went behind and took care of Lawrence. He and I were the only ones left."

Lawrence told Dwain Esper of the *Star-News*, "I could almost feel the ball in my hands, it was so close. It was a perfect pass. Troy had me pegged all the way. But that Purdue fellow made a tremendous play."

McKay, who was to become famous as a gambler on the field, said, "We had no thought of playing for a tie. Even if we had tied it up, Purdue could have worked Griese's short passes to the sidelines after we kicked off, and they could have moved within range of a field goal. We put Sherman, Lawrence and Ray Cahill on the right side. Sherman and Cahill criss-crossed in the end zone and Law-

USC coach Johnny McKay

Rod Sherman catches TD pass for USC

Indiana coach Johnny Pont advises his players

In order to break from the official routines, Tournament president H.W. Bragg took Grand Marshal Everett Dirksen to Santa Anita's race track one afternoon. When Senator Dirksen excused himself from their box after each race, Bragg assumed Dirksen was visiting the pari-mutuel window. Dirksen appeared more jolly each time he came back. To cash in on some of his companion's good fortune, Bragg followed Dirksen after the seventh race. As they passed the turf club's "fountain of lively water," the bartender beamed, "Shall I mix you another one, Senator?"

H.W. "Hoot" Bragg

rence flared to the right. Troy threw the ball perfectly, but that Catavolos played it beautifully."

1968
The Juice Makes a Splash

A rosy-faced, amiable Santa Claus type and Los Angeles oil executive, H.W. "Hoot" Bragg, was president of the 1968 Tournament. Bragg had only one choice for his grand marshal—Senator Everett Dirksen of Illinois. Although the senator's face was pale, his heart was glowing. Pasadena loved him.

Bragg was fascinated by Dirksen's affection for people. "We were running a little late to attend the Chrysler reception prior to the Big Ten dinner at the Palladium," recalled Bragg.

"We stopped in front of the Palladium on Sunset Boulevard, and I warned the senator not to stop for autographs and the usual handshaking because we were due inside. He said, 'Fine, don't worry.' Then he got out of the car and walked to the glass ticket-sales window and shook hands with a gray-haired sixty-year-old gal. He said to her, 'Now put your mouth up to the round hole in the glass and give me a kiss.' She promptly did. This caused a great applause from the people milling around outside. Then Mr. Dirksen explained to his wife that the lady might live in Illinois someday and he needed a vote everywhere he could find it.

"I also recall a great evening after the Grand Marshal Ball in his honor at the Huntington when we attended a meatball party at the Overland Club. Since he was very tired, he suggested he stay only thirty minutes. We arrived at 10:15 p.m. and he was still visiting and exchanging stories with Maudie Prickett at 2:45 in the morning. Before leaving the party, the senator shook hands with everyone

Senator Everett Dirksen

and called them by their first and last names, which, in itself, is a pretty hard thing to do, especially after Overland Club hospitality."

Bragg said the senator was never off schedule during his entire stay in Pasadena and wrote all of his speeches on a cloth napkin with a felt pen about two minutes before giving them.

Bragg was a president with foresight. Five months before New Year's Day, at an annual guess-the-team contest gathering of Tournament people, "Hoot" predicted it would be Indiana against USC in the Rose Bowl. Johnny Pont's amazing Indiana "Cinderella Kids" made his prediction come true by staging a series of startling comebacks in Big Ten thrillers to qualify as national champion USC's opponent on January 1. Each team had lost one game during the season.

The seventy-ninth annual Tournament of Roses was a special occasion, for it marked the first time the parade and game telecasts were beamed by satellite to other parts of the world. Bragg had become cognizant of the international acceptance of the Tournament when he visited Thailand with Henry Kearns as guests of Thanat Khoman. During a garden reception, Thai children pasted flowers on a wall to spell out, "Welcome, Pasadena Tournament of Roses."

Bragg had first ridden in the Rose Parade in 1914. He was a three-year-old boy riding on the fire truck driven by his father. In 1929 he was an usher in the Rose Bowl. He threw a handful of tickets away in excitedly trying to gesture Roy Riegels when he ran the wrong way.

A chilly but clear day greeted Queen Linda Strother and her court for their reign on January 1, 1968, a day that will be remembered as "The Great Indiana Invasion." More than twenty thousand Hoosier rooters came to Pasadena, their bright red dominating the west side of the Rose Bowl. Hoosier red was not dominant on the field, however.

The Juice Puts on a Show: USC 14, Indiana 3

O.J. Simpson had a boyhood dream of playing in the Rose Bowl. It remained his driving goal throughout his two-year USC playing career. When he had transferred from San Francisco City College to become a Trojan, he consoled his depressed future teammates after they suffered that disheartening 14–13 loss to Purdue in the 1967 classic. "Don't worry about it," O.J. said after the game. "We will be back next year."

The Trojans were back the next year, and O.J. made the difference. Led by his two touchdowns and 128 yards in twenty-five carries, USC turned back the young Indiana challengers, 14–3, in a game that did not excite the experts.

The 102,946 spectators enjoyed the performance, however, while young In-diana quarterback Harry Gonso and his sophomore pals made the Trojans work to win. Paul Zimmerman of the *Times* praised the Trojan defense for the victory. "The USC defense shut off quarterback Gonso's option plays, adjusted to the sprint-out pass and Coach Johnny Pont's belly series where the quarterback fakes to the fullback, slides along the line, and pitches back or keeps the ball," wrote Zimmerman in his last Rose Bowl story before retiring from an eminent sports-writing career.

Veteran television commentator Paul Christman, himself a great player in his day, said after his first broadcast of a Rose Bowl game that an injury to Gonso in the fourth quarter, when the Hoosiers were making a comeback bid, prevented a wild finish and denied Indiana a shot at another dramatic victory.

The Trojans took advantage of the Hoosier strategy of keying on Simpson by mixing in the forward pass with more-than-usual use of fullback Dan Scott as a runner to the inside. The strategy paid off. Simpson scored twice on short runs, and all the Hoosiers could get against USC was a 27-yard field goal by Dave Kornowa. "We knew Indiana had quick linebackers," said Trojan quarterback Steve Sogge, "so we figured if we ran Dan Scott, who lines up directly in front of Simpson, we would gain an extra step. That extra step helped a lot."

1969
Thanks for the Memories

The president of the 1969 Tournament was Gleeson L. "Tige" Payne, a handsome, tall, athletic-looking insurance executive. Payne selected Bob Hope as his grand marshal for "A Time to Remember" milestone in the great history of Pasadena's famed classic. Hope was a

Hoosier cheer leaders

The 1969 Rose Bowl was the second of seven Rose Bowl confrontations between USC and Ohio State—the most meetings of any pair of schools through the Tournament's first one hundred years. The scores:

1955	Ohio State 20, USC 7
1969	Ohio State 27, USC 16
1973	USC 42, Ohio State 17
1974	Ohio State 42, USC 21
1975	USC 18, Ohio State 17
1980	USC 17, Ohio State 16
1985	USC 20, Ohio State 17

At the Kiwanis Kickoff Luncheon, Ohio State's Woody Hayes was asked what he feared most about USC. "Not a damn thing!" he bellowed. The way the Buckeyes beat up on the Trojans, Woody was, for once, correct.

popular choice. He had to hurry back from his annual Christmas tour of entertaining troops in Vietnam to join Payne in leading one of the most beautiful parades ever to pass through Pasadena.

The assembled one-and-one-half million spectators greeted the Hopes on this day of happiness. As Bob passed the networks' cameras, he said, "I would have been Rose Bowl queen, but my wig fell off during the semifinals."

The eightieth Tournament, with Queen Pamela Anicich reigning, was staged on a beautiful, warm, summer-like day.

Gaiety was the mood, after Hope had broken all pregame tensions with a rib-

O.J. Simpson rolls against Ohio State

tickling talk at the Kickoff Luncheon the day before. "It was nice of Tige Payne to recall my boxing career. I was known as Rembrandt Hope—I was on the canvas so much," said the comedian, who then added such quips as:

"You know Everett Dirksen was grand marshal last year. The parade will go faster this year. I don't have to sell albums . . . They didn't need a float for Dirksen. They just frosted his hair. He looks as if he were electrocuted and lived. . . .It's a great honor to be grand marshal. Some of the past men honored were General Eisenhower, Chief Justice Warren and Richard Nixon. I think I'll go to Whittier while I'm over this way and see the manger Nixon was born in . . ."

Four of the great names of American intercollegiate football rode the National Football Foundation's float: Dr. Jerome "Brud" Holland of Cornell; Ernie Nevers of Stanford; Fritz Crisler of Minnesota, Princeton and Michigan; and Morley Drury of USC. This was part of the foundation's observance of football's one-hundredth year. Television surveys claimed ninety-eight million people saw this float and the others in the parade, which was beamed via television to many parts of the world.

Floats from San Diego, City of Commerce and San Gabriel depicted two hundred years since the beginning of California. Many organizations celebrated their birthdays with floats: Loyal Order of Moose, eighty years; Demolay, fifty years; Odd Fellows and Rebekahs, one hundred and fifty years; and National Restaurant Association, fifty years.

With the temperature in the high seventies, the Buckeyes of Ohio State, who had trained with hot blowers providing California conditions in their field house in Columbus, put on a tremendous display of hard hitting, solid football and stamina to defeat Simpson, Sogge and company, 27–16, before 102,036 stunned spectators, including President-elect Nixon, who flew to the stadium via helicopter which landed on Brookside Golf Course west of the stadium.

At Nixon's side during the game was ex-coach of renown Bud Wilkinson, appointed to the "cabinet" for the day as "minister of football." Nixon was so thrilled by the spectacle of seeing one hundred thousand American flags displayed during the singing of the National Anthem that he congratulated the Tournament for its patriotism.

The flags were secured and paid for through the efforts of three Pasadena men—Art Neff, Bob Mulvin and Marv Gray—and distributed by military personnel, Boy Scouts and volunteers to every person who entered the stadium. Americans watching the telecast in foreign countries were thrilled.

Two-time grand marshal Bob Hope and President Gleeson L. "Tige" Payne in 1968 festival

Dream Game:
Ohio State 27, USC 16

Before the 1969 game, Dick Cullum, accepted football authority from the Midwest and columnist for the *Minneapolis Tribune,* said: "This isn't Indiana that USC is playing. Ohio State is a great football team. Watch out."

Trojan followers should have known, as January 1, 1969, approached, that there was trouble ahead when Ohio State's sophomore-studded team swept through a nine-game season undefeated and qualified to battle once-tied USC for the national championship. Ohio State went into the game ranked number one in the polls. USC was number two. It was indeed a dream game.

The Trojans paved the way for their doom, as Dwain Esper so perfectly de-

scribed it in his *Star-News* story, by throwing two costly interceptions on bids for touchdowns and by losing the ball three times on fumbles—five turnovers that reversed the trend of the game completely, despite another workhorse display of staying power by O.J. Simpson. In contrast, Ohio State had no interceptions and never lost a fumble.

Simpson fumbled the ball away twice and Steve Sogge once. Each threw it away on potential touchdown plays. One of Sogge's fumbles set up a Buckeye touchdown and one of Simpson's set up another. These mistakes offset a brilliant 80-yard touchdown run by O.J., as well as his 171 yards gained while carrying the ball twenty-eight times and his eight pass catches that were good for 85 yards more. After a display of skill like this, it was sad for the Trojans to watch their Heisman Trophy hero suddenly come up with greasy fingers.

When Grand Marshal Bob Hope's driver went to start his car to begin the 1969 parade, nothing happened. The battery was dead—possibly victim to a gadget overload, which included TV set, radio receiver and transmitter and audio equipment. A jump-start kept the car running smoothly until Holliston Avenue, where the battery conked out completely. Five scruffy teenagers pushed the stricken vehicle to Victory Park, where Hope gave them his own Rose Bowl game tickets. Imagine the surprise of Tournament Manager Max Colwell at the stadium when he saw five barefooted young men in the grand marshal's seats. He was further surprised when they said, "Bob Hope gave us the tickets."

Ohio State's Leo Hayden breaks through USC defense

USC's 10–0 lead on a 21-yard Ron Ayala field goal and O.J.'s 80-yard dash deteriorated when Ohio State got its inside running game functioning, a blasting attack that the Trojan defense could not stop. Sophomore quarterback Rex Kern earned player-of-the-game honors by directing and executing this attack as he ran and passed the Trojan defense into a state of futility. Big Ohio State ground-gainers were fullback Jim Otis and halfback Leophus Hayden. Simpson's great run, in which he broke off left tackle, cut back and outraced the Buckeye defense, was the last Trojan gem of the day.

A 69-yard Ohio comeback drive culminating in an Otis thrust for the score and a 26-yard field goal by Jim Roman three seconds before the half time gun tied it up and signaled a "Roman Holiday" after intermission.

As Simpson and Sogge took turns handing the ball to the Buckeyes, Ohio State scored again on a 25-yard Roman field goal, a Kern touchdown pass to Hayden and a 16-yard looper from Kern to Ray Gillian. Meanwhile, the Trojans blew scoring chances by throwing two interceptions before Sogge connected on a

spiral to Sam Dickerson for a disputed touchdown deep in the end zone. Joint possession, according to college football rules, becomes a touchdown for the offense if the receiver at least touches one foot in the end zone while retaining partial possession coming down. This Dickerson may have done, as substantiated by excellent Associated Press photos, although the fans thought they had witnessed nothing more than two players and the ball spurting out of the end zone. The play was the topic of argument for days, the touchdown small consolation for a Troy that had fallen in a jittery performance against a team that hit harder, forced mistakes and came to win.

Ohio State line coach Lou McCullough said his team set up its defense to avoid giving Simpson the cutback. "USC took away our wide game," added Hayes. "But they did it at a price. We were able to curl our receivers around their front for passes and we were able to run inside. Even when we were down 10–0, I knew we could come back. I knew our offense would roll. And I also felt Simpson would not break away again."

"Tying before the half time gun was a big lift for us. It gave us the momentum and it took that away from them," said Kern, who not only was player of the game, but also dated the Rose queen, who soon decided to enroll at Ohio State. "That's the first time I ever saw a touchdown when the ball was rolling on the ground," said Hayes, who couldn't forget the disputed USC touchdown.

Then Woody headed for Vietnam to show the troops the pictures of how Ohio State continued to be a power in the Rose Bowl.

He was to return to face his greatest Rose Bowl challenges.

THE 1970s

THE SPACE AGE

1970
Moon Men

After the excitement of the first manned landings on the moon in 1969, C. Lewis Edwards, president of the 1970 Tournament, made a moon shot in reverse. He brought the "moon men" to Pasadena.

Astronauts Charles Conrad, Richard Gordon and Alan Bean—recently back from the Apollo 12 mission to the moon—kept their date with Edwards and arrived amid the thundering applause of the three thousand football fans attending the Kickoff Luncheon the day before the big game.

The smiling astronauts, loudly cheered in every Pasadena appearance, led the parade as grand marshals in three separate automobiles. They loved the role. President Edwards made an inter-

When the Apollo 12 astronauts were introduced at the 1970 Kickoff Luncheon, Commander Charles Conrad said, "The moon will probably put Disneyland out of business if we can find a way to get the kids up there. The moon is good news for golfers. You can hit the ball a country mile, and with no atmosphere there is no way you can hook or slice. As for football on the moon, you'd have to make a lot of changes in the rules."

When the committee of 1970 Tournament officers visited Washington, D.C., a rose sticker was observed on Conrad Hilton's lapel in the portrait gracing the lobby of the Statler-Hilton Hotel. Who put it there? The mystery has not been solved, although somebody pointed out that Tournament president C. Lewis Edwards was the only member of the group tall enough to reach the picture.

The Apollo 12 crew: Conrad, Gordon and Bean

esting observation. "From my vantage point near them, I could tell that they were setting the pattern of our parade. Everybody was happy all along the route. This was the happiest parade I have ever seen, and it was the astronauts who set the mood of good will."

Queen Pamela Dee Tedesco was crowned before three thousand people in what coronation chairman Alexander Gaal called "the most impressive coronation we have ever had." Queen Pamela had a rose planted in her honor in the shadow of the Rose Queen Fountain in the center of Wrigley Gardens at Tournament House in Pasadena. It marked the first American planting of the new hybrid tea rose, Interflora, which was developed by Universal Rose Selection of Meilland, France.

A total of 84,803 seats in grandstands constructed along the parade route were sold to the public for up to $8.50 each—a price which was to rise another two-and-a-half times by the late 1980s.

It was a particularly colorful parade in 1970, and the city of Los Angeles won the Sweepstakes prize with a float depicting an exotic bonsai planter in the midst of an Oriental garden and pool.

The Farmers Insurance Company float, "Holiday in the Park," was made up of twenty thousand dark red Forever Yours roses, but a little dog named Rosey turned out to be the sweetest rose of all. Charles Manos, a *Detroit News* reporter, bought the four-month-old pup from the Detroit Humane Society and gained a trip to Pasadena for Rosey and himself when Farmers Insurance agreed to let the pair ride on a park bench on the float.

Rosey flew to Pasadena by air freight, but flew home first class because she had been such a big hit in the parade when she waved her tail to millions. Manos re-

USC's Wild Bunch: Gunn, Smith, Scott, Cowlings and Weaver

ported that she stood on her hind legs when the float got near the television cameras. "What a ham," he remarked.

Mrs. J. Lambert Roberts of Pasadena especially enjoyed the 1970 parade. Its theme "Holidays Around the World" was an idea she had submitted. She was a second-time winner in the annual theme-idea contest. In 1957 she had suggested "Famous Firsts in Flowers."

Debut of da Bo:
USC 10, Michigan 3

At the Kickoff Luncheon the day before the game, USC's coach John McKay was asked about his controversial offense. He replied, "If Michigan didn't show up, we wouldn't score eighteen points." One of his assistants, Craig Fertig, told the Los Angeles Jonathan Club, "I was told I could have sixty minutes to review the season. I'll stand here for fifty-eight minutes and do nothing. Then I'll talk for two minutes." Of course, Fertig was referring to USC's season of not being productive until the final two minutes of most games. The Trojans changed the pattern against

Michigan, however. They played it to the hilt all the way.

Despite McKay's remarks, Michigan did show up, but without its head coach, Bo Schembechler, who had complained of stomach pains all week, went to St. Luke's Hospital with a mild heart attack and had to remain in Pasadena for three weeks to recuperate. Michigan players told Will Watson of the *Star-News* that the loss of Schembechler hurt them; it wasn't the same without the coach to talk to on timeouts. Michigan played under Jim Young, Bo's assistant.

Although the Michigan team wore Pasadena-made uniforms (the maize and blue was "spic and Spanjian" in its garb manufactured by the Spanjian Company), the Wolverines couldn't handle McKay's "Wild Bunch"—the name given to the Trojan front five-man line. The reason? In this game, McKay came up with a six-man line, adding big Tony Terry, and the strategy checked Michigan's running game. The original "Wild Bunch" were Jimmy Gunn and Charlie Weaver at ends, Al Cowlings and Tody Smith at tackles, and Bubba Scott in the middle.

C. Lewis Edwards

Bob Chandler scores on a pass from Jimmy Jones

USC athletic director Jess Hill handled 1970 VIP Rose Bowl seats when university president Norman Topping was in Seattle on business. Near game day, Hill was home shaving when his wife announced, "The president's calling you from Washington." Believing it to be President Topping in the state of Washington, Hill asked to have him call back later. "No!" she said. "Not *that* president. It's President *Nixon.*" His face literally a-lather, Hill took the call. Nixon could not attend the Rose Bowl, so he wished USC good luck.

At the 1970 Kickoff Luncheon Michigan coach Bo Schembechler was introduced with one of the shortest poems ever written:
Oh goodie,
No Woody!
Gung ho,
Here's Bo!

Even the Michigan "Touchdown Pup" couldn't score a touchdown on this New Year's Day. In its famous nose-dribble act between halves, the Michigan mascot ran out of bounds on the 5-yard line.

It cannot be said the Trojans won, 10–3, only on defense, however. The Trojan offensive unit, often criticized in 1969 for offensive breakdowns up until the last two minutes of their games, did just fine. USC had six scoring chances to Michigan's four and outgained the Wolverines 323 yards to 289.

USC scored first on a 25-yard field goal by Ron Ayala, who had kicked a last-second field goal to beat Stanford earlier in the season. Michigan tied the game on a kick by Tim Killian. Then, in the third quarter, Jimmy Jones threw a 13-yard pass to Bob Chandler which the fleet USC receiver took on the Michigan 20. Chandler pivoted away from Michigan's Brian Healy and then escaped Barry Pierson's desperation grab near the goal line to score the winning touchdown. Ayala

kicked the point to make it 10–3.

Dwain Esper in the *Star-News* described McKay's victory strategy: "John McKay deduced early in his Rose Bowl preparation that Michigan liked to run. Consequently he reconstructed his defense to meet this team tendency—and oh, how it paid off! McKay's answer was a 'sixty-one' defense, fundamentally a six-man line with one linebacker."

McKay said that his strategy "was to try to get Michigan to play us left-handed." He succeeded. Michigan needed long passes by quarterback Don Moorhead at the finish, but had to be content mostly with short ones to his great tight end Jim Mandich, who caught eight.

Clarence Davis and Mike Berry carried the running load for USC and churned up enough yardage to keep the attack going with Jones's well-placed spot shots to his receivers offering a change.

Punter Ayala may have made the play that saved the day for USC. With three minutes to play, he stood in midfield to punt. The pass from center was high over his head. He leaped, batted it down, caught the ball, and kicked it from amidst the charge of Michigan's rushing giants, Cecil Pryor and Mike Keller. This kick, which stopped on Michigan's 8-yard line, put them too far back to go all the way with a late offensive.

Loel Schrader, *Long Beach Press-Telegram,* wrote: "Doubtless the Wolverines missed the presence of their dynamic young coach, who had masterminded the 24–12 victory over Ohio State in his first year at Ann Arbor. But the story of this game lay in USC's ability to stack up Michigan's running attack and force Michigan to be content with nothing more than aerial 'gimmies' of the short variety, plus the return to early season form by Trojan quarterback Jimmy Jones."

1971
The Power of Prayer

The 1971 Tournament of Roses marked the reign of Lewis the Second—A. Lewis Shingler, who succeeded C. Lewis Edwards. Shingler was an institutional fund-raiser by trade, but a Tournament of Roses worker by first love. During twenty-three years of Tournament service he chaired five committees and served on nine.

For seventeen years Shingler had been a Pasadena auto salesman. "I started selling cars here with Henry Kearns in 1936. He went pretty far, didn't he?" Shingler said of the president of the Export-Import Bank of the United States.

Shingler's grand marshal was evangelist Billy Graham. Hinting that the Tournament of Roses had placed him in charge of the weather, Dr. Graham and his wife, Ruth, were happy to see that Pasadena enjoyed one of its finest sunny

days for the pageant. The theme of the Tournament was "Through the Eyes of a Child." When Graham spoke before three thousand football fans at the Kiwanis Kickoff Luncheon, he said, "The strife in the world would end if people everywhere viewed the world through the eyes of a child." Graham could not arrive in Pasadena in time for the Grand Marshal's Ball, so actor Robert Young, who had learned his trade at the Pasadena Playhouse, filled in for him.

The queen of the 1971 Tournament was Kathleen Denise Arnett, a Pasadena City College sophomore from Los Angeles. The other members of her court were Janet Kay Hagemeier, Cynthia Lee Coleman, Christine Marie Hartwell, Debbi Ann Gilmore, Patricia Hartman Burch and Paula Kay Hubbard.

The Sweepstakes float winner in the parade was called "Georgia—Wonderland of Fun." It featured attractive southern belles posed in swings beneath two majestic oak trees fashioned of flowers. The highlight of the entry was a pair of peacocks in all their magnificence perched in the trees, creating a picture of the scenic wonders and serene atmosphere of Georgia as a place of pleasure and enjoyment.

"Cinderella," drawn by six white ponies, took the Grand Prize for the Farmers Insurance Group. The two parts of this entry were synchronized to depict Cinderella going to the ball down an avenue of graceful trees.

The President's Trophy went to the "Birds and Bees," the seventeenth annual entry of the Florists' Transworld Delivery Association. The wings and arms of both species moved mechanically, and more than fifty thousand roses were used to blanket the float, which depicted a flower garden fifty feet long, eighteen

Billy Graham

The 1971 Tournament president A. Lewis Shingler was a genuine Southerner, from Georgia. To many Californians all Southerners sound the same, so many associates assumed he was a Texan. His stock answer to that calumny always was the same: "Fellows, I've spent only one day of my life in Texas and that was in leaving." As it turned out, January 1, 1971, wasn't a bad day for his original home state. The Sweepstakes prize in the parade went to the float "Georgia—Wonderland of Fun."

Lewis Shingler

South Pasadena's Jack Schultz, Stanford safety man and co-captain, hung around the Rose Bowl as a child, hoping someone would take him in. A star for Stanford in 1971, it was his interception that set up the winning touchdown drive. "I never got inside the bowl until today," said Schultz afterwards. "I always wondered what it was like. Now I know. It's great."

Stanford's Steve Horowitz kicks a 48-yard field goal

feet wide, and sixteen feet high. Seventeen huge flowers were covered with different varieties of roses.

Mission Impossible: Stanford 27, Ohio State 17

Woody Hayes brought in yet another Ohio State team, this time heavily favored to beat John Ralston's Stanford aggregation. At a Big Ten dinner at the Palladium in Hollywood, Peter Graves, of the hit TV series, "Mission Impossible," said, "I assure you this Ohio State team will not self-destruct." However, Stanford turned out to be extremely destructive by rallying with two fourth-pe-riod touchdowns that overcame a 17–13 Buckeye lead and gave the Indians a 27–17 triumph that thrilled the record 103,839 spectators viewing the game in warm sunshine.

The victory could be interpreted as a triumph for Dr. Graham. When he learned that the Ohio State team had spent the night before the game at a monastery in the foothills of the San Gabriel Mountains above Pasadena, Stanford's coach John Ralston said, "Billy Graham will be on our side."

Indeed, Stanford surprised Ohio State early, with an end-around reverse that sprang Eric Cross for a 41-yard gain. This

Bob Moore's catch sets up a Stanford TD

Rex Kern gains a big one for Ohio State

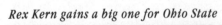

Stanford's Randy Vataha

165

Coach Johnny Ralston celebrates second-straight upset

set up Jackie Brown's 4-yard touchdown sprint, giving Stanford a 7–0 lead. The first of two field goals by Steve Horowitz gave the Indians a 10–0 margin.

Ohio State then opened up with its own powerful ground attack, which featured Rex Kern's pitchouts and keepers to the outside. Kern netted 129 yards in twenty carries. John Brockington and Leo Hayden also provided solid punch, and Ohio State climbed to a 17–10 lead.

In the third quarter, Horowitz set an all-time Rose Bowl distance record for field goals by connecting on a 48-yard attempt to cut the Buckeye lead to 17–13. However, Ohio State's ground power was asserting itself and the Buckeyes had a fourth and inches to go on Stanford's 19. If successful in this fourth down try, Ohio State appeared to be capable of moving in for a fourth-quarter score that would have clinched the game. The Buckeyes called on Brockington to punch the right side, but Ron Kadziel, Stanford linebacker, met him head-on for a yard loss. Stanford took over, and

with new vigor the Indians completely took charge of the football game.

Jim Plunkett, the Heisman Trophy winner who completed twenty of thirty passes for the day in an amazing demonstration of accuracy and sharp play-calling while facing one of the nation's top defenses, started to connect to little rabbit Randy Vataha and leaping Bob Moore, and it wasn't long before Stanford had its 27–17 victory margin. Moore made an "impossible" catch by leaping between two defenders for a Plunkett pass on the 4-yard line to set up another touchdown sprint by Brown. Vataha scored on a 10-yard catch to clinch it.

Wells Twombley of the *Los Angeles Herald Examiner* described the Woody Hayes who finally met with the press long after the game was over: "Finally, the tomb opened. There was W. Woodrow Hayes. He looked centuries older. His head was down like a man in prayer. Yes, he'd been beaten by a great team. Yes, Plunkett was a great quarterback. 'But Rex Kern was outplaying him until the third period,' said Woody. 'They beat us on two plays—that mad dog pass to Moore and when they held us on fourth down and inches . . . The only way you defend against Plunkett is to do exactly what we didn't.' In middle age, the great ogre from Columbus has discovered something he never knew he had—a sense of good sportsmanship. He was taking defeat as gracefully as he knew how.''

1972
The Joy of Music

John J. Cabot was the first president of the 1972 Tournament—for less than an hour. On the night of January 21, 1971, he succumbed to a heart attack at Tournament House after being inducted into office. His vice president, Virgil J. White immediately became the new president, a year before he would have assumed the office.

The theme for the 1972 Tournament was "The Joy of Music." Appropriately, Tournament president White named as grand marshal popular orchestra leader Lawrence Welk, who achieved fame with champagne music and the popular expression, "a-one-a and a-two-a."

Before the Michigan-Stanford football game, Welk told several thousand Kick-off Luncheon fans, "It's going to be around a-one-a and a-two-a game." He was almost, but not quite correct. Actually, the 1972 Rose Bowl game was more of a "three-a"—in the form of a last-second field goal off the accurate toe of Rod Garcia in the second-straight Stanford upset.

The 1972 Tournament queen was Margo Lynn Johnson, a Vancouver, British Columbia native. In keeping with the music theme, Margo majored in music at Pasadena City College and was an ac-

complished singer with a musical group called the Sandpipers. Her coronation at the Pasadena Civic Auditorium was an impressive affair coordinated by E. Milton Wilson and featuring the Pasadena High School choir singing "Joy to the World." Each boy carried a candle into the darkened auditorium.

The parade was as beautiful as the typically sunshiny day, and, appropriately, strains of "What the World Needs Now Is Love" established the mood for the President's Trophy–winning float, Bank of America's stunning basket of pink roses drawn by a pair of hovering white doves.

"Put a Little Love in Your Heart," said the Compton float, which won the Queen's Trophy for its portrayal of a white dove of peace nestling on a bed of yellow roses. Glendale's "Icy Wonderland" won the Sweepstakes. Los Angeles Dodger pitcher Don Sutton—named San Fernando Valley's Athlete of the Year—rode aboard the Glendale float. "I felt like Willie Shoemaker riding a winner," he later quipped.

The Locke High School band, directed by Don Dustin and Frank Harris, featuring the Saints' soul routines, shared the high school band marching championship, televised over NBC, with the Houston, Texas, Spring Branch band, directed by Jack D. Miles. The Locke story is one of success through inspiration. In 1968, eighty students had to march in old used uniforms donated by another school. The "Soulful Saints" became an instant hit, and through many school and community projects they purchased handsome new uniforms and appeared in many areas, including Honolulu, where they were described as "the black band in blue Hawaii."

The Michigan and Stanford bands feuded during their practices at UCLA.

John J. Cabot

John J. Cabot, who was president of the 1972 Tournament for less than an hour, had been a lifelong resident of Pasadena. His interest in the Tournament went back to 1925, when he was an altar boy while the Notre Dame football team was in town. Knute Rockne himself gave Cabot and his friends tickets to the Rose Bowl game.

Virgil White

Young Bill Radock, a Stanford freshman, had a problem of loyalty at the football game. His brother Bob was a member of the Michigan band and his father, Michael, was vice president of the University of Michigan. Bill bought two tickets—one on the Stanford side and one on the Michigan side and reportedly sat in both at intervals to keep family peace.

Three members of a prize-winning band from Texas in the 1972 parade paid a price for being responsible citizens. They had been at Disneyland only ninety minutes when they saw a man pick someone's pocket. After notifying security, they spent the day filling out reports and answering questions while fellow band members toured the park and performed in the Disneyland parade. They also missed the Rose Parade New Year's Day— apparently because they had missed too many practices.

George Cavander, Michigan band director, said his group had been stoned and spat upon by some members of the Stanford band—which David Ruiz, Stanford band manager, quickly denied. While the Michigan band was awesome in its formal marching technique and musical excellence, the Stanford band displayed a more liberal approach to football entertainment. "We don't want to be rigid and present a strict disciplinary performance," stated Ruiz. "We provide relaxed showmanship that everyone can enjoy rather than be awed by it."

Cardinal Rules: Stanford 13, Michigan 12

Shortly before the 1972 Rose Bowl, Ohio State grad Jim Wilce of Pomona, a member of the Southern California Big Ten Club, issued what he described as "Lincoln's Pasadena Address" to spur the Wolverines on. Referring to the 1902 game, in which Michigan had smashed Stanford, 49–0, to begin Tournament of Roses football, Wilce wrote:

"Three score and ten years ago, our Michigan forefathers brought forth to the western part of our continent a new style of battle, conceived in brilliance, and dedicated to the proposition that all armies are not created equal. They were engaged in a great war with all the tribes of the Stanford Indians, testing whether that group, or any other group so contrived and non-dedicated, could endure against the awesome powers from the eastern lands of might and right.

"Before the war was ended, 49 times had the war-keeper struck a point for the brave Wolverines while never did his pen touch the column of the totally vanquished Indians. . . . Now they are to meet again on this same battlefield strewn with roses. We speak with malice

towards none, and with charity for all, but this world in the West must be shown, before memory dims again, that a battlefield can be littered with Big Red remnants. . . ."

Wilce's prophecy did not come true as Stanford avenged the Great Massacre of 1902. The *Los Angeles Times* headed its story, "Gracias, Garcia! Stanford Does It Again on Field Goal."

Dwain Esper of the *Star-News* wrote:

"In many respects this was a carbon copy of Stanford's victory over Ohio State the year before. . . . Blond Don Bunce emulated his quarterbacking predecessor Jim Plunkett in carting away player-of-the-game honors. And, like Plunkett, he did it with his passing arm with twenty-four completions in forty-four attempts. . . . Bunce was joined by running back Jackie Brown, a spectacular group of receivers and a defense that refused to be intimidated by a sledgehammer Michigan attack. Time and again, Jeff Siemon, Randy Potle, Pete Lazetich and their mates hurled back Wolverine thrusts."

Michigan scored first in the game on a 30-yard field goal by Dana Coin.

A Stanford goal-line stand kept the score at 3–0 until well into the third quarter, when Garcia tied it up with a 42-yard field goal.

In the fourth quarter, Michigan scored on a short plunge by Fritz Seyferth, culminating a 71-yard power drive. Trailing 10–3, Bunce retaliated with his own air game, but didn't score. But the next drive did pay off, featuring a 31-yard run by Brown. Fullback Jim Kehl took a direct snap from center and handed the ball forward between Brown's legs in a trick Johnny Ralston maneuver. Brown soon ran 24 more for a touchdown that tied the game.

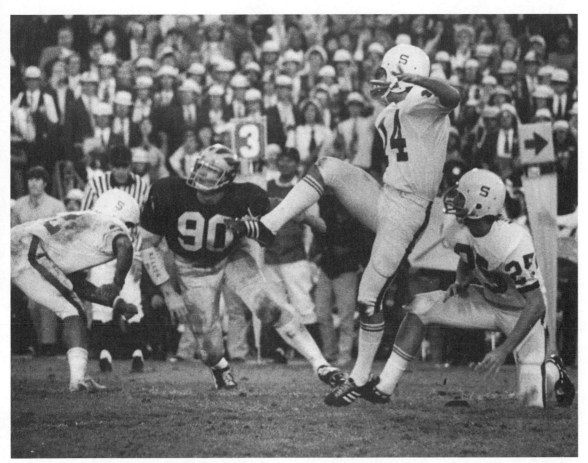

Rod Garcia's winning field goal for Stanford

In 1972, because of heightened sensitivity to native Americans, Stanford dropped the nickname "Indians" that it had used since 1930 and went back to the name "Cardinals," which had been the university's nickname at the turn of the century.

The Michigan football team found its East Los Angeles practice field too wet to use, thanks to heavy rains on top of a heavy watering by the groundskeeper during an earlier drought period. Coach Bo Schembechler took his team a hundred miles north to Bakersfield, where they were hosted by Bakersfield Junior College officials.

The game may be best remembered for the Rose's Bowl's most stunning "wrong-way run" since Roy Riegels's famed 1929 sprint—a run that seemingly handed Michigan a 12–10 victory before Stanford pulled it out, 13–12.

With the score tied, 10–10, with four minutes to play, Stanford sophomore Jim Ferguson tried to run Michigan's missed field goal attempt out of the end zone. He ran the ball out, then got nailed by Michigan's Ed Shuttlesworth and was driven back into the end zone. The officials ruled a safety, although it appeared to many that Ferguson's momentum had been caused by Michigan and the play should have been ruled a touchback. In any case, Michigan gained a 2-point advantage, 12–10.

Stanford stopped Michigan after the post-safety free kick. Stanford unleashed an attack with well-placed passes against a "protect" Wolverine defense. Bunce connected to Bill Scott, John Winesberry, Miles Moore, Reggie Sanderson, and Winesberry again to get to Garcia's range where their last precious timeout was used to set up Garcia's field goal, held by Steve Murray shortly before the gun barked. Bedlam reigned.

Michigan gained 264 yards rushing in the game and only 26 yards passing. Stanford, on the other hand, had 290 yards passing and 93 rushing.

Ralston's victory gained for him the head coaching job with the National Football League's Denver Broncos—a job he said he took because it was the next logical challenge.

Meanwhile, Bo Schembechler told Dick Robinson of the *Star-News:* "It's a helluva thing to lose a Rose Bowl game after we had it won. After we got the safety, all we needed is one first down, and we couldn't get it. We couldn't come up with the big play all day."

The Garcia comments are best told by

Ed Shuttlesworth nails Stanford's Jim Ferguson for safety

Jim Ferguson's disastrous attempt to run Michigan's failed field goal attempt out of the end zone gave Michigan a safety and the lead— just as Roy Riegels's wrong-way run had cost California a safety in the 1929 game. The man who hit Ferguson said, "You better go dig yourself a hole." He had a lonely walk back to the sidelines. "I could see the eyes of 56 players and 103,000 fans asking me, 'Why did you do that?' And then I thought of the millions seeing it on TV. I didn't think of Riegels until I got to the sidelines. Suddenly I asked myself: 'Am I going to spend the rest of my life with this on my mind?' "

reporting a monthly meeting of the Southern California Big Ten Club at which Garcia was invited to be the guest of honor. Young Garcia awarded to Tournament of Roses president White the shoe he actually used to make the winning kick. White, an antique collector by trade, responded, "I shall always consider this one of my prize possessions. You can bet this trophy will never be offered for sale."

Garcia, who later tied the NCAA 53-yard record for field goal distance against USC in a 1974 game, told the Big Ten Clubbers: "I wear a size eight shoe. Yes, I was twitching a bit when it came time to run out and kick. It was a difficult position for me from the right side of the field as I had to twist my kick back with my soccer style to go between the posts. I always aim to the right of the posts to protect in case I don't meet the ball squarely. I don't kick with my toe. I make contact with the top of my foot. I learned how to play soccer in Chile and the Canary Islands where we lived before coming to Southern California. My dad trained me how to kick. I went to Stanford from La Mirada High when USC said they wanted somebody who could do other things besides kick."

1973
True Grid

A former Glendale High School football player who played on Howard Jones's great USC teams was named grand marshal by Tournament president Otis Blasingham. He grew up as Marion Michael Morrison and was later known as "The Duke" or "True Grit." To most people, however, he was simply John Wayne.

When Mrs. Delmar R. Beck of Pasadena earned two Rose Bowl tickets, two parade tickets, and two places at the Distin-

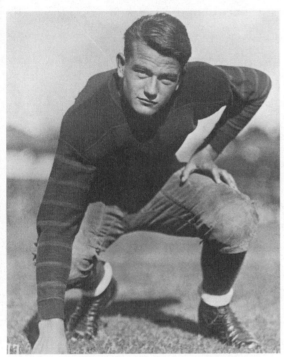

John Wayne when he was a USC player named Morrison

guished Guests luncheon for suggesting "Movie Memories" as the theme of the eighty-fourth Tournament of Roses, Blasingham quickly picked Wayne as the grand marshal.

Born in Pueblo, Colorado, and raised in the Pasadena area, Otis Blasingham joined the Tournament of Roses Association in 1946 and worked his way up the ladder of service on virtually every committee. He dedicated his term as president "to improve some of the fences around here—I think Pasadena has taken the Tournament for granted." Blasingham told the *Star-News* writer Margaret Stovall that he wanted people in Pasadena to admire their festival as much as the rest of the world admires it.

Blasingham crowned Salli Noren of Altadena, a Pasadena Community College student, the 1973 Tournament queen.

Noren, the daughter of Everett and Lois Noren, was the niece of former major league baseball star and Oakland Athletics coach Irv Noren.

Increased and improved aluminum seating in the Rose Bowl raised the huge Arroyo Seco oval's capacity by 3,076 seats to 104,699, making the Rose Bowl the largest stadium in the United States.

During Pasadena's many pregame festivities, the new Big Ten commissioner, Wayne Duke—not to be confused with "Duke" Wayne—told a Rotary Club audience he hoped the day would never come when the people who stage the Rose Bowl, and the Big Ten and Pacific conferences, would disturb their pact and return to the "bowl jungle" of bidding for teams in the open market. In declaring he hoped the pact between the Big Ten and Pac Eight would continue forever, Rose Bowl sports committee member Lay Leishman said, "There isn't a bowl game in America that would not take our package just as it is."

If the New Year's Day weather in 1973 had a place in "Movie Memories," it could only have depicted *Typhoon*. Gales of twenty to forty miles per hour blew through the night, easing off only somewhat for the parade and the game.

"Kismet," the city of Lakewood float, featuring a garden pavilion plus a princess and her ladies-in-waiting, won the Sweepstakes prize. Occidental Life Insurance Company received the Grand Prize for beauty, and the President's Trophy went to Baskin-Robbins Ice Cream for its "many-flavored" display of roses.

Three Yards and a Cloud of Dust: USC 42, Ohio State 17

"The Trojans simply exploded in the second half," said *Star-News* football expert Dwain Esper, of USC's 42–17 tri-

In working with the network television people in 1973, President Blasingham found that everything in the parade had to be timed to the split second. "You don't get any sleep the final week, and the television people don't realize we are a bunch of amateurs. It's bad if a float is too early and it's bad if a float is too late. I was standing there with a CBS man. We were six seconds off. He moaned, 'What am I supposed to do with six seconds?' I almost told him."

Ohio State's inflammable coach, Woody Hayes, lost his cool at the 1973 game. He grabbed the camera of *Times* photographer Art Rogers, and bashed it into Rogers's face before the game because he thought his privacy was being invaded along the sidelines. Rogers filed a complaint; months later the case was settled out of court. Bud Furillo of the *Herald Examiner* wrote, "General Hayes came to Los Angeles prepared to make the world forget Napoleon and left acting like Major Hoople, the buffoon in the funny papers."

Grand Marshal John Wayne arrives at game with Otis Blasingham

John McKay

umph over the Ohio State Buckeyes.

The game featured the power dives of fullback Sam Cunningham, who zoomed like a missile over the bunched Buckeye line four times for touchdowns. McKay used a human torpedo to destroy the fortress of Napoleon Hayes.

The always-amusing Jim Murray of the *Times* commented:

"Woody Hayes's team made touchdowns like a guy laying carpet. They had all the razzle-dazzle of Princeton-Rutgers in 1869. Woody's team was so slow, pigeons kept trying to light on them. I have seen guys move faster on canes. . . . Sam Cunningham gets touchdowns the same way we get to the moon. He lifts off, orbits the line of scrimmage, and then does a flaming reentry and splashdown in the end zone. . . . Woody Hayes kept sending in plays. He mixed

his attack well. He sent the fullback left, he sent the fullback right and he sent the fullback center."

John Hall of the *Times* summed up the afternoon's barbecue equally well:

"Mike Rae to Lynn Swann may not replace Doyle Nave to Al Krueger in Pasadena passing lore. Anthony Davis may not have broken a bigger run than O. J. Simpson pulled on the Buckeyes on New Year's of 1969. Sam Cunningham may not be the most popular MVP. Richard Wood may not be the 'baddest' sophomore linebacker, though he got ten tackles, and Dave Brown may not be the greatest center in the fifty Rose Bowls that have come and gone. But you put them all together—along with Chuck Anthony, who got tackles, offensive linemen Pete Adams and Mike Ryan, tight end Charles Young and steady defensive

Sam Cunningham scores one of his record four touchdowns

A football fan, Gary D'Angelo, studied the post-college careers of the 1973 Trojan Rose Bowl team. His findings suggest this squad may have been the most talented Rose Bowl team of all time— as measured by pro success. Twenty-three Trojans went into pro football.

bulls John Grant, Dale Mitchell, Jeff Winans, Monte Doris and James Sims—and the USC club that buried proud Ohio State, 42–17, in Monday's Rose Charade is just about what Coach McKay said it was—'the best I've ever had.' "

Cunningham's four touchdowns were the most ever scored by one man in the Rose Bowl. Anthony Davis carried twenty-three times for 157 yards. Quarterback Mike Rae completed eighteen passes in twenty-five attempts for 229 yards and a touchdown. Tight end Charles Young and flanker Lynn Swann caught six passes apiece. The Trojans used a basic "fifty" attack to crack open the Buckeyes after a 7–7 first half.

The Trojans felt they could beat anybody. Religious dedication developed this team, such stalwarts as Brown, Ryan, and Adams told a Fellowship of Christian Athletes gathering. Ryan put it this way:

"We found the answer this year to becoming a solid unit with purpose when we joined in religious appreciation. It transformed us from a floundering group into a true undefeated winner."

Anthony Davis prances for Trojans

1974
Happiness Is . . . Revenge

After his football and public relations disasters of the 1973 Tournament, Woody Hayes returned in 1974 to lead his Ohio State team to one of its greatest triumphs. His previous year's troubles were re-created briefly and then forgotten by almost everybody. He even made a few friends along the way.

Tournament president Edward Wilson named Charles M. Schulz, creator of the *Peanuts* comic strip, grand marshal of the eighty-fifth Tournament of Roses. The Tournament theme, "Happiness Is—" was suggested by Mrs. Kathy DeAr-

mond of Canoga Park in the annual contest, which drew ten thousand entries. The theme celebrated Schulz's book, *Happiness Is a Warm Puppy*.

When Wilson first asked Schulz to be grand marshal, the cartoonist was reluctant to accept the honor because, as Wilson learned, Schulz truly believed his characters were more interesting than the man who created them.

Twenty-three years of Tournament service had led to Wilson's being named the eighty-fifth president. Reared in Pasadena, Wilson joined the Tournament of Roses Association in 1950. He served on twenty-six committees and held twelve

Charles Schulz shows logo to President Ed Wilson

Pat Nixon, Ronald Reagan and Nancy Reagan

Rube Samuelsen was not in the press box for the 1974 Rose Bowl game. The veteran sports writer died a few weeks before the eighty-fifth Tournament. A memorial in his honor was established at the new Pasadena Presbyterian Church. As a Pasadena sports editor from 1929 to 1962, he was nationally known as the major Rose Bowl authority. His column "Rube-Barbs" was universally accepted as the Rose Bowl bible, and he published a book of Rose Bowl stories in 1951.

chairmanships during his service before becoming president—a position his father, Elmer Wilson, had held in 1955. The younger Wilson was director of marketing for United California Bank, and his department had been responsible for the commercials that raised Sandy Duncan to fame on TV and then in films.

The 1974 Tournament queen was Miranda Barone, a hazel-eyed, brown-haired seventeen-year-old high school student. The daughter of Sebastian and Nancy Bar-

one, Barone was the first Rose queen born outside of North America. She had come to America as a small child with her parents from Catania, Sicily. Comedian Jack Benny was the host at her coronation.

The eighty-fifth Tournament marked the retirement of Max Colwell as executive secretary and manager after twenty-one years in the office. In appreciation of his long and able service, the executive committee of the Tournament

Rube Samuelsen

William Lawson

Pete Johnson crashes over for Buckeyes

named him manager emeritus and appointed him a consultant. Colwell also received the Arthur Noble Medal—the highest award annually given to a Pasadena citizen for community service .

William Lawson, a long-time member, succeeded Colwell as Tournament manager, and Walter Hoefflin, son of a former president, became his assistant.

After a heavy all-night rain, the skies cleared in time for the 1974 parade, which was staged in brisk weather. "There was a chill in the air, skies were bluer and clearer than ever and the aroma of roses and stirring band music filled the air as the sixty-one flower-bedecked floats glided down Colorado Boulevard to fulfill the theme of happiness," wrote Vera Danielson in the *Star-News*.

"Happiness Is . . . Love" was the theme of the Kodak float, which won the Grand Prize. The St. Louis float was the Sweepstakes winner, and Spokane, Washington, took the Queen's Trophy.

Students at Linda Vista Primary School in Pasadena, members of Mrs. Janet Cooke's resources class, distinguished themselves during the pre-1974 float activities by building their own miniature floats from flowers.

Eldon Fairbanks, head of equestrian activities in the annual Rose Parade, reported that 1974 set a record for tonnage and numbers of horses in the spectacle. In addition to the usual steeds in the parade, two giant floats were pulled by monsters of the equestrian world—the traditional St. Louis float drawn by the eight huge Clydesdales from Anheuser-Busch company and the Milwaukee entry with a forty-hitch team of Belgian draft horses.

Same Script, New Ending: Ohio State 42, USC 21

Woody Hayes, when interviewed by reporters at the airport upon Ohio State's arrival, made it clear immediately that he hadn't come to Pasadena to talk about the previous year.

Hayes said he considered it a "great tragedy" that reporters wanted to review past problems or make something of the recent dispute which followed the selection of Ohio State as the Big Ten's representative instead of Michigan. Michigan had outplayed Ohio State in a tie game that left the two schools deadlocked for the Big Ten title.

Under new Big Ten rules, which permitted the return of the last year's Rose Bowl representative, Big Ten athletic directors had chosen the Buckeyes over the Wolverines, much to Michigan coach Bo Schembechler's disgust. The explanation Big Ten directors gave was that Ohio State, in their opinion, had the best chance to defeat USC. An injury suffered by Michigan's quarterback obviously influenced the selection.

Surprised that they were picked, but happy for the new chance to avenge previous failure, the Ohio State players came to Pasadena with determination. It was a Big Ten crusade to end recent Pac Eight dominance—and Coach Hayes admirably led his forces in every act, every preparation and every bit of strategy.

The 42–21 Ohio State victory over USC before 105,267 spectators prompted the *Star-News* headline, "Ohio State Turns USC Greene in Rose Bowl." This game wasn't a rout. But it was a knockout.

The reference to "Greene" played on the fact that Ohio State quarterback Cornelius Greene opened the eyes of the grid world with a selective aerial game that paved the way for the running and bolting of backs like Archie Griffin, Pete Johnson and Greene himself.

Although the first pass he tried was intercepted, Greene completed six of his next seven. On four of Ohio State's touchdown drives, Greene passes provided the vital ingredients.

Statistics show that USC out-downed Ohio State, 27–20, and Ohio State led in total yardage, 449–406. USC had enough offense, but its defense eventually gave way.

Hayes revealed that Greene hadn't passed in the Michigan game because he had had a bruised thumb. His thumb was okay on January 1, 1974, however.

Little Chris Limahelu, who had kicked a last-second field goal to defeat Stanford during the regular season, blasted a school record 47-yarder for a 3–0 USC lead. He missed another of that length after an interception.

Ohio State came back with an 80-yard drive featuring a timely Greene to a Fred Pagtac aerial shot and a scoring plunge by fullback Pete Johnson, the first of this husky freshman's three for the day.

A 42-yarder by Little Chris cut the Buckeye lead to 7–6, and a unique left-handed Anthony Davis pass to J. K. McKay, son of the coach, followed by a Pat Haden-to-McKay two-pointer, sailed USC ahead, 14–7. Greene passes and the

One of college football's most noted traditions is Tommy Trojan riding USC's magnificent white charger out of the stadium tunnel as the Trojan band plays its fight song. The original Tommy Trojan was Arthur Gontier. In 1954, when USC's Airedale mascot, Tirebiter, died, Gontier and others rented a horse and costume. When their volunteer rider backed out, Gontier got the job because he was the only committee member who had ever ridden a horse. His inaugural ride around the Coliseum track went badly and people laughed at him. "It was so humiliating I never revealed my identify," he later admitted.

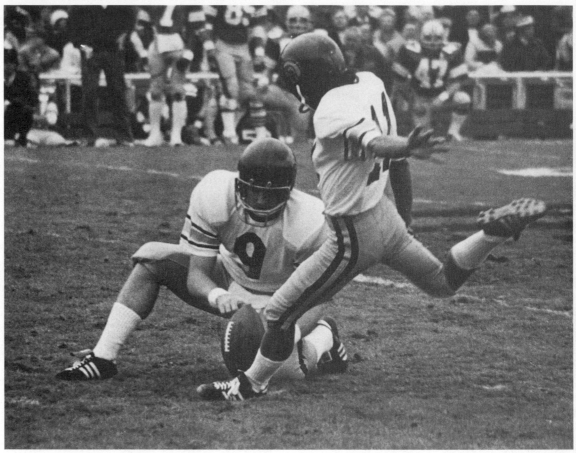

Chris Limahelu kicks USC field goal

Johnson bolt tied it up, 14–14, just before the intermission.

After stopping the Buckeyes by causing them to fumble deep in USC territory after intermission, USC put on a drive that featured Haden aerials to Lynn Swann and Davis draws. Rod McNeil almost blew it with a pop-fly fumble, but fullback Manny Moore recovered at the Buckeye 2, from where Davis dove over.

Ohio State came back to score with Johnson again, but Pasadena's own Charlie Phillips blocked the extra-point try to leave the USC lead 21–20.

A line-drive punt by Arcadia's James Lucas was fielded by Ohio State's Neal Colzie, who scooted from his 35 to USC's 9. Johnson's bolts set up Greene for a scoring keeper.

Haden, who had a twenty-one for thirty-nine passing day, tried to rally USC, but his receivers were "just missing" this day. Ohio State's defense was mighty tough by now, too. The rest of the game was all Ohio State. There came a typical drive, and the last touchdown was a 47-yarder by Archie Griffin that sent thousands of Buckeye fans into ecstasy.

Greene was named Player of the Game, although Griffin with 149 yards,

Johnson with three touchdowns, and linemen like All-American John Hicks on offense and end Van DeCree on defense were also too much for USC, as was jumping receiver Pagtac, who caught all of the Greene bullets on his chest.

Post-game comment lauded Hayes and the Buckeyes, proof the West Coast can tell it like it was:

Tom Singer, *Herald Examiner:* "Woody Hayes, charming coach of the Ohio State Buckeyes, launched his campaign to become the new guru of the Love Generation."

Bud Tucker, *San Gabriel Tribune:* "Known in this part of the world as the snarling and unsociable buffoon, Hayes marched in oozing sweetness. . . . Wet-eyed Woody alternately spoke of the greatness of Winston Churchill and the potential of our youth and the softness of motherhood."

Jim Murray, *Times:* "Like the guy who didn't find out about girls until he was forty, Woody's team went slightly wild when they did learn the pass was legal—and that everybody was doing it."

Dick Robinson of *Star-News* quoted USC players as saying that the Buckeyes were better than Notre Dame, which was the eventual national title selection, but Hayes told local sports writer Terry Johnson: "You know I am a little biased, but today I'd certainly say we were number one in the nation."

1975
The Master of Suspense

The eighty-sixth Tournament of Roses year was a tragic one. For the second time in just a few years, a Tournament of Roses president died soon after taking office. Carl H. Hoelscher succumbed to a heart attack only a few weeks into his presidency. A local clothing merchant,

Hoelscher was born in Nebraska on New Year's Day, and had come to Pasadena at the age of six. He had been active in Pasadena civic affairs and Tournament duties for many years.

Hoelscher was succeeded as president of the Tournament by his life-long friend, Paul Bryan, who moved up from vice president a year sooner than he had expected. Bryan's ascendancy to the presidency represented years of Tournament participation. In 1930, his wife Gabrielle had ridden on a parade float with her sister, Queen Holly Halsted. Bryan himself had chaired committees on decorating and floats several years.

Bryan selected the theme "Heritage of America," suggested by Mrs. William Barton of Arcadia—who had almost missed the submission deadline—for the 1975 parade. His goal was to make the parade a tribute to his friend Hoelscher and to the country as a whole.

Bryan's grand marshal was baseball great Hank Aaron, who had recently broken Babe Ruth's all-time career home run record. Aaron called his selection "a particular honor for me because Jackie Robinson, who came from Pasadena, was my idol. This is the greatest tribute that can be placed on any American, and it makes me proud to be an American." Aaron and his wife, Billye, had never seen a Rose Parade before in person and were very impressed.

The queen was Robin Carr of San Gabriel. She was joined by princesses Kathryn Andrews, Melanie Charvat, Beverly Chapman, Patricia Linne, Carolyn Coates and Janet Marcellus on the royal court. Carr later was to become Miss California and a runner-up in the Miss America contest at Atlantic City.

The morning parade ran off smoothly under crystal azure skies before a mil-

Hank Aaron

Carl Hoelscher

Paul Bryan

In 1975 Lathrop Leishman relinquished chairmanship of the Tournament of Roses Football Committee, a post he had held since 1945, to Bill Nicholas, the director of the Los Angeles Coliseum operations. Of Leishman, *Star-News* editor Charles Cherniss wrote, he "is a man who has probably devoted as much or more time to his community as he has his career and personal interests. Lay is essentially his own man, more interested in doing good and seeing the community advance than in publicity or recognition for himself."

lion-and-a-half viewers on the Pasadena streets. The previous day's winds died down and the temperature was a crisp fifty-five degrees.

The South enjoyed a double triumph in the 1975 Tournament of Roses. It not only had a native son as grand marshal but the the Sweepstakes Trophy—the parade's greatest award—went to the state of Georgia for its float, "The Colonial Dream." The Grand Prize, highest award to commercial entries, went to Farmers Insurance Group for its "Knight of the Forest." Theme prize went to Long Beach for its "Proclaim Liberty Throughout the Land."

Two unique groups appeared in the parade: the Navajo Indian group from Window Rock, Arizona, and the 126-member Ohio State Fair youth choir. Not a single member of the latter group played an instrument. The members' music was all in their vocal chords. Carrying backpacks with loudspeakers and amplifiers, they sang their way along the 5 ¼–mile parade route.

Southwest Indians, colorfully costumed, have ridden on horseback in many Rose Parades, but the Navajo group was the first to march the parade route playing instruments. Their music was traditionally Navajo, based on legends.

The Arcadia High School Apaches, winners of twenty-seven sweepstakes awards in band competitions over nine years, was one of the most popular aggregations, along with the Pasadena City College Lancers, appearing in their forty-third Rose Parade.

Rubber Match:
USC 18, Ohio State 17

The 1975 football game marked the seventh visit of Ohio State's Woody Hayes. After winning his first three games—the

first going back to 1955—he had lost two of the next three. With a Rose Bowl mark of 4–2 he, along with his 1975 rival, John McKay of USC, threatened to equal the all-time Rose Bowl record of five wins set by Howard Jones. Woody's luck ran out, however, as the 1975 and 1976 games were to show. In each of those games a victory would have given him the national championship.

"Biorhythms" were the rage around that time, and someone worked it out on a biorhythm calculator that Hayes would not explode in Pasadena, but would be slightly below his norm for good decisions. The first point turned out to be true, although Coach McKay also was supposed to be less than sharp according to his physical and intellectual cycle. *Star-News* editor Keith Murray checked the coaches out on his Biomate, but only the Hayes "no explosion" prediction turned out to be true in USC's 18–17 comeback victory. Hayes was a calm man and took his defeat well—for him.

The game itself was a thriller. Little 140-pound Chris Limahelu opened the scoring when he kicked a 30-yard USC field goal. After a series of comical turnovers on both sides, Champ Henson bucked over to give the Buckeyes a 7–3 edge. Limahelu then connected on a 39-yard field goal that cut the Ohio State lead to 7–6. When the Buckeyes were called offside on the scoring play, McKay confounded traditional football wisdom by choosing to take the penalty instead of the three points so USC could go for a go-ahead touchdown. The unusual gamble failed, however, leaving the Buckeyes with a 7–3 half time lead. McKay would think more wisely later.

McKay's daring decision moved Allan Malamud of the *Herald Examiner* to write, "Johnny McKay does not remind

Shelton Diggs catches winning 2-point pass while falling

USC's Pat Haden

me of Bud Wilkinson, Vince Lombardi, Frank Leahy or anybody else who ever drew a play on a blackboard. His style is more like Alfred Hitchcock. USC didn't hire a football coach in 1960. It hired a master of suspense.''

In the second half, USC's Jim Obradovich scored on a 9-yard pass from Pat Haden before Cornelius Greene darted in with a short gainer to make it 14–10 Ohio State. Tom Klaban's 32-yard field goal made the Buckeye lead 17–10.

USC then drove for victory. Allen Carter gained 75 yards on eighteen carries for the day, many of his biggest in the winning drive. The game was won when Haden fired a 36-yard pass to McKay, a play ordered by the senior McKay, and Haden threw a 2-point pass to Shelton Diggs with 2:03 left to play, sending the 106,721 spectators into hysterics.

Of McKay's coaching, the *Star-News* sports editor wrote, ''Coach McKay, a river boat gambler, gambled again at the finish and won. Coach McKay can thank son John and Haden, who in one precarious minute paid Coach McKay in full for four years of rent accrued when Haden

Of the third-straight USC–Ohio State Rose Bowl matchup, Jim Murray of the *Los Angeles Times* wrote, "As exciting as the game was—it was one of the Rose Bowl classics—the game left a dimension to be desired. Newness. By 1980, these two teams will have each other's moves down so pat it will look like Veloz and Yolanda. The Rose Bowl should not be an annual rematch."

Pat Haden aims for McKay and connects with winning TD

Sam Akers stepped down, in 1975, as Tournament public relations director, a position he served with dignity and high journalistic standards for fifteen years. He was succeeded by Forest W. "Frosty" Foster of San Marino. For most newspapers, Akers had been like a staff writer, he was so dependable in news coverage.

The 1975 Tournament year marked William Lawson's first full campaign as Max Colwell's successor as festival manager. After more than two decades as a Tournament volunteer he was in line for the Tournament presidency; however, he resigned as treasurer to accept the career managerial post and left the building construction industry. He had been associated with twenty committees since 1949, had chaired ten committees and had been on the policy-making executive board since 1969.

lived with the McKays during the McKay-Haden conquests at Bishop Amat High School. Yes, Coach John is off the hook. Had Ohio State won, arguments would have raged for days over the judgment of McKay's call before the half when he turned down three points."

Terry Johnson of the *Star-News* reported that Anthony Davis, injured early in the game, was happy because the game proved he was expendable. "USC showed it can win without Anthony Davis," A.D. happily told Johnson. "Allen Carter picked up the slack."

The year 1975 began beautifully for Johnny McKay—and it ended that way. But the USC coach experienced a rough time in between. The Rose Bowl win gave him both the U.S. Coaches national football championship and a lifetime

Rose Bowl record of 5–3—equal to Howard Jones's record win total.

The following season, after his team defeated Notre Dame to roll up seven victories in a row, the news leaked out that McKay had agreed to become coach of the new NFL Tampa Bay Buccaneers in 1976. He admitted it was all true—that the pro challenge and financial opportunity were more than he could refuse. USC then dropped successive games to Cal, Stanford, Washington and UCLA, and didn't qualify for its "annual" Rose Bowl trip in 1976. Instead, it got a Liberty Bowl bid to play once-defeated Texas A&M in Memphis. USC won the game as a pre-Christmas going-away present for McKay and a lifter for the squad that was to play under new Trojan coach John Robinson in the 1976 campaign.

THE FLOATS

The original floats at the turn of the century were horse and buggy units with individual flowers tied to the carriages with string.

In the early 1900s, young Pasadenan Isabella Coleman attached bunches of flowers to floats, pioneering the contemporary techniques that have brought so much beauty and animation to the parades. In 1929, Coleman's concept of pasting flower blossoms on the structures was adopted. She also pioneered changes in power design, chassis construction and mechanical animation.

According to Tournament rules, a float is a self-propelled or horse-drawn vehicle completely decorated with fresh foliage and other vegetation, either dried or fresh. All visible surfaces must be covered, including top surfaces and wheels. A typical float may use a hundred thousand flowers and up to a million petals.

The first requisite in float construction is a stripped-down automobile, jeep or truck chassis, rebuilt with an extra-large radiator to stand the parade pace of 2½ miles per hour. Over the chassis is placed a metal or wooden frame that is no more than sixteen feet high, eighteen feet wide and fifty feet long. Variances must be approved. The final shaping is done with one-inch chicken wire that is sprayed with a polyvinyl material, a process known as "cocooning." Papier mâché is used for more detailed shapes. The float is then painted and flowering begins five or six days before parade morning. Some of the more delicate flowers are placed only a few hours before the parade. Roses, gardenias and orchids are placed in water vials or tubes sunk into the skin of the float.

Eighteen trophy winners are picked by the judges on the basis of design, style and decoration. The top award is the Sweepstakes Trophy. The floats are commercially, community or organization-sponsored.

Electronically operated mechanisms make it possible for flowery eyes to blink, arms to move and any other movement of parts the project may require. Usually there are two operators of each float, a driver who often must use the pink line on the pavement as his steering guide and a mechanism operator who also can serve as a "spotter." The driver works from cramped quarters, often lying on his side in a small compartment just a foot above the pavement. The spotter rides in an advantageous position under the foliage, often a considerable distance from the driver. The man with the "eyes" communicates with the driver either by telephone or by voice, if they are close enough to hear each other.

Sixty Tournament volunteers comprise the trouble-shooter squad on scooters that shepherd the big creations down the parade route. They must make quick decisions on calling tow equipment at the time of mechanical failures.

Twenty-five corporations enter floats costing from $50,000 to $200,000 each in the parade to gain a few seconds of exposure before the television cameras and the spectators on Pasadena streets. They believe it offers a better chance to display the company image or leave a better impression than they would gain on a commercial bought for the same price.

Communities, countries and organizations enter floats for prestige. For example, Korea, host of the 1988 Olympic Games, entered a float for the first time in the 1988 parade—to focus the world's eyes on Korea's assets.

One veteran float builder who has created many trophy winners is Rick Chapman of Festival Artists. "With the advent of television, more is expected from a modern

ansteel's spacecraft rocks over parade route

float," says Chapman. "Once the static float that looked good was enough, but now it must move and articulate."

Chapman admits it is a risky business creating animation and mechanical surprises. "Sponsors must realize, everything can fail without warning," he says. "On the great big scary ones, they've got to trust my integrity to make it function."

Over the years only a handful of companies have assembled almost all the floats. Recently, five new companies have entered the Rose parade float building business, bringing the total of creators of floral wonders to eleven.

Through the years, many firms and corporations in the United States have entered floats. Through the showmanship of its public relations director R. M. "Dick" Pittenger, the Farmers Insurance Company gave impetus to having celebrities ride on its floats.

Another successful float presenter for many years was the Chrysler Corporation under the direction of J. R. "Jack" Barlow. The Chrysler "Thanks for the Memory" float in 1969 was a tribute to Bob Hope, grand marshal, and featured such movie stars as Dorothy Lamour, Rosemary Clooney, Barbara Eden, Lynda Bennett and Jerry Colonna. In 1970 when astronauts Charles Conrad, Richard Gordon and Alan Bean were grand marshals, Chrysler entered "The Eagle with Wings" float, a tribute to the lunar landings of Apollo 11 and 12.

Pasadena's Pioneer Float Builder

Isabella Coleman began designing floats in 1909 and entered the 1910 parade when her father suggested she put her horse and buggy in the competition.

"In those days people tied flowers to the wheels of their buggy and the body with wire and string," she explained. "I decided to fasten flowers in bunches. I believed bunches of flowers were prettier and more natural than flowers on a string. With my horse 'Queen' prancing in front of my buggy, we took second place in 1910."

With Queen, Coleman won first place in the horse-drawn vehicle in 1912. This led to her being hired to construct the realty board's float in the commercial division in the 1913 parade. It won first place. In 1915 she created the city of Los Angeles float, which won the Sweepstakes award because it

Party time, says Lawry's Garfield the Cat

was loaded with beautiful flowers. Isabella put so many flowers into the display, she lost $300.

The job that made Coleman famous was the Aimee Semple McPherson float in 1925—a floral display of McPherson's Angelus Temple.

"I remember discussing the float plans with her while I was eating a fudge sundae at the Biltmore Hotel," said Coleman. "She was a gracious lady, very charming and wonderful to work with. We won first prize because she gave me approval to spend for the flowers we needed."

Coleman said a development in float-making that became important to the future took place in 1929 when, instead of weaving the flowers, they were pasted to the surface of the float, making more lifelike creations possible.

Low chassis was the next development of importance in float building, she explained. "By going low and bringing the float down to the pavement, we enabled people to see its beauty more clearly," she declared. "We used airplane wheels instead of old high wheels. Then we designed floats to be driven forward instead of backward. I was the first to use vials to display flowers more realistically. My favorite flower to work with was the mum. Roses were the most difficult to work with. Another major development during my career was the creation of the cocooning process for the presentation of lifelike objects. Eventually we could put material on the frame with a 'fan' or 'blower.' "

Before her career ended, Coleman gave the following summation of successful float presentation: "Every float needs a climax. I always tried for that. A float is a stage. You can do anything. The future is unlimited. But they should never get too high above the pavement. I always wanted to keep my floats low."

Poseidon, the Greek god of the sea

Rand McNally's Lincoln float

weet Switzerland float in 1987 parade

American Savings' barbershop quartet

Rose Parade Trophies

Sweepstakes, *most beautiful*
Theme, *use of theme*
Queen's, *use of roses*
President's, *best floral*
Grand Marshal's, *creative design*
Princesses', *small float*
Directors', *craftsmanship*
Mayor's, *originality*
Pioneers', *romance of California*
International, *international subject*
Anniversary, *life in the U.S.A.*
Governor's, *emphasis on city*
Founders', *self-built*
Coleman, *most unusual*
Animation, *best animation*
Humor, *best humor*
Judges', *whimsicality*
Special, *special merit*

(Grand Prize was formerly
awarded to top commercial entry.)

1976
UCLA's Great Rally

A brand new football success story was born on January 1, 1976. It had been seeded in the years when Dick Vermeil was an assistant coach under four proven masters—Tommy Prothro, George Allen, Johnny Ralston and Chuck Knox. The young Napa Valley man—like the wine in his home area—got better with age. He was named by UCLA athletic director J. D. Morgan to succeed Pepper Rodgers as the UCLA coach for the 1974 season. Just one campaign later, at age thirty-nine, Vermeil led the Bruins to a decisive Rose Bowl win over the number-one team in the nation, Ohio State.

The Buckeyes weren't helped by the fact that an Ohioan was president of the Tournament of Roses in 1976. Akron born Ralph Helpbringer had served the festival since 1954, chairing such committees as television and radio, float construction, float entries and queen selection. Known by the nickname "Speedy," Helpbringer brought to the 1976 festival a philosophy he described as, "In our world of problems, it is good for everyone everywhere to see something that is beautiful, not irritating."

The 1976 Tournament officially kicked off America's 200th birthday. Appropriately, the Tournament theme was "America, Let's Celebrate." The idea was submitted by Mrs. Max Younkin of La Cañada—one of six thousand entries. The Bicentennial thirteen-cent stamps reproducing Archibald M. Willard's century-year old *Spirit of '76* painting, were sold for the first time in Pasadena. This caused a collectors' stampede at the Pasadena post office.

For his grand marshal, Helpbringer chose Kate Smith, whom he called a legend, forty-four years a star, with her fa-

Grand Marshal Kate Smith

mous songs "When the Moon Comes over the Mountain" and "God Bless America." When Smith accepted the honor, she said, "I am happy to say that I'm singing for my fifth generation. I've sung to my grandmother's generation, my mother's generation, mine, my nieces, and now their children's. And I warmed up as an amateur singing to my great grandmother's friends."

Prior to the UCLA–Ohio State game, Smith thrilled the crowd of 105,464 under sunny skies by doing an exciting rendition of the national anthem and "God Bless America" in conjunction with the UCLA choir and band. After a full morning of parading and festivities, Smith was too tired to remain in the bowl for the football game but retired to her hotel,

During the 1976 parade, a wheel fell off the Occidental float. As it rolled toward the curb, a child ran out to try to capture it. Equestrian Montie Montana—one of the Tournament's old-time stalwarts—who was prancing on his horse right behind the float used his rope to lasso the lad, much to the amusement of the crowd lining the curb.

Pasadena was jolted at least three times during the 1976 Tournament. Jolt number one came when the city first allowed beer to be sold in the Rose Bowl. The second jolt was a mild 4.2-magnitude earthquake which struck during the parade. The third jolt was the biggest: UCLA's upset of Ohio State. UCLA coach Vermeil had predicted his team "would jolt the world" on January 1—he was right.

With his wife, Betty, Tournament president Ralph Helpbringer rode in an old-fashioned car in one of Pasadena's most popular parades. He amused the thousands along the parade route by lifting his pants leg to reveal his special "Bicentennial Salute"—a pair of red-white-and-blue socks, complete with stars—the most risqué act a Tournament president ever committed. The socks were a gift from fellow Tournament worker, Frank Hardcastle.

Ohio State's two-time Heisman Trophy winner Archie Griffin eludes Trojan tacklers

where she watched the action on TV.

The 1976 queen was Anne Elizabeth Martin, a freshman at Pasadena City College and graduate of La Cañada High School. Her court included Martha Anna Carnahan of Pasadena, Edythe Elaine Roberts of Pasadena, Lisa Marie Pedersen of Sierra Madre, Carol Lynn Hennacy of Pasadena, Caren Denise Ashton of Arcadia and Margaret Ann Charvat of Pasadena. Margaret was the sister of Melanie Charvat of the 1975 court—the first sisters in the court in successive years.

Twenty-one former Rose queens at-tended the annual queen's luncheon, sponsored by Eastman Kodak. The participants included May McAvoy Cleary (1923), Holly Halsted (1930) and Sally Stanton (1941).

With New Year's Eve temperatures hovering near freezing, thousands of people, as usual, spent New Year's Eve sleeping along the boulevards of the parade route. Little fires in trash cans helped keep the all-nighters warm until the sun came up.

In the parade, the Sweepstakes trophy went to the "Sunday Band Concert" float entered by the Credit Union National Association. It depicted a typical American small-town park and lakeside, festooned with gladioli, camellias, orchids and thousands of other blooms. P. T. Barnum's home town of Bridgeport, Connecticut, entered a float in the parade depicting a circus scene, as a tribute to the circus founder. The first Mormon Church float was the first church-sponsored float in many years.

Canada had its biggest representation ever: four floats, two bands and a contingent of the Royal Canadian Mounted Police. Among the many spectacular bands was the U.S. Marine Corps in its twenty-fifth appearance and the Musicale Municipal de Genève from Switzerland, the first European band in the festival.

Meanwhile, the Ohio State–UCLA football showdown started to gain momentum at the annual Big Ten dinner staged at the Palladium for the Buckeye football team. Some two thousand midwestern football fans attended the function sponsored by the Southern California Big Ten Club, headed by former Michigan All-American Al Wistert.

The featured entertainers at the dinner were comedienne Phyllis Diller, who came on the stage wearing a multicolored sequined mini-dress ("My Christmas tree exploded") and former Ohioan Bob Hope, who declared, "I am happy to return for the rerun"—meaning, of course, what was becoming Ohio State's annual visit to Pasadena. Bob quipped: "This is the Hayes Bowl . . . Woody spent this afternoon with the USC football team trying to help them get Rose Bowl tickets. . . . I used to think the Big Ten were my toes. . . . I haven't seen such scrambling as Corny Greene does since the last payday of the World Football League. . . . Hey, Buckeyes, if you lose to UCLA, they're sending you home on a skateboard. . . ."

Hope also counseled Ohio State's coach: "Stay calm, Woody. We want you with us for many more years"—in reference to the heart attack Hayes had had a few weeks after the 1974 Rose Bowl game. In 1976, however, the veteran coach was destined not to remain calm.

The Biggest Upset of Them All?
UCLA 23, Ohio State 10

At the Kiwanis Kickoff Luncheon at the new Pasadena Conference Center, 250-pound UCLA nose guard Cliff Frazier told how the Bruins planned to defend against the Buckeye attack.

"Sometimes we'll send our defense right and sometimes we send our defense left, and the whole time we're gonna keep me right in the middle," grinned Frazier. Cliff made thirteen tackles the next day, the most in the game.

Coach Dick Vermeil told cheering luncheon fans, "I'm certain of one thing. We've prepared and worked hard for this. I'm an optimist." UCLA's 8–2–1 record didn't suggest it could handle the top-ranked Buckeyes, however.

"Many people think we'll have trouble getting up for the game because we beat UCLA 41–20 when we played during the season," said Archie Griffin, who won a historic second Heisman Trophy shortly before coming to Pasadena. "But this is the Rose Bowl. We'll be high. We don't have to depend upon any other team to get the national championship. It's up to us."

Asked whether his 11–0 Buckeyes were his best team ever, Woody Hayes replied, "I'll let you know at four o'clock tomorrow."

Woody never let anyone know. After his Buckeyes were upset, 23–10, before

Ralph Helpbringer

In late 1975 USC beat Texas A&M in the Liberty Bowl and on January 1, 1976, Michigan lost to Oklahoma in the Orange Bowl in what were the first Pacific and Big Ten appearances in bowls other than the Rose Bowl since the Pacific–Big Ten pact had begun in 1947. The conferences tried the "second bowl" idea amidst Tournament misgivings that it was wise.

Wendell Tyler on the loose for Bruins

UCLA's victory in 1976 came exactly ten years after the last UCLA Rose Bowl team defeated Michigan State, 14–12. The parallels between the two upsets were striking. Just like Ohio State in 1976, in 1966 Michigan State had defeated UCLA during the regular season and come to Pasadena number one in the country, only to be upset.

Dick Vermeil

105,454 sun-baked and surprised fans, Woody walked across the field to congratulate Vermeil while the final action was still taking place. Then Hayes locked himself in his dressing room for an hour without meeting with the press. He also told his players not to talk to reporters. Later, in a private interview with Columbus sports writer Paul Hornung, Woody said, "We got out-played and out-coached. What else is there to say?"

UCLA's John Sciarra completed thirteen of nineteen passes, two of them for touchdowns, to become the Player of the Game, as selected by Bill Schroeder and his committee for his United Savings–Helms Hall of Fame.

The game presented one of history's most stunning reversals of form in the two halves. In the first half, UCLA gained only 9 yards rushing and 39 yards passing. Ohio State seemed to gain at will in the first half when it out-first-downed the Bruins 11–2. UCLA, the team that couldn't make a first down the first twenty-six minutes, came back to roll up seventeen first downs in the second half, when the Bruins scored three spectacular touchdowns and a field goal. Ohio State, which had a yardage advantage of 174–48 in the first half, was outgained for the game, 414–298.

Ohio State hit the Bruins with a powerful offense and bruising defense for the first thirty minutes, but walked off the field at intermission with a mere 3–0 lead on Tom Klaban's 42-yard field goal. The Bruin defense, although pushed around, made big plays when necessary to hold the Buckeyes to 3 points on four scoring chances—penetrations to UCLA's 25, 33, 32 and 21.

Then, inspired and encouraged because they were down only 3–0, Vermeil's fighting Bruins returned to outplay Ohio State in every phase of football: running, passing, catching, blocking, tackling and good old fight. Helping the Bruins reverse the story was the UCLA coaching staff's adjustment of offense, which took advantage of Ohio State's using its free safety to rush Sciarra. When confronted with one-on-one coverage, UCLA receivers got into the open for short passes and long runs.

The Bruins won on Brett White's 33-yard field goal, a 16-yard touchdown catch of a Sciarra bullet by Wally Henry, who then took a sharp pass and ran 67 yards for a touchdown, and a long Wendell Tyler touchdown run. After Pete Johnson battered through for a Buckeye tally that kept Ohio State hopes alive, Tyler killed Ohio dreams by scoring on a startling 54-yard dash with just three minutes and forty-two seconds left.

Speedy UCLA halfback Tyler, who played with a wrist that had been in a cast until ten days before the game, carried the football twenty-one times for 172 yards. Although he had fumbled repeatedly in the season finale against USC—when UCLA lost eight fumbles—he didn't fumble once in the Rose Bowl.

In the Bruin defensive-line action, nose guard Frazier was mighty, but so were men like Manu Tuiasosopo, Terry Tautolo, Dale Curry, Raymond Burks and Raymond Bell, who got better as the game progressed and caused all kinds of trouble for Griffin and Greene.

Two-time Heisman Trophy winner Archie Griffin finished with 93 yards in seventeen carries. With a record four Rose Bowl starts behind him, his name also went into the Rose Bowl record books with career marks of seventy-nine carries and 412 yards rushing. UCLA's Henry also tied records with two touchdown receptions and the longest-ever touchdown pass play.

Reporters were shut out of the Ohio State locker room after the game, but Griffin talked to Dick Robinson of the *Star-News* as he walked to the team bus. "This is definitely the toughest defeat of my life," he told Robinson. "We lost because we didn't execute. We were expecting the defense they showed us, but in the second half they seemed to get our count system down and they started shifting just before the snap. It hurt us."

Terry Johnson of the *Star-News* had no trouble getting quotes in the UCLA locker room. Coach Vermeil told him, "I didn't say anything at half time. We didn't have any pep talks. We spent the whole time making technical adjustments. When we went with the short passing, we forced their front seven to be more conservative. That opened our running game, too. When we were down only 3–0 at half time, the players knew they could win. I would like to say to some Northern California writers who didn't think we belonged in this game that they can go to hell. I was proud of Tyler because his wrist had to be hurting."

The victory was the sixth Pac Eight win in the last seven years of interleague bowl play. Could this be the same West that had lost twelve of the first thirteen games in the series?

They loved UCLA's 1976 victory in John Sciarra's hometown of Alhambra, adjoining Pasadena. Warner Jenkins, publisher of the *Alhambra Post-Advocate* wrote, "The Sciarra home on Glenaven Avenue has to be the happiest house in town. When I talked to Mrs. Sciarra a couple of weeks ago, she predicted UCLA would win. Mom was right. When I attended the Kickoff Luncheon, Sciarra looked like a midget alongside the visiting guests. Today he owns Alhambra. Give him the keys to city hall."

Roy Rogers and Dale Evans rode horseback in several Rose Parades, but in 1977 they went the distance in a Stutz Bearcat. When asked why he didn't ride a horse, Rogers replied, "Did you ever try riding a horse and smiling for five miles?" Roy and Dale had also ridden on many floats during the 1950s and early 1960s. Roy recalled the year "they had to lift us seventeen feet off the ground to set us on top of two horses made of rosebuds. Once the parade started, we couldn't get off for the entire five hours. And we had just had about a gallon of coffee before they lifted us up there."

Dale Evans and Roy Rogers arrive at game with Carl Wopschall

Carl Wopschall

1977
The Good Life

Carl E. Wopschall, a lifetime Pasadenan, war veteran, and son of a Pasadena mayor, became the eighty-eighth Tournament of Roses president. Wopschall became a "Tournament man" early in life. As a youngster he received free coffee and doughnuts in return for helping to paste flowers on the floats. A Tournament volunteer since 1948, Wopschall had joined the executive committee in 1971. He was a USC law graduate and a' past president of the Pasadena Bar Association, as well as past commander of Pasadena American Legion Post No. 13.

From the more than three thousand suggestions received from the public, Wopschall selected "The Good Life" as the theme of the 1977 Tournament. The winner, Pamela Rubel of Altadena, received two tickets to the parade, the football game and the distinguished guest luncheon. "I had this theme in mind long before I became president," said Wopschall. "I feel it is a positive way to begin 1977."

Wopschall's choice for grand marshal was the parade's first husband/wife team—movie stars Roy Rogers, the King of the Cowboys, and Dale Evans, the Queen of the West. "No one exemplifies our theme more than Roy and Dale," said Wopschall. "Throughout their forty-year show business career, they have continually given a slice of the 'good life' to millions.''

Diane Ramaker, a Pasadena City College sophomore, was 1977 Rose queen. Her mother, Joyce, and her father, Gene, an engineer in the public works department in Pasadena, disclosed that their daughter had an early "in" to the Tournament mansion, since her fiancé, Bill Stimson, was the grandson of the architect who designed the Wrigley house.

Sharing Ramaker's court were princesses Debbie van den Broek of South Pasadena, Margaret Price of La Cañada, Lori Japenga of La Cañada, Carol Newell of Arcadia, Cheri Peoples of San Gabriel and Pamela Pastis of San Marino.

The city of Glendale won the parade's Sweepstakes Trophy. In keeping with the theme "The Good Life," its float symbolized "Life Is Beautiful" through use of an elegant white peacock.

There were twenty-two marching bands in the parade. Traveling farthest was the Union-Endicott High School marching showband from Endicott, New York. Other bands came from Lawrenceburg, Indiana; Boulder, Colorado; Gary, Indiana; and San Antonio, Texas. There were also the usual number of California musical organizations.

Two hundred and sixty horses marched in the parade. For the first time in Tournament history, thoroughbred racehorses carrying renowned jockeys made their way down Colorado Boulevard. The jockeys were Ralph Neves, Donald Pierce, Sandy Hawley and Robyn Smith.

Bo Who?
USC 14, Michigan 6

Bo Schembechler, Michigan coach, back for the third time and winless in Pasade-

na, promised, "This will be a classic game. We know USC is great and we are ready to play our best game. The winner should be national champion." The sixty-third Rose Bowl football game was a classic, thrilling the crowd of 106,182 as USC upset highly regarded Michigan. The victory did not give USC the national championship as Schembechler predicted, because undefeated Pittsburgh was hailed as the clear-cut king after beating Georgia in the Sugar Bowl.

John Robinson was the new USC coach in a year of coaching changes that found Robinson replacing John McKay and thirty-one-year-old Terry Donahue bringing UCLA to the Pac Eight title showdown with USC. Donahue carried on amazingly well for Dick Vermeil, who went from UCLA to the NFL's Philadelphia Eagles, whom he led to the Super Bowl in 1981.

Dr. John R. Hubbard, president of USC, virtually called the 14–6 USC victory over Michigan the day before at the annual Kiwanis Kickoff Luncheon attended by four thousand fans at the Pasadena Conference Center. "I learned one thing during my biology class when I attended college," he said, "a horse is a helluva lot faster than a wolverine."

The Trojans did turn out to be faster— and very much better with the passing game, as USC quarterback Vince Evans became the star of the game with a fourteen-for-twenty passing show. Called a failure at quarterback when he had completed only 31 percent of his passes in 1975, Evans completed 51 percent during 1976.

Coach Robinson said there was only one word to describe the feelings his team had for Michigan after studying their films: "Fear."

The Michigan-USC game attracted the return of Fritz Crisler, known to many as

An Arkansas woman who visited Pasadena in January 1977 said, "The most amazing thing about living in Pasadena is that the people have such a good life they can even change the weather." The weather was, indeed, on the miraculous side that year. Rain poured for several days before both the Rose Bowl and the following week's Super Bowl. Then, suddenly, the skies cleared and the sun emerged long enough for each game to be played.

The Rose Bowl was the venue for three major levels of competition, each of which pitted a California team against a midwestern team. Prior to the Michigan-USC game, Bakersfield City College defeated Ellsworth, Iowa, in the renewal of the Junior Rose Bowl. Then, after Schembechler and his Wolverines went home, the great Midwest suffered its third-straight disappointment when Oakland drubbed Minnesota, 32–14, in the first Super Bowl played in the Rose Bowl, on January 9.

Charlie White rips one for Trojans

Charlie White goes high in gaining 144 for day

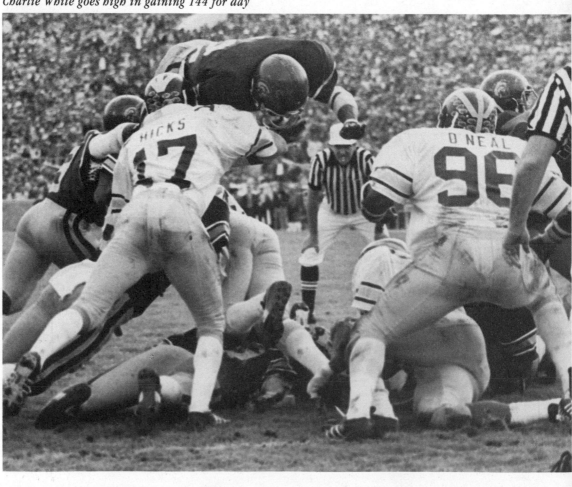

the Debonair Duke of Earlville, Illinois, and to others as the coach of the Michigan team that trounced USC, 49–0, in the 1948 Rose Bowl game. But even the presence of Crisler, who celebrated his seventy-eighth birthday during his vacation on the West Coast, could not save Schembechler's Wolverines, who had drubbed Ohio State to earn the Pasadena shot after four years of Buckeye reign.

As advertised, Michigan had the option running attack to cause USC problems, especially in the first half; but Michigan lost because it could not match USC through the air offensively or defensively. USC made eleven of twenty third-down conversions. Evans was accurate and his receivers caught balls in every conceivable manner—leaping, straight on, or while sprawled on the ground. Shelton Diggs caught eight passes, set up two Trojan touchdowns and figured in three of the other four USC scoring chances which fell short.

After a strong start, great USC running star Ricky Bell, had his "bell rung" early in the game and was kept out of action thereafter. Star receiver Randy Simmrin was reduced to spot action, although effective in that role, by a previous injury. However, freshman running back Charles White—later to lead the NFL in rushing—filled in for Bell and gained 114 yards in thirty-two carries.

USC made the big plays, just as Coach Robinson's team had made them throughout the season while winning eleven straight after an opening loss to Missouri when the team obviously was unprepared and chesty. When Robinson came back to USC, where he had assisted John McKay before interning for a year with the pros in Oakland, he said his plan was to take what the enemy gave. Michigan slowed the Trojan ground at-

tack, so Evans hit them through the air.

Rob Lytle's short touchdown buck gave Michigan a 6–0 lead, but Walt Underwood, Trojan lineman, blocked Bob Wood's conversion try. USC came back to score on a fake rollout by Evans and again on a 7-yard dash by White with Glenn Walker converting both times.

Michigan couldn't rally, although it tried with Jim Smith making a miracle catch to set up a late chance. USC punished quarterback Rick Leach, who completed only four of twelve passes. The game ended with USC in possession but with a center pass going 20 yards to nowhere as the clock ran out.

Said John Hall in the *Times:* "It wasn't a bad snap. Coach Robinson explained that the Michigan nose guard, in desperation, punched the ball with his fist. For Michigan, it was a pretty good idea. Nothing to lose. It went like shot, but it was illegal. The official saw it. The penalty would have been called, but since the game was over, USC refused it."

Jim Murray, *Times:* "A major swindle was perpetrated on the Tournament of Roses committee. I want an immediate house-to-house search from Ann Arbor to Columbus. The real Big Ten champions are locked in a closet some place, bound and gagged. They must think we are awful rubes to accept these guys they suited up and sent here in their place."

The USC victory was especially sweet for Marv Goux, the faithful Trojan assistant coach who developed "Goux's Gorillas." Goux is the all-time Rose Bowl participation champion. He appeared in eleven Rose Bowl games—twice as a player, in 1953 and 1955, eight times as an assistant to McKay, and once as an assistant to Robinson.

On January 9, the National Football League's Super Bowl game was played in

The Pac Eight became the Pac-10 with the acquisition of Arizona and Arizona State in 1977, following a movement to invite them led by USC president John Hubbard and UCLA chancellor Charles Young. The move was labeled a money-saver due to the close proximity of the schools, thus eliminating much travel expense to play other teams.

The 1977 Super Bowl in Pasadena was such a success that the National Football League announced shortly afterwards that it would return its championship game to the Rose Bowl in 1980. While civic officials revealed they wanted to stage the event as often as possible, Tournament of Roses officials remained silent about future Super Bowls coming to the stadium that had been paid for out of Rose Bowl game funds.

A victory ride for USC's Coach John Robinson

Vince Evans proves an elusive USC quarterback

the Rose Bowl—ten years after Pasadena had turned the professionals away. It was not, however, the idea of the Tournament of Roses to hold the Super Bowl game at the Rose Bowl in January. The Oakland Raiders ran over the Minnesota Vikings, 32–14.

The city of Pasadena fathers wanted the classic and got it. Former mayor Donald F. Yokaitas, Mayor Tim Matthews, City Manager Donald F. McIntyre, his assistant Jim Crain and other city officials offered the Rose Bowl facilities for the game to the National Football League for

$60,000 rental. In addition, Pasadena derived $50,000 in ticket tax and $30,000 in concessions profit. After expenses, the city netted somewhat over $80,000.

After opposing the Super Bowl's coming to Pasadena in 1966, the *Star-News* supported the 1977 deal. By then, the climate had changed. Everybody needed more income. The colleges were fumbling with financial problems. Communities like Pasadena were fighting lack of funds to carry on steps needed for continued community progress. It clearly didn't seem practical any longer for the city of Pasadena to let a huge stadium sit idle for a whole year except for one big game. Nor did it seem fair for the colleges to expect Pasadena to keep out pro football when the colleges realized how tough it was to balance the books.

"Pasadena sleeps 364 days a year," had once been the claim of critics who coined such phrases as "Little Old Lady from Pasadena." But when two nationally significant events like the Rose Bowl game on January 1 and the Super Bowl game on January 9 attracted more than two hundred thousand fans and were viewed by more than one hundred fifty million on TV, while the Rose Parade attracted another million spectators on the streets of Pasadena, it was generally agreed this city was the hub of the good life in California as the year 1977 began.

1978
Bo's Unlucky Town

By January 2, 1978, two of the most successful Midwest football coaches of all time—Woody Hayes of Ohio State and Bo Schembechler of Michigan—had the distinction of being the "losingest" coaches in Rose Bowl history. By then each had suffered four defeats in the New Year's Day classic. Schembechler's Rose Bowl record fell to 0–4 when his Wolverine team, though 14-point favorites, suffered a 27–20 loss to Washington in the 1978 game.

Bo should have known before then that Pasadena was his unlucky town. On his first visit in 1970, he had suffered a heart attack and his team lost to USC, 10–3. In 1972, it rained so steadily he took his team to Bakersfield to practice. Again he lost, this time to Stanford, 13–12. In 1977, USC ripped his Wolverines, 14–6. Two weeks before the 1978

Gerald Ford as a Michigan player

game, Schembechler arrived at Los Angeles International Airport just as weeks of sunny seventy-to-eighty-degree days were turning to rain and steady overcast. "There's that big black cloud again," remarked Bo as he came down the ramp behind his nine-year-old son Glenn Schembechler II.

That "big black cloud" hardly left during Michigan's entire damp stay. Although game day was warm and dry, it still was dark for Michigan.

Meanwhile, Harrison R. "Bud" Baker Jr., a real estate developer and appraiser, had become president of the eighty-ninth Tournament. His election capped twenty-nine years of service.

The Tournament and the football game staged during Baker's regime were spectacular affairs. An estimated 1.5 million people packed the parade route in Pasadena, with 125 million more watching on television. Although it rained almost daily for a week prior to January 2, the Sunday-Monday holiday weekend enjoyed delightful weather. Typical of Pasadena luck in recent years, the rains returned on January 3 and more than ten inches of moisture were measured for the pre- and post-Tournament storms. Arthur D. Welsh, vice president in charge of weather, carned his 1979 Tournament presidency with a magnificent job of control over the elements.

Former U.S. president Gerald Ford was grand marshal and enjoyed the day—at least until the football game, in which he saw his alma mater go down to defeat. Ford was the fourth U.S. president in Tournament history to be grand marshal, following Herbert Hoover, Dwight D. Eisenhower and Richard Nixon.

The queen of the 1978 Tournament was Maria Lynn Caron of La Cañada-Flintridge, a student at Pasadena City College—which early the preceding December won the Junior Rose Bowl football game by trouncing Jones County Junior College of Mississippi. Caron's court consisted of Lou Ellen Harryman, Elizabeth Ann Jacobs, Kathleen Alice Graves, Colleen Kettenhofen, Devon Marie DeGrazio and Brenda Ann Handy.

Luaine Scheliga, reporting the parade for the *Star-News,* said she was impressed by the U.S. Cavalry from Arizona with its authentic uniforms from the 1880s and the All-Ohio State Fair Youth Choir from Zanesville, Ohio, which am-

plified its songs with portable audio packs.

Eastman Kodak won the Grand Prize with a whimsical play on nature's creatures. The two theme winners dipped into history—the "Hayride" by the city of St. Louis with its Clydesdales, and an ornate Victorian house depicted in the Winchell's Donut House entry.

Washington's Governor Dixie Lee Ray was a story herself during Tournament festivities. She came down from Olympia with an entourage of motor vehicles and lived in her motor home parked near the Rose Bowl. She was often seen walking her pet poodle, Jacques.

A fire which gutted the old Taylor Hotel along the parade route provided a show for parade all-nighters.

Dog Eat Dog:
Washington 27, Michigan 20

The 1978 game marked the first time since 1965 that a team other than USC, UCLA or Stanford represented the Pacific conference in the Rose Bowl when Don James led his Washington Huskies into Pasadena. The Big Ten, however, continued to be monopolized by Michigan and Ohio State—the only conference schools to go to the Rose Bowl since 1969.

At the Big Ten Club dinner a few nights prior to the game, Bob Hope received a Michigan sweater from Wolverine alumni secretary Bob Foreman. Hope promptly predicted that the impending Wolverines vs. Huskies confrontation would be dog eat dog. Phyllis Diller also gave the Wolverines a grin that remained until Washington wore it off.

Warren Moon, the Washington quarterback, received the 1978 Player of the Game Award selected by the Citizens Savings Athletic Foundation under the direction of Bill Schroeder and Braven

Harrison "Bud" Baker

Marian Martin, known as "Magnolia," "Buttercup" and "Marian the Librarian," who retired from the Tournament in 1978 after eighteen years of service, was known for keeping everyone in the Tournament family in stitches. One evening she took a phone call and realized she couldn't answer the questions. She was heard to say to the caller, "I'm just the cleaning lady here. Why don't you call back in the morning?"

The 1978 grand marshal, former U.S. president Gerald Ford, had played center for Michigan teams which were undefeated in 1932 and 1933, but big losers in 1934—when he was named most valuable player. A 1934 teammate remarked that Ford was named most valuable player that year "because the other athletes felt Jerry was one guy who would stay and fight in a losing cause." That 1934 team had plenty of losing causes: It won only one game of eight, while being outscored, 143–21.

President Gerald Ford says "Let's play ball"

Dyer Jr. Moon scored two touchdowns, passed to speedy receiver Bob Gaines for another and rocked Michigan with twelve timely passes in twenty-three attempts for 188 yards. Gaines was his chief target with four big catches, including a 28-yard touchdown reception that made the score 24–0 in the third quarter. Washington's Steve Robbins kicked two field goals and was three-for-three in conversions.

Michigan was hurt by its own mistakes. For example, early in the game, a Michigan punt was nullified and Washington got possession in midfield because a low, bouncing center snap forced kicker John Anderson to touch one knee to the ground while reaching for the ball. Moon promptly fired passes to Joe Steele and Gaines to set up his own keeper sweep for the game's first touchdown.

A 62-yard Moon-to-Gaines pass set up Robbins's first field goal, and another Moon-to-Gaines pass plus the running of Ron Rowland led to Moon's over-the-top touchdown which left the lead 17–0 at half time. After a surprise fourth down pass from the Washington punter to Kyle Stevens shocked Michigan with a 46-yard gain, Washington almost increased the lead before Dwight Hicks's interception saved Michigan further distress.

That distress did come, however, early in the third quarter when Michigan couldn't score after a Mike Jolly interception and runback put the ball on the Washington 12. Moon then engineered a drive from his 3 that ended with a touchdown pass to Gaines.

Native Californian Curt Stephenson surprised the world, including the Washington defense, by getting open on the sidelines for a bowl record 76-yard touchdown catch and run that cut the

Player of the Game Warren Moon

While Bo Schembechler was losing his fourth Rose Bowl game on January 2, 1978, Woody Hayes and his Buckeyes were getting trounced by Alabama, 35–6, in the Sugar Bowl. Bob Hope said Hayes belonged in the Sugar Bowl "because Woody is a sweet guy."

score to 24–7 on Greg Willner's conversion. Robbins's second field goal upped Washington's lead to 27–7. Then Michigan awakened.

A 78-yard drive culminated in a short Russell Davis tally. Soon Rick Leach completed a 32-yard pass to freshman Stan Edwards for another score. A bad center snap gummed up the conversion.

Washington's Spider Gaines takes a breather

Michigan kept coming. Leach's first-down pass to Edwards was off the mark enough to force him to juggle trying to recoup. The play came with the Wolverines having a minute-and-a-half to work the ball in from the 8-yard line, including three timeouts to stop the clock. The ball rolled off Edwards's hands over his shoulder pads where Michael Jackson picked it off for an interception. The Michigan defense held, so the Wolverines gained a new chance from midfield following the punt. But Leach's pass intended for Edwards was intercepted over the shoulder by Nesby Glasgow, final

death for Michigan, which, had it scored, would certainly have gone for two points—which would have given it a 28–27 victory.

Jackson explained how his game-saving interception came about:

"I was about three steps behind Edwards and thought he was going to catch the ball. It hit him in the hands. Then I saw the ball bounce up and hit his helmet when I was about two steps away. At that time, I was just trying to make the tackle, but when I saw the ball go up, I felt I could get to it."

After yet another Pac-10 win, Allan

Don James rides from the stadium in triumph

Malamud of the *Herald Examiner* said the game result proved again that the Pac-10–Big Ten pact had outlived itself as the game was no longer a match. But Bob Oates of the *Times* countered, "If Michigan keeps working on its passing, the next game will be closer."

One reason why Malamud's suggestion to end the Pac-10–Big Ten pact was ignored was that the Rose Bowl continued to dominate the television ratings. Even with the Cotton Bowl having the battle for the national championship between winning Notre Dame and dethroned Texas, NBC's Rose Bowl telecast topped the ratings of the four major bowl games again. The Rose Bowl had 29.2 percent of the TV sets in the nation and 46 percent of the sets in use—about 70 million viewers. The Cotton Bowl had a 23.4 rating, 45 share or 58 million viewers. The Orange Bowl, which presented Arkansas vs. Texas, at night had 27.1 and 41, while the Sugar Bowl (Alabama vs. Ohio State) going head-to-head with the Cotton Bowl drew a 10.3 and 20 share.

Four *Star-News* reporters rode on Occidental Life's "Good News 1928" float, which depicted an old-time newspaper office. Feature writer Belinda Busteed, who rode with Keith Murray, Larry Palmer and Brent Howell, described what it was like to ride in the parade: "You may not see much of the parade while riding on a float, but you learn a lot about waving. People wave in circles. People wave with vigor. People wave with their fingers apart, together, flopping or wiggling. People wave their babies' hands. People sweep the air. People wave in unison. For best results, we found the best way to wave back was to establish eye contact with an engaged waver and direct waving at that person. This takes the strain out of smiling at everybody for 5 1/2 miles."

When Lathrop Leishman was named grand marshal of the 1979 Tournament, he said, "I stood on this very same turf 55 years ago when the Bowl first began. It had 57,000 seats, cost $272,000, and now it stands debt free. I won't need a lot of drivers to get me places. I know my way around and won't get lost. I know where to park, and I won't need four rows of seats at the game—only enough for my family." Leishman recalled driving his father, William, to the 1920 parade in their decorated touring car. "My father wore a tall silk hat," said Lay. "I will not wear a silk hat come January 1."

1979
Lathrop's Reward

Arthur Welsh did not delay in making two significant decisions as the 1979 Tournament president. He named Lathrop "Lay" Leishman grand marshal of the 1979 festival. And he announced that the theme of the ninetieth Tournament would be "Our Wonderful World of Sports," as proposed by Marie Terry of Altadena.

Welsh transformed the annual coronation into a garden party that attracted several hundred people for a luncheon on the Tournament grounds. Welsh said he hoped in the future the Tournament parade would attract more floats from foreign countries, including Pasadena's sister cities, Ludwigshafen in Germany and Mishima in Japan. Appearing in the 1979 parade were floats from Puerto Rico, British Columbia, Calgary, Quebec and Mexico.

The "Wonderful World of Sports" theme drew many sports notables who appeared in the parade. The Atlantic Richfield float, "Return to Olympia," which featured six former Olympic gold medal winners in person, had six oversized replicas of classic Greek Olympic sculptures covered in gladioli and carnation petals with red ti leaves. The flame of the Olympic torch was created by using hundreds of rapidly spinning "flippers," tied through an intricate network of gears and attached to the float's drive chain. Riding the float, which won the Governor's Trophy for commercial entry best depicting the parade theme, were Olympic champions Bob Mathias, Bill Toomey, Parry O'Brien, Wilma Rudolf, Donna DeVarona and John Naber.

Among other sports stars riding floats were Bruce Jenner, Tracy Austin, Tom Lasorda, Stan Musial, Jesse Owens, Bob

Arthur Welsh

Lemon, Donna Caponi Young, Jim Plunkett, Linda Fratianne, Bob Chandler, Vince Evans, John McKay Jr., John Sciarra, Don Bunce, Raul Ramirez and more. Jockey John Longdon fell off a mechanical horse on one float and suffered an arm injury that pained him more than any misfortune he had suffered while riding thousands of mounts during his long racing career.

The Order of the Sons of Italy float captured the coveted Sweepstakes Trophy for the most beautiful entry. This float depicted a fierce race between two forty-foot-long gondolas floating atop a cameo-like frame.

Queen of the 1979 Tournament was Catherine Mary Gilmour of La Cañada-Flintridge, a student at La Cañada High School. Her court consisted of Lisa Kathleen Gage, with Kathleen Caroline Looney, also from the same school; Suzanne

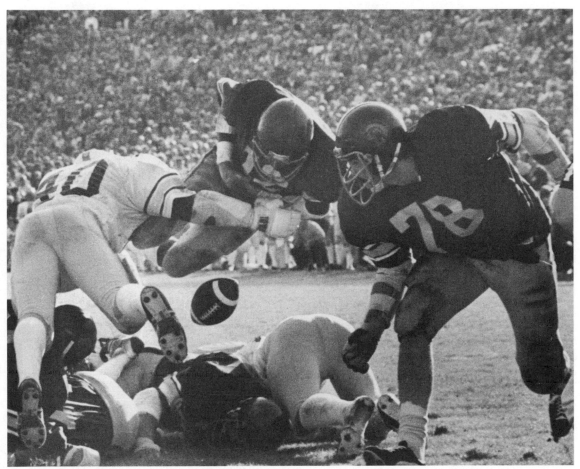

Did Charlie White score for USC before losing the ball?

The legendary Woody Hayes was permanently removed from the Rose Bowl scene shortly before the 1979 Rose Bowl game. Ohio State's athletic director Hugh Hindman fired him for punching a Clemson player in the Gator Bowl game played in Jacksonville, Florida, two days before the Rose Bowl game. Hayes had a 4–4 record in Rose Bowl play since his first appearance in 1955.

By the mid-1970s Surl Kim was booking tourists from all parts of the United States for Tournament events. A noted Los Angeles area travel man, Kim was bringing ten thousand travelers a year to the Pasadena festival, for which he leased an entire stand for the busloads of parade fans he brought in.

A Pasadenan, Mary Ellen Lewis, revealed a novel hobby in 1978. Since 1969 she had taken roses left over from Tournament float-making, dried them and sent them to a monastery in Terre Haute, Indiana.

Thelma Simone from Arcadia High School; Robin Elaine Townsend of Sacred Heart Academy; and Melissa Jo Young and Julianne Lucille Hageman from Pasadena City College. A field of 832 young women entered the original competition.

The 1979 festival was the first in more than two decades that was not favored by Max Colwell's presence. The previous October he had died at the age of seventy-five, leaving a void in the Tournament that was impossible completely to fill.

Bo's Not-So-Wonderful World of Sports: USC 17, Michigan 10

The University of Michigan returned to the Rose Bowl for a ninth time—Bo Schembechler's fifth as head coach. Although Bo had pledged, "We'll keep coming back until we do it right," he lost in Pasadena a fifth straight time, thus becoming the losingest coach in Rose Bowl history, dethroning Woody Hayes.

Tragedy struck the Michiganders when they encountered John Robinson's Trojans. The loss came despite the pregame statement of movieland's Knute Rockne, the one and only Pat O'Brien, at the annual Big Ten Club dinner at the Palladium: "How can you lose when God is on your side?"

The 17–10 USC victory, achieved before 105,629 fans under sunny skies, "wasn't a pretty game offensively,"

Perhaps the best study of Woody Hayes was revealed by Anne Hayes, his wife: "It certainly hasn't been a calm and peaceful marriage, but it has been darn interesting. I don't think I'd want to be married to anybody else. I have to fight 85 to 100 football players for attention, but that's better than one skinny blonde. I don't get upset when I am at a game and some fan yells at Woody and calls him an SOB. Why should I? I've called him that myself. Mellowing isn't the right word for the Woody of today. His basic beliefs are still the same. But styles change, and I think he's gradually learned to accept them. He's just changed his approach."

wrote Terry Johnson in the *Star-News*. "What it was was a classic display of defense on both sides."

Rick Leach, the Michigan quarterback playing in his third Rose Bowl, tended to throw too high. His overthrows led to two USC interceptions that produced ten Trojan points. The other seven came on a disputed touchdown by White.

Leach, named coplayer of the game with USC's Charles White, completed ten of twenty-two passes, but he threw two of them to Trojan defensive backs Ron Lott and Dennis Smith. Lott's return set up a 9-yard touchdown pass from Paul McDonald to Hoby Brenner, and Smith's return set up a 35-yard field goal by Frank Jordan, the hero of USC's late season victory over Notre Dame.

Michigan's scores came on a 36-yard field goal by Greg Willner and a 44-yard scoring pass from Leach to Roosevelt Smith. Leach made quite a comeback after his early failures, but his biggest comeback came a week later in the Hula Bowl in Hawaii. Ditto for fullback Russell Davis, who scored six times in the East-West game.

The play the experts discussed most was a touchdown blast by White that gave USC a 14–3 lead in the second quarter. Sparked by some key gains by USC fullback star Lynn Cain, USC had second and goal on Michigan's 3. White dove over left guard and headed for the end zone. Ron Simpkins of Michigan, a capable linebacker, made a stab at White and stripped the ball. The ball bounced on the 1, where Mark Braman recovered it for Michigan. Although Michigan players argued that White had not broken the plane of the goal line before fumbling, line judge Gilbert Marchman, a Big Ten official, signaled touchdown. The umpire indicated White hadn't scored, but

referee Paul Kamanski of the Pacific conference accepted his line judge's opinion and made the touchdown official. In the opinion of many observers, White had scored, but the ball hadn't.

The dispute that raged reminded Rose Bowl veterans, like Mal Florence of the *Times*, that Art Murakowski of Northwestern scored in a similar manner in the 1949 game, leading to California's defeat.

Loel Schrader of the *Long Beach Independent* said in his column: "Two guys in striped shirts tried to imitate the Marx Brothers. Or maybe Laurel and Hardy or Abbott and Costello. One zebra, line judge Gilbert Marchman, signaled touchdown, and umpire Don Mason pointed fumble recovery by Michigan. An earthquake that followed in the area a little later couldn't have been more unsettling."

Schrader added, "It's a good thing W. W. Hayes wasn't gracing the Pasadena scene this day."

Columnist Ken Gurnick of the *Valley News* wrote: "Even Charles White had trouble keeping a straight face about 'the fumble.' He said he landed on the ground, saw the referee's hands go up in the corner of his eye and he let go of the ball." The headline above Gurnick's story read, "A White Lie for Charles?"

Mike Waldner of the *Daily Breeze* explained Michigan's defensive tactics: "Michigan had two missions. It wanted to take away USC's favorite play, the pitch to the tailback, also known as student body right or left, and it set out to swarm quarterback McDonald. Michigan's basic defense includes three down linemen, four linebackers and four deep backs. Michigan brought outside linebackers Jerry Meter and Tom Seabron up to the line where they became standing defensive ends. Strong safety Gene Bell often crept up to the line to become an additional linebacker.''

Valley News sports editor Frank Mazzeo disputed White's explanation, noting that the line judge wouldn't have been in Charlie's view ''and Charlie would have had to see the signal through his helmet.''

Bob Keisser of the *Herald Examiner* quoted Michigan players as saying ''it was no touchdown.'' His sports editor Allan Malamud added, ''If the mark of a national champion is to be both good and lucky, USC should be fitted for the crown immediately.''

John Hall of the *Times* added, ''Even God seemed to be angry over White's touchdown as an earthquake was felt in the bowl.''

USC adjusted. The Trojans discarded the pitch, went to a two tight-end offense and began blasting quick hitting plays. But USC didn't adjust its passing game, being greedy and continuing to send its receivers deep. They should have been more patient and thrown short more often instead of long.

The victory by 12–1 USC over 10–2 Michigan led to a debate on the national championship, which ended in a draw. The United Press International coaches' poll awarded the title to USC when Alabama, defeated early in the season by USC, upended previously undefeated Penn State in the Sugar Bowl, 14–7. But the writers' poll conducted by Associated Press gave the crown to Alabama. ''There was no doubt in Pasadena who was number one. It was USC by a landslide,'' observed Dave Daniel of the *Santa Monica Outlook.* ''The dispute just proves there should be a national tournament,'' said the *Outlook's* columnist Mitch Chortkoff.

Not much to toot about for Michigan

Michigan coach Schembechler praised USC, and USC coach Robinson lauded Michigan, but Bo told Gary Rausch of the *Long Beach Independent,* ''I love coming to the Rose Bowl, although I am tired of losing press conferences.''

Schembechler had created some ill feeling in Tournament circles by taking his team to a four-day preliminary stay in Newport Beach near the ocean before coming to the Huntington Sheraton in Pasadena. Rose Bowl officials felt slighted when Schembechler suggested he wanted to give his players a change in scenery to break the monotony. But Bo insisted he meant nothing degrading and he affirmed love for Pasadena—if he ever could win in the Rose Bowl.

USC finished the year with eight straight victories and claimed its eighth national crown. The victory gave USC an 18–6 all-time record in all bowl games and a 16–6 mark in Pasadena, best of any team in the history of the Rose Bowl. White, who carried thirty-two times for 99 yards against Michigan, ran his yardage for his first three seasons at USC to 4,195 yards, the highest total in Pacific conference history.

Once again the Rose Bowl telecast led the New Year's Day ratings despite the fact the Sugar Bowl duel between Alabama and Penn State was advertised by the ABC network as being "for the national championship." The Rose Bowl had a 23.3 rating, followed by the Orange Bowl (Oklahoma-Nebraska) 22.8; the Sugar Bowl with 21.7; and the Cotton Bowl (Notre Dame–Houston), fourth, 12.5. Combined CBS and NBC Tournament of Roses parade ratings totaled 34.7, however, to lead the day.

All football ratings were down from the previous year, however. The Rose Bowl had been 29.2 in 1978, when it reached 70 million people in 20 million homes.

Ron Lott scoots with interception

THE 1980s

PAC-10 TAKES THE LEAD

J.D. Morgan

Frank Hardcastle

Frank Hardcastle's tenure as Tournament president fell between those of two men whose fathers had previously been presidents. Hardcastle didn't seem to mind. When he was named president, he said, "I am happy to prove that one does not have to be born here or be the son of a past president to become head of this wonderful organization." Hardcastle was born in Swarthmore, Pennsylvania, and came to Pasadena to enter the insurance business.

1980
The Music, Man

A debonair and charismatic graying Frank Sinatra sat atop the back seat of a rose-strewn antique auto with his wife Barbara. The grand marshal and his fair lady blew kisses to one-and-a-half million people who lined the boulevards of Pasadena to view the ninety-first Tournament of Roses parade under balmy, sunny California skies on January 1, 1980.

"You are gazing at the happiest man in the country at this moment . . . because I have been asked to be the marshal of this parade," said America's popular crooner who was chosen by Tournament president Frank Hardcastle to epitomize the parade theme, "Music of America." In Hardcastle's words, "No person could better exemplify our theme than Ol' Blue Eyes, a man who is gentle at heart and a real humanitarian."

The 1980 Tournament year was exciting from the very start. In January, 1979, president Art Welsh received his "walking papers" and turned over the chief executive post to Hardcastle. Mike Ward's AAA Towing Service was called to move Welsh's buggy from the private parking place at Tournament House. During the parade, Hardcastle, his wife, Irene, and their family rode in a fire engine commemorating his days as a volunteer fireman when he lived in New Jersey before coming to Pasadena as an insurance executive.

From an initial group of eight hundred candidates, a Pasadena City College co-ed, Julie Raatz, was named queen of the ninety-first Tournament. Julie's ascension to the Tournament throne marked a sudden upturn in the fortunes of her family, whose Pasadena home had burned down the previous December. Joining Raatz on the court were Mindy

Frank Sinatra at Kickoff Luncheon

Margett, Judy Bacic and Linda Deal of Arcadia, Mary McCoy and Liz Matioli of San Marino and Sue Davis of South Pasadena.

The day couldn't have been more pleasant as Pasadena again became the pageant capital of the world while newspapers, magazines, radio and television carried the story of fun, beauty, love, flowers and peace to mankind.

A new record 21,822,000 households, forty-nine percent of the total television market, witnessed NBC's Rose Bowl telecast. Three networks carried the parade to an estimated 125 million viewers. *Pasadena Star-News* reporter Becky Bartindale captured the spirit when she wrote, "Smiles were abundant and hands clapped to the myriad tunes as 59 floral floats, 24 bands and 185 equestrians paraded by." Bartindale told how the parade went on despite such unusual mishaps as a small fire inside one float, quickly extinguished; the toppling over of a flowered poodle during a gust of wind, a derrick hoisting it back into place; and an equestrian getting thrown when his mount balked, the rider courageously returning to the saddle.

Julian Loewe of the *Star-News* described "Baubles, Bangles and Beads" as a stunning mirage of flowers from the community of Mission Viejo. This float emerged the coveted Sweepstakes winner as the most beautiful entry. The float was inspired by the memorable 1953 operetta *Kismet*.

For the second time, the Rose Bowl was the scene of the pro football's Super Bowl—just three weeks after the 1980 Rose Bowl game. The Pittsburgh Steelers won their fourth championship by defeating the Los Angeles Rams, 31–19, as 103,985 sunbathers in the Rose Bowl and millions more in television audiences viewed the action.

Victory from the Jaws of Defeat:
USC 17, Ohio State 16

A last-minute 17–16 victory gave USC an all-time Rose Bowl record of 17–6 and cut to 18–16 the lead the Big Ten had built over Pacific conference teams since the two leagues began their Rose Bowl pact in 1946. For the Pac-10 it was the fifteenth victory since 1960.

USC, its 10–0–1 season record marred only by a 21–21 tie with Stanford, bumped Associated Press's number-one-ranked Ohio State, coached by Earle Bruce, from national title contention. This left undefeated Alabama atop both the sportswriters' AP and coaches' UPI polls after New Year's Day.

Eric Hipp's 41-yard field goal gave USC first blood, 3–0, in the first quarter. The Trojan defense—including Myron

Lapka, who had downed nine Diamond Brady cuts at the Lawry's "beef bowl" a few days earlier—put on a tremendous second quarter goal line stand that prevented the Buckeyes from scoring after an Art Schlichter–to–Gary Williams bomb had placed the ball on the 2.

Southpaw Paul McDonald then pitched a 53-yard touchdown pass to speedy Kevin Williams for the latter's twenty-first career touchdown to make the score 10–0. The first of Vlade Janakievski's field goals for Ohio State cut it to 10–3. Charles White had a chance to put USC well in front when he tore up the middle for 45 yards, only to fumble within scoring range when hit by Todd Bell. This save inspired Ohio State. Three plays later, Schlichter connected on a 67-yard scoring strike to Williams for a 10–10 count at intermission.

Ohio State took the lead in the third quarter when Janakievski connected on a 37-yard field goal. USC's bid to regain the lead was foiled when McDonald's pass to James Hunter on the Ohio State 1 was nullified by an official call against Rick Rakhshani, another receiver, for offensive interference in the end zone. The violation gave the ball to the Buckeyes.

In the final quarter, Janakievski boosted the Ohio State lead to 16–10 with a 24-yard field goal. After sputtering through the air following retaliation on the ground that advanced to Ohio State's 24, USC gained its last chance from its 17-yard line with five minutes and thirty-one seconds remaining.

Instead of passing as expected, USC decided to rip on the ground. Despite a split nose smeared with blood, White broke for 32 yards, then a 28-yard gain. Five plays later, USC was on the 1. White soared over the top to climax one of the great Rose Bowl drives of all times.

Of his experience as 1980 grand marshal, Frank Sinatra said, "My career hasn't meant much to my grandchildren, but now I am in the big time with them because they have seen me in the parade."

John Robinson

Earle Bruce

Although John McKay, with 127 career USC victories, and Howard Jones with 121, remained the school's all-time leaders, John Robinson's third Rose Bowl victory kept him even with Jones's unbeaten Rose Bowl record, and his victory gave him a four-year winning percentage of 87.5% (42–6–1), which let him surpass Gloomy Gus Henderson's 46–7–0 (86.8%) record.

Ohio State's Art Schlichter rolls out to pass

Anthony Munoz, a giant offensive tackle who went down with a knee injury in the opening Trojan victory of the year at Texas Tech, returned to action to help open the holes that enabled Charlie White and the Trojans to blast 83 yards in eight ground plays in the final five minutes to snatch victory. White gained 70 yards in six carries during the drive to erase a 16–10 deficit. Trojan place-kicker Eric Hipp qualified for the Rose Bowl "Hall of Toes" instead of hips by perfectly placing the extra point between the crossbars after White torpedoed one yard over the Buckeye defense for the winning touchdown.

Terry Johnson of the *Star-News* quoted USC coach John Robinson as stating, "Charlie White is the greatest football player I have ever seen." White was named Player of the Game in the Citizen's Savings Athletic Foundation sports writer poll conducted by Bill Schroeder and Braven Dyer Jr., after he gained a record 247 yards on thirty-nine carries.

The statistics supported the wisdom of Robinson's strategy to go infantry-style at the finish. Throughout the game, USC had success running the ball and wound up with 306 yards rushing against 234 yards passing. Ohio State had its best fortune through the air, 297 yards passing compared to its ground total of 115. Talented sophomore Schlichter completed eleven of twenty-one passes. His top receivers were elusive and sure-handed Doug Donley who caught four and Gary Williams with three. USC southpaw McDonald ended his career with eleven for twenty-four via the skyways, his problem being that his passes didn't connect inside the 20 when he switched to the air after mainly getting there on the ground. Frank Mazzeo of the *Valley News* praised the USC defense "for bending

Charles White

The 1980 Tournament marked the retirement of William G. Lawson after six years as executive secretary and manager. Lawson had been in line for the presidency in the early seventies, but resigned as a volunteer officer to become the manager. "I'd rather serve several years as manager than be president for one year," he explained. Lawson was succeeded by Walter Hoefflin, son of Walter Hoefflin Jr., the 1965 Tournament president. Hoefflin served a single year.

with the best of them and mustering the intestinal fortitude that got USC to Pasadena." Rick Talley of the same paper called the final Trojan punch "a drive to remember in a Rose Bowl to remember."

Talley asked White to explain how he could run off two big ground gains from the 17, and Charlie replied, "My fullback, Marcus Allen, blocked the middle linebacker, and I was off to the races." McDonald added, "If Charles didn't break those runs, we'd have had to go back to the pass, but we would have scored somehow."

1981
A Family Affair

The Tournament of Roses seems to be in the Davidson family's blood. Millard Davidson, who once played trombone in

Lorne Greene and Millard Davidson

Leslie Kim Kawai, the first minority queen in Tournament history, was the granddaughter of a Japanese carpenter, Toichiro Kawai, who came to California in 1898 and helped assemble the Japanese Tea Gardens in San Marino. Kawai's aunt, Kimiko Kawai, and four other young Japanese women rode on the float entered by the Imperial Hotel of Tokyo in the 1916 parade.

the Rose Parade for the Pasadena City College band, was the Tournament's 1981 president. His son, Jim, blew the same trombone in the 1981 parade. Davidson's father, the late John S. Davidson, headed the Tournament in 1957. "Dad was long active in the association and I kind of grew up understanding and being around the Tournament of Roses," Davidson recalled. "My first recollection is sitting on a curb in East Pasadena watching the parade when I was seven or eight. And I can remember helping my dad set up barricades the day before the parade."

President Davidson enjoyed huge success in staging the ninety-second Pasadena festival. After "guaranteeing" beautiful weather that continued for many days before and after January 1, Davidson and his wife Jeanette headed a spectacular parade that attracted 1.3 million spectators. Jiles Fitzgerald, describing the parade in the *Star-News,* reported that the crowd's rowdy mood from the night before, when 350 arrests were made, "changed into a cheerful, exuberant attitude, cheering and clapping as the 61 floats, 24 bands and 238 equestrians passed by."

Davidson chose veteran actor and environmentalist Lorne Greene as his grand marshal to lead the theme "The Great Outdoors." Greene, known as television's Ben Cartwright on the popular series "Bonanza," had often appeared in previous Rose Parades along with his "Bonanza" son, Michael Landon, and other fellow actors. Marilyn Ludwig of Panorama City, California, suggested the theme for the parade—one of 4,500 entries that had been submitted.

The queen of the 1981 Tournament court was another Pasadena City College coed, Leslie Kim Kawai. The selection committee headed by Bob Hemmings also picked princesses Julie Allen, Monica Lichter, Rebecca Miller, Janet Park, Lourdes Vita and Julie Vogel.

Pasadena City College's marching band, appearing in its fifty-first parade as the official band, was headed by Raul Ramirez, a drum major who got his start marching in a Juarez, Mexico, samba-jazz band as a youngster.

The city of Mission Viejo float won the coveted Sweepstakes award in the parade for a second consecutive year. The winning float in the non-commercial division, "Summertime," was a tableau of ten thousand roses and orchids depicting a leisurely boat ride through a bayou beneath a canopy of butterflies. Winner of the Grand Prize, highest award for commercial entries, was Avon Products for its depiction of "Autumn Splendor," featuring two ring-necked pheasants. The third major award, the Theme prize, went to "High Sierra," a gracefully sculpted image of three deer leaping over the snow, entered by the Reno-Sparks Convention Authority.

The last float in the parade, a whale over a hundred feet long called "Monarch of the Sea," accompanied by its thirty-five-foot baby, ended the show in an exciting manner.

A Team That Knew How to Win: Michigan 23, Washington 6

Five Pac-10 schools—USC, UCLA, Oregon, Oregon State and Arizona State—were declared ineligible for the conference championship and bowl play because of scholastic violations. The disqualification of half the conference's teams set the stage for a potentially embarrassing situation in which a sixth-place team could go to the 1981 Rose Bowl. Washington prevented the conference from being embarrassed by winning the title outright with a 9–2 record.

It may not have been a banner year for President Jimmy Carter. Not only did he get swept out of office, he broke his collarbone while skiing. However, another Carter enjoyed great success on New Year's Day. Anthony Carter, all 155 pounds of him, joined Player of the Game Butch Woolfolk in leading Michigan to a 23–6 victory over Washington in the 1981 Rose Bowl game. The victory was coach Bo Schembechler's first in Pasadena after five Rose Bowl defeats.

When Schembechler arrived in Pasadena on Christmas Day, he told his team that the eighties were a "new decade, men, a new decade." Bo insisted that his 9–2 team was different from the others as "this one knows how to win."

The Wolverines led, 7–6, at intermis-

sion although Washington had appeared stronger in the first half with numerous scoring opportunities. In the second half, Bo's team convinced the 104,863 sunbathers in Pasadena's seventy-five-degree paradise that it knew the formula for victory. As Roger Murray of the *Star-News* pointed out, Michigan got the ball to Carter in the second half. Quarterback John Wangler wasn't "going" to him in the first thirty minutes. Schembechler explained, "I think John thought he was forcing it if he went to Carter who was closely guarded. At half time, we told Wangler to 'force it.'"

In the second half, Carter contributed key plays that set up a field goal and two touchdown drives. The lean and speedy

Michigan's great Anthony Carter

After Bo Schembechler won his first Rose Bowl game in six tries, the *Herald Examiner*'s Melvin Durslag called him "the happiest .167 hitter alive." Durslag credited part of Michigan's victory to a false fire alarm that had rousted the team at 2:30 in the morning at the Huntington Sheraton Hotel two nights prior to the game. He suggested that the disturbance had "helped the Wolverines, whose forces five previous times obviously suffered from an excess of rest."

While USC's John Robinson didn't come back to Pasadena as a coach in 1981, he did appear as a chauffeur for Schembechler on numerous occasions—an act of close friendship.

The University of Michigan won *two* bowl games against Pac-10 teams in 1981. After defeating Washington, 23–6, in Pasadena on New Year's Day, Michigan defeated UCLA, 33–14, in the following December's Bluebonnet Bowl in Houston. Washington, meanwhile, returned to the Rose Bowl on January 1, 1982, and beat up on Iowa.

Bo Shembechler finally wins one

WIDE WORLD PHOTOS

wide receiver caught five passes for 68 yards, including a 7-yard touchdown reception. He also sped 33 yards on four pitchouts. Durable tailback Butch Woolfolk's 182 yards in twenty-six carries and Wangler's twelve pass completions in twenty attempts helped the Wolverines to take total control of the game.

The victory continued Michigan's streak of twenty-two straight quarters in which opposing teams did not score a touchdown. Field goals of 35 and 26 yards by Chuck Nelson were all quarterback Tom Flick's otherwise splendid Washington offense could tally.

Coach Don James's Huskies had good opportunities in the first half, including a fourth down shot on the Michigan 1-yard line by potent running back Toussaint Tyler. However, Tyler was smacked while trying to go over the top and got separated from the football. After his Huskies had gained 269 yards in the first half without scoring a touchdown, James told Mal Florence of the *Los Angeles Times,* "That's when we lost it. We needed 20 points out of those chances to have a chance to win."

The victory made Schembechler ecstatic. "I feel good after those frustrating years," he said. "I don't want to be number one in the nation. That honor belongs to Georgia for winning twelve straight. All I want is to be number one in the Rose Bowl. I got tired hearing how we couldn't win here. We haven't played a bad game in all six. Fate just went against us before today."

As John Hall pointed out in the *Times,* fate was with "Schembechler and Michigan this day." Hall cited ten key moments that went Michigan's way on a day when Washington started out as the better team and had Michigan on the run. Included in Hall's list were an offensive

Huskies' Toussaint Tyler leaps over the top

After a long and rowdy New Year's Eve in which an estimated four hundred thousand people roamed downtown Pasadena's streets, a hot-selling T-shirt read, "I Survived the Rose Parade in 1981." According to police spokesman Rocky McAlister, "The warm weather made people not want to cuddle up and sleep with people they like, so they roamed about to fight with those they didn't like." The weather climaxed a week during the hottest December on record when temperatures were reaching eighty-five degrees.

pass interference penalty that nullified a 52-yard pass gain from Flick to Aaron Williams, a line drive punt by Michigan's Don Bracken that skipped 73 yards, Tyler's fumble while attempting to go over the top at the goal line and a second-half fumble by Michigan's Kyle Stevens that settled in the hands of Washington's Mike Reilly—whose touchdown play was disallowed by a quick whistle.

Although admitting that Michigan was impressive in the second half, Jim Murray of the *Times* wrote, "Michigan was like a guy who comes home with two black eyes, a broken nose, torn ear and his teeth in a cup and says, 'Guess what? I won.' "

Actually, many insiders from Ann Arbor credited a change in Schembechler's

Anthony Carter zips away

Although for the first time in years the 1981 Rose Bowl earned slightly lower television ratings than the Orange Bowl and Sugar Bowl, NBC gave the Rose Bowl a new television contract worth $7.2 million for rights to the 1983 game. This figure was more than double that of the previous two years because of a bidding war with CBS and ABC. This huge figure for television combined with gate receipts of more than one hundred thousand tickets at $25 apiece to make the Rose Bowl a $10 million package. J.D. Morgan, 61, longtime UCLA athletic director, a strong Rose Bowl booster and leader to 30 NCAA championships at UCLA during his career, died of a cardiac deficiency after a long illness.

1982
Jacque Frosh

Plating company executive Harold E. Coombes Jr. succeeded Millard Davidson to become president of the 1982 Tournament. He had worked in Tournament activities for thirty-four years. In January 1981 he gave the 1982 parade its theme name of "Friends and Neighbors" to reflect the international interest of the Tournament.

After an all-night rainstorm, the skies cleared at dawn and an estimated one million spectators witnessed the ninety-third Rose Parade led by Grand Marshal Jimmy Stewart, who rode in a 1932 Packard. Stewart admitted to wearing long johns during the parade. President Harold Coombes rode in a 1908 Buick.

The queen was Kathryn Ann "Katy" Potthast, of Pasadena, a senior at Flintridge Preparatory School. Her court included princesses Jamie Lee Werk of Arcadia, Lisa Anne Beltrami of La Cañada, Monica Lynn Gordon of Altadena, Mary

training schedule with contributing to the victory formula. Instead of coming west two weeks before the game, Michigan didn't arrive until Christmas Day, thus avoiding tiring extracurricular activity on the scene of battle. A new indoor training facility in Ann Arbor made possible home workouts while outdoor temperatures were below zero.

Washington's defeat was especially painful to two Pasadena-area athletes, tight end David Bayle and defensive tackle Scott Garnett of the Huskies, who had hoped their return to the Rose Bowl where they had performed with Pasadena City College and Muir High School, would have a happier ending. Washington coach Don James also was frustrated by the result, but he was cheered by a new five-year contract from athletic director Mike Lude that included a raise from $50,000 to $65,000 a year.

Continued on page 231

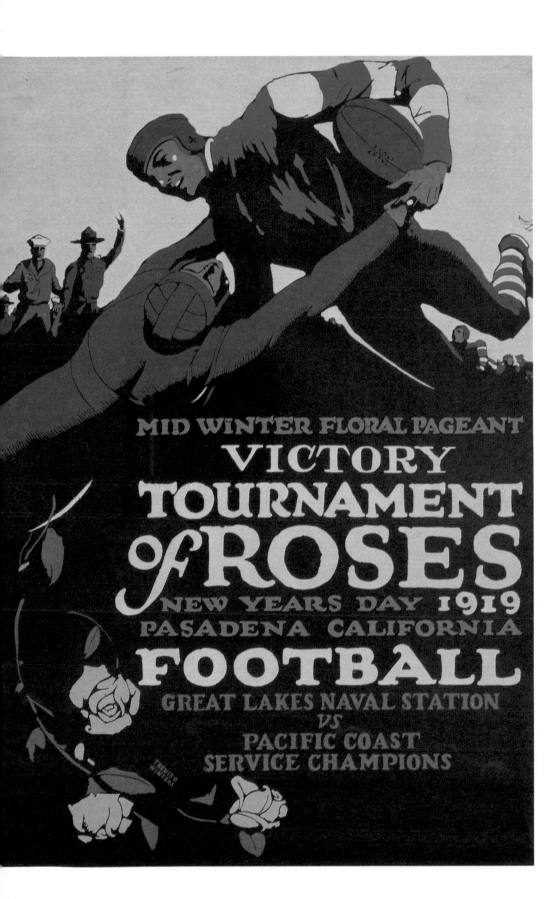

MID WINTER FLORAL PAGEANT
VICTORY TOURNAMENT of ROSES
NEW YEARS DAY 1919
PASADENA CALIFORNIA
FOOTBALL
GREAT LAKES NAVAL STATION
VS
PACIFIC COAST SERVICE CHAMPIONS

1902	Michigan 49, Stanford 0
1916	Washington State 14, Brown 0
1917	Oregon 14, Pennsylvania 0
1918	Mare Island Marines 19, Camp Lewis Army 7
1919	Great Lakes Navy 17, Mare Island Marines 0
1920	Harvard 7, Oregon 6
1921	California 28, Ohio State 0
1922	California 0, Washington & Jefferson 0
1923	USC 14, Penn State 3
1924	Washington 14, Navy 14
1925	Notre Dame 27, Stanford 10
1926	Alabama 20, Washington 19
1927	Stanford 7, Alabama 7
1928	Stanford 7, Pittsburgh 6
1929	Georgia Tech 8, California 7
1930	USC 47, Pittsburgh 14
1931	Alabama 24, Washington State 0
1932	USC 21, Tulane 12
1933	USC 35, Pittsburgh 0
1934	Columbia 7, Stanford 0
1935	Alabama 29, Stanford 13
1936	Stanford 7, SMU 0
1937	Pittsburgh 21, Washington 0
1938	California 13, Alabama 0
1939	USC 7, Duke 3
1940	USC 14, Tennessee 0
1941	Stanford 21, Nebraska 13
1942	Oregon State 20, Duke 16
1943	Georgia 9, UCLA 0
1944	USC 29, Washington 0
1945	USC 25, Tennessee 0
1946	Alabama 34, USC 14
1947	Illinois 45, UCLA 14
1948	Michigan 49, USC 0
1949	Northwestern 20, California 14
1950	Ohio State 17, California 14
1951	Michigan 14, California 6
1952	Illinois 40, Stanford 7
1953	USC 7, Wisconsin 0
1954	Michigan State 28, UCLA 20
1955	Ohio State 20, USC 7
1956	Michigan State 17, UCLA 14
1957	Iowa 35, Oregon State 19
1958	Ohio State 10, Oregon 7
1959	Iowa 38, California 12
1960	Washington 44, Wisconsin 8
1961	Washington 17, Minnesota 7
1962	Minnesota 21, UCLA 3
1963	USC 42, Wisconsin 37
1964	Illinois 17, Washington 7
1965	Michigan 34, Oregon State 7
1966	UCLA 14, Michigan State 12
1967	Purdue 14, USC 13
1968	USC 14, Indiana 3
1969	Ohio State 27, USC 16
1970	USC 10, Michigan 3
1971	Stanford 27, Ohio State 17

1972   Stanford 13, Michigan 12
1973   USC 42, Ohio State 17
1974   Ohio State 42, USC 21
1975   USC 18, Ohio State 17
1976   UCLA 23, Ohio State 10
1977   USC 14, Michigan 6
1978   Washington 27, Michigan 20
1979   USC 17, Michigan 10
1980   USC 17, Ohio State 16
1981   Michigan 23, Washington 6
1982   Washington 28, Iowa 0
1983   UCLA 24, Michigan 14
1984   UCLA 45, Illinois 9
1985   USC 20, Ohio State 17
1986   UCLA 45, Iowa 28
1987   Arizona State 22, Michigan 15
1988   Michigan State 20, USC 17

The Teams

Big Ten Teams
Illinois (3–1) 1947, 1952, 1964,
   1984
Indiana (0–1) 1968
Iowa (2–2) 1957, 1959, 1982, 1986
Michigan (5–7) 1902, 1948, 1951,
   1965, 1970, 1972, 1977–79,
   1981, 1983, 1987
Michigan State (3–1) 1954, 1956,
   1966, 1988
Minnesota (1–1) 1961–62
Northwestern (1–0) 1949
Ohio State (5–7) 1921, 1950, 1955,
   1958, 1969, 1971, 1973–76,
   1980, 1985
Purdue (1–0) 1976
Wisconsin (0–3) 1953, 1960, 1963
Pac-10 Teams
Arizona State (1–0) 1987
California (2–5–1) 1921–22,
1929, 1938, 1949–51, 1959
Oregon (1–2) 1917, 1920, 1958
Oregon State (1–2) 1942, 1957, 1965
Stanford (5–5–1) 1902, 1925,
   1927–28, 1934–36, 1941,
   1952, 1971–72
UCLA (5–5) 1943, 1947, 1954,
   1956, 1962, 1966, 1976,
   1983–84, 1986
USC (18–7) 1923, 1930, 1932–33,
   1939–40, 1944–46, 1948,
   1953, 1955, 1963, 1967–70,
   1973–75, 1977, 1979–80,
   1985, 1988
Washington (4–5–1) 1924, 1936,
   1937, 1944, 1960–61, 1964,
   1978, 1981, 1982
Washington State (1–1), 1916, 1931

The California Gridiron   Price · One Dollar

JANUARY 1 · 1949

ROSE BOWL

BION ATKINSON

NORTHWESTERN vs CALIFORNIA

USC quarterback Rodney Peete in the 1988 Rose Bowl

Michigan State, 1954
Neal, Earle (0–0–1)
  Washington & Jefferson, 1922
Neyland, Robert (0–1)
  Tennessee, 1940
Oosterbaan, Ben (1–0)
  Michigan, 1951
Owens, Jim (2–1)
  Washington, 1960–61, 1964
Perles, George (1–0)
  Michigan State, 1988
Phelan, James (0–1)
  Washington, 1937
Pont, John (0–1)
  Indiana, 1968
Price, C.M. Nibs (0–1)
  California, 1929
Prothro, Tommy (1–2)
  Oregon State, 1957, 1965
  UCLA, 1966
Ralston, John (2–0)
  Stanford, 1971–72
Robinson, E.N. (0–1)
  Brown, 1916
Robinson, John (3–0)
  USC, 1977, 1979–1980
Rockne, Knute (1–0)
  Notre Dame, 1925
Sanders, Red (0–2)
  UCLA, 1954, 1956
Schembechler, Bo (1–7)
  Michigan, 1970, 1972,
  1977–79, 1981, 1983, 1987
Shaughnessy, Clark (1–0)
  Stanford, 1941
Smith, Andy (1–0–1)
  California, 1921, 1922,
Smith, Larry (0–1)
  USC, 1988
Stanton, W.L. (0–1)
  Camp Lewis Army, 1918
Stiner, Alonzo (1–0)
  Oregon State, 1942
Sutherland, John (1-3)
  Pittsburgh, 1928, 1930,
  1933, 1937
Taylor, Charles (0–1)
  Stanford, 1952
Thomas, Frank (2–1)
  Alabama, 1935, 1938, 1946
Thornhill, Claude (1–2)
  Stanford, 1934–36
Tollner, Ted (1–0)
  USC, 1985
Vermeil, Dick (1–0)
  UCLA, 1976
Voights, Bob (1–0)
  Northwestern, 1949
Wade, Wallace (2–2–1)
  Alabama, 1926–27, 1931
  Duke, 1939, 1942

Waldorf, Pappy (0–3)
    California, 1949–51
Warmath, Murray (1–1)
    Minnesota, 1961–62
Warner, Pop (1–1–1)
    Stanford, 1925, 1927–28
Welch, Ralph (0–1)
    Washington, 1944
White, Mike (0–1)
    Illinois, 1984
Wilce, J.W. (0–1)
    Ohio State, 1921
Williamson, Ivan (0–1)
    Wisconsin, 1953
Yost, Fielding H. (1–0)
    Michigan, 1902

Players of the Game

1902	Neil Snow, Michigan
1916	Carl Dietz, Washington State
1917	John Beckett, Oregon
1918	Hollis Huntington, Mare Island
1919	George Halas, Great Lakes Navy
1920	Edward Casey, Harvard
1921	Harold Muller, California
1922	Russ Stein, Washington & Jefferson
1923	Leo Calland, USC
1924	Ira McKee, Navy
1925	Elmer Layden, Notre Dame & Ernie Nevers, Stanford
1926	John Mack Brown, Alabama & George Wilson, Washington
1927	Fred Pickhard, Alabama
1928	Coff Hoffman, Stanford
1929	Ben Lom, California
1930	Russ Saunders, USC
1931	John Campbell, Alabama
1932	Erny Pinckert, USC
1933	Homer Griffith, USC
1934	Cliff Montgomery, Columbia
1935	Dixie Howell, Alabama
1936	Jim Moscrip & Keith Topping, Stanford
1937	William Daddio, Pittsburgh
1938	Vic Bottari, California
1939	Al Krueger & Doyle Nave, USC
1940	Ambrose Schindler, USC
1941	Pete Kmetovic, Stanford
1942	Don Durdan, Oregon State
1943	Charles Trippi, Georgia

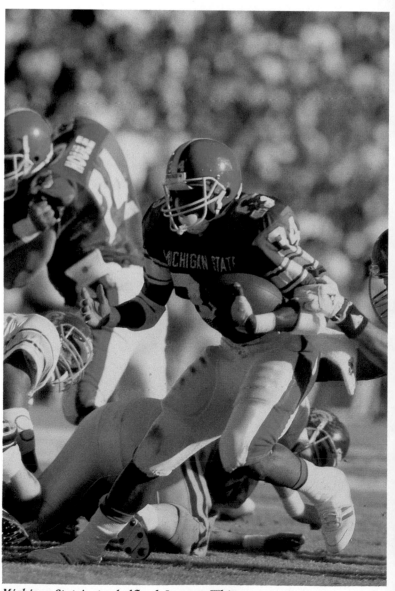

Michigan State's star halfback Lorenzo White

The 74th Rose Bowl Game®

USC vs Michigan State

January 1, 1988 Pasadena, California $4.00

1944	Norm Verry, USC
1945	James Hardy, USC
1946	Harry Gilmer, Alabama
1947	Claude Young & Julie Rykovich, Illinois
1948	Robert Chappius, Michigan
1949	Frank Aschenbrenner, Northwestern
1950	Fred Morrison, Ohio State
1951	Donald Dufek, Michigan
1952	William Tate, Illinois
1953	Rudy Bukich, USC
1954	Billy Wells, Michigan State
1955	Dave Leggett, Ohio State
1956	Walter Kowalczyk, Michigan State
1957	Kenny Ploen, Iowa
1958	Jack Crabtree, Oregon
1959	Bob Jeter, Iowa
1960	Bob Schloredt & George Fleming, Washington
1961	Bob Schloredt, Washington
1962	Sandy Stephens, Minnesota
1963	Pete Beathard, USC & Ron VanderKelen, Wisconsin
1964	Jim Grabowski, Illinois
1965	Mel Anthony, Michigan
1966	Bob Stiles, UCLA
1967	John Charles, Purdue
1968	O. J. Simpson, USC
1969	Rex Kern, Ohio State
1970	Bob Chandler, USC
1971	Jim Plunkett, Stanford
1972	Don Bunce, Stanford
1973	Sam Cunningham, USC
1974	Cornelius Greene, Ohio State
1975	Pat Haden & J. K. McKay, USC
1976	Paul Sciarra, UCLA
1977	Vince Evans, USC
1978	Warren Moon, Washington
1979	Charles White, USC & Rick Leach, Michigan
1980	Charles White, USC
1981	Butch Woolfolk, Michigan
1982	Jacque Robinson, Washington
1983	Don Rogers & Tom Ramsey, UCLA
1984	Rick Neuheisel, UCLA
1985	Jack DelRio & Tim Green, USC
1986	Eric Ball, UCLA
1987	Jeff Van Raaphorst, Arizona State
1988	Percy Snow, Michigan State

Highest Point Totals

49	Michigan, 1902
49	Michigan, 1948
47	USC, 1930
45	Illinois, 1947
45	UCLA, 1984
45	UCLA, 1986
44	Washington, 1960
42	USC, 1963
42	USC, 1973
42	Ohio State, 1974
40	Illinois, 1952
38	Iowa, 1959
37	Wisconsin, 1963
35	USC, 1933
35	Iowa, 1957

Teams Ranked No.1 in the Nation Going into the Rose Bowl Game

1955	Ohio State
1958	Ohio State
1961	Minnesota
1963	USC
1966	Michigan State
1968	USC
1968	Ohio State
1973	USC
1975	USC
1979	USC

The Graveyard: Teams Whose Perfect Seasons Ended in the Rose Bowl

1919	Mare Island (10-0)
1921	Ohio State (7-0)
1930	Pittsburgh (8-0)
1931	Washington State (9-0)
1932	Tulane (11-0)
1933	Pittsburgh (8-0)
1936	SMU (12-0)
1938	Alabama (9-0)
1939	Duke (9-0)
1940	Tennessee (10-0)
1947	UCLA (10-0)
1949	California (10-0)
1950	California (10-0)
1966	Michigan State (10-0)
1971	Ohio State (9-0)
1972	Michigan (11-0)
1976	Ohio State (11-0)
1980	Ohio State (11-0)

The 1988 Rose Bowl game: Michigan State vs. USC

Laird Hildeburn of San Marino, Holly Rose Kenney of South Pasadena and Carole Marshall Owen of Pasadena.

Thousands of Iowa fans were in the crowd, many of them drenched by the pre-parade rain. The Benevolent Order of Elks captured the Sweepstakes prize with the float "Elks Serve Children Everywhere." It depicted children riding on carousel animals. Avon Products captured the Grand Prize for commercial entries a second straight year. Its "Beauty of the Orient" float presented a flowered Kabuki dancer standing in a Japanese garden. Among the novelty floats were a roller coaster that sent youngsters into a loop and a floral float pulled by a team of elephants. The tires of the roller coaster float split when they rolled over a set of railroad tracks, but workers jacked up the front and changed the tires so the vehicle could continue.

USC, the all-time Rose Bowl king with a 17–6 record in Pasadena and an overall 20–7 post-season mark, was banned from bowl games for two years when the NCAA placed it on probation, principally for player ticket sale violations. USC joined Oregon as the second Pac-10 team placed on probation.

A Double Mugging: Washington 28, Iowa 0

After arriving in Southern California, assistant Iowa football coach Jim Fox and his brother were robbed in the parking lot of a hotel. Their Iowa team experienced an even nastier mugging when the Hawkeyes met up with the University of Washington's "James Gang" in the 1982 Rose Bowl. The victory was the Washington Huskies' second in three appearances during a five-year span under Don James's guidance.

The Hawkeyes could not say that they

Jimmy Stewart

hadn't been warned. At the Big Ten Club's annual Dinner of Champions staged for the Iowa team, comedian Bob Hope had tried to warn the Hawkeyes. "The Washington Huskies got ready for you by training on Mt. St. Helens during its eruption," said Hope.

Despite the rough treatment Iowa received in Pasadena, Coach Hayden Fry said his team enjoyed the visit. "People keep asking me about distractions—things like Disneyland and Universal Studios," said Fry. "They aren't distractions. They are positive things. And the media has given us most positive coverage."

The Huskies blasted a big hole in the Iowa defense en route to victory. Some Caltech students engineered a prank that would have blasted a hole in the Rose Bowl turf, had it succeeded. An elaborate helium-hydraulic device designed to send a balloon aloft during the middle

One of the first acts of Harold E. Coombes Jr. as Tournament president was to eliminate the annual contest to choose a Tournament theme. "We did so to give the float builders more time to fulfill our goal of a finer, more beautiful parade each year," said Coombes. "The theme contest delayed them until March."

Harold Coombes

The Tournament's new manager in 1982, Jack French, had been executive director of the Pasadena chapter of the American Red Cross since 1976. Before that he was manager of economic development for the Pasadena Chamber of Commerce and manager of special business development for the *Star-News*. French named William Flinn the new director of Tournament public relations and retained Forest "Frosty" Foster as assistant manager.

Washington's 28–0 trouncing of Iowa in 1982 inspired such comments as:

"The most interesting part of the game was that the Iowa coach had a mustache. . . . Fry also had a bag full of trick plays, few of them working well."—Jim Murray, *Times*.

"Iowa dream ends with a crash heard as far away as Des Moines."—Mark Heisler, *Times*.

"Perfect weather for a mugging. This time the guys in black shirts were the victims."—Terry Johnson, *Pasadena Star-News*.

And this confession by Iowa's coach to Allan Malamud of the *Herald-Examiner*: "The world just witnessed an old-fashioned rump kicking."

Iowa punter Reggie Roby gets off a beauty

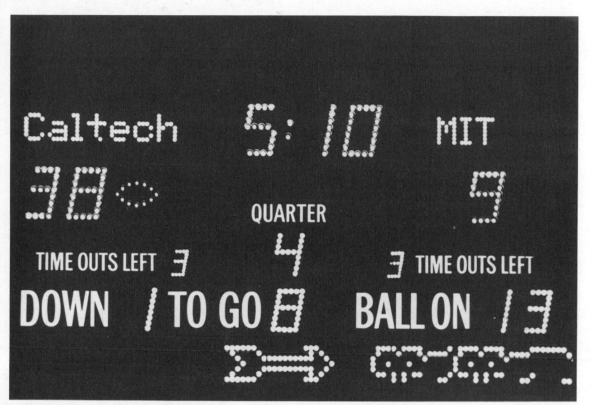

Caltech students rig scoreboard in 1984

After a dispute over seating arrangements between Chancellor Charles Young and the Los Angeles Coliseum, UCLA signed a five-year lease with the city of Pasadena to play its home games in the Rose Bowl. It launched a six-game home slate with a 35–14 triumph over Long Beach State before 45,396 spectators. It was estimated that the agreement would net Pasadena an annual revenue of $130,000 to $200,000.

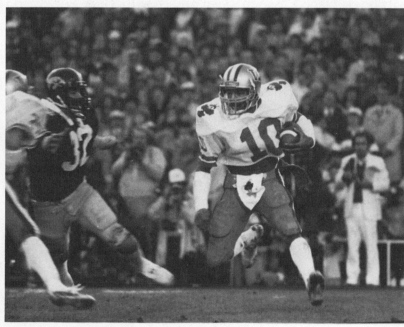

Rick Neuheisel eludes Illini tacklers

of the game was discovered buried in the field the previous night by Rose Bowl manager Bill Wilson and his crew.

Led by the first freshman ever named player of the game, Jacque Robinson, and sophomore quarterback Steve Pelluer, Washington stunned the crowd of 105,611 with a decisive conquest of Iowa. The victory was the West's thirteenth in the sixteen games played since Jim Owens and an earlier version of the Huskies had proved the Big Ten could be had back in 1960. The Big Ten's lead in the Rose Bowl series was cut to 19–17.

Robinson, who had advanced from fourth string to Rose Bowl star, set up or scored three of the Huskies' four touchdowns by gaining 142 yards on twenty carries. End Paul Skansi made four receptions for 69 yards as Pelluer completed fifteen of twenty-nine passes. On defense, Mark Jerue had thirteen tackles.

Georg N. Meyers of the *Seattle Times* came to the following conclusions: "To be embarrassed by an anonymous substitute tailback with a roly-poly boyish face and the fleet heels of a sprinter was cruel and inhuman punishment. . . . The whisper in the coaching profession is that if you give Don James three weeks to prepare for an opponent, he will find a way to win—even if it is the Pittsburgh Steelers or a team dressed to look like them."

1983
Donahue Debuts

Career college fund-raiser Thornton H. Hamlin assumed the Tournament presidency for 1983 and selected as the Tournament theme "Rejoice."

"My reward and satisfaction comes from being part of a unique display of that which is beautiful, dramatic, exciting, warm and friendly amidst a world beset with tension, struggle and depres-

Don James

Hayden Fry

Player of the Game Jacque Robinson

sion," said Hamlin. "The Tournament helps the world smile when it may want to cry. We advertise happiness, not gloom." This philosophy was behind his choice of "Rejoice" as the theme. It was also behind his choosing television actor and former football star Merlin Olsen as his grand marshal. In Hamlin's words, "Merlin represents the dignity of human endeavor under God."

Olsen had the distinction of being the first grand marshal also to serve as TV broadcaster during the Rose Bowl game when he worked with Dick Enberg on the NBC telecast.

Queen of the Tournament was San Marino High School senior Suzanne Gillaspie, who was shocked by her selection because she considered herself "too short, just another girl on the block." Other members of her court were Shandrea Denise Gilcrest and Monica Elena Auzenne of Pasadena, Laurie Anne Matlock of La Cañada, Dawn Marie Wilson of Arcadia, Mary Hernandez of San Gabriel and Heather Lee Hall of Sierra Madre.

The parade's 1983 Sweepstakes Trophy went to "Sweet Days of Love," a float featuring two swan boats in giant seashells. This best non-commercial entry was sponsored by the Orange County community of Mission Viejo. The Grand Prize for the most beautiful commercial entry went to Transamerica Occidental Life Insurance Company for "Triumph," which depicted the legend of St. George slaying a dragon. Sixty floats, 230 horses, twenty-two bands and four thousand marching musicians made their way along the five-and-a-half-mile route to receive the applause of 1.4 million onlookers in Pasadena and millions more watching the parade on television throughout the world.

Human-powered floats made a debut in the 1983 parade. Fifty-five people carried the Atlantic Richfield display of flags representing nations that were to compete in the 1984 Los Angeles Olympics. Honda also had a human-powered float, an airplane-shaped 7,500-pound construction.

A great highlight of the parade was human cannonball Braun Reinhold, who shot seventy feet out of a howitzer into a net aboard an Avco-sponsored float that climaxed the ninety-fourth Tournament

Merlin Olson

of Roses parade on the sunny first day of 1983.

Two accidents caused interruptions. One float damaged a traffic pole while trying to negotiate the first turn at the corner of Orange Grove and Colorado. Another float caught fire and was quickly routed to a side street as smoke billowed skyward. There were no injuries, just time lost in parade movement.

The eighty-voice United States Naval Academy Glee Club was a feature of the 1983 Tournament festivities, as a prelude to the Army-Navy game that was to be played in Pasadena in 1984. Pasadena backers of the first Army-Navy game to be played on the West Coast transported and housed the entire cadet corps from Annapolis and West Point. Navy won, 42–13, before a crowd of 81,347.

Bo Takes Another Beating:
UCLA 24, Michigan 14

Although Michigan's Bo Schembechler predicted at the Big Ten Club of Southern California's annual dinner that "UCLA better be damn good if they think they are going to beat us . . . no matter what happens, we will eventually win it," the Wolverine mentor lost his sixth game in seven Pasadena appearances. Bo also was confident at the Kickoff Luncheon when he said:

"Every Michigan player is going to perform with every ounce of his strength because this is the greatest game he ever could play in . . . it never becomes old, it never becomes boring, it is a challenge to us every time."

"Bo's fired up," commented Terry Donahue, the young UCLA coach who was making his first Rose Bowl appearance as a head coach. Previously, he had played for UCLA in the 1966 game.

Michigan paid a price for basing too

Thornton Hamlin

The day after the parade an estimated two hundred thousand people crowded around the floats on Sierra Madre Boulevard. Laura Nicholson of the *Star-News* wrote, "The over-all feeling among the post-parade fans was that the floats were beautiful, the parade was wonderful and the congestion in the small area where the floats were parked was awful." A visitor from Waverly, Minnesota, Hubert Humphrey's summer home, suggested having the Rose Parade in Waverly. "There's plenty of room there."

One person came to the post-parade to do more than gaze at the flowers. Beverly Hills perfumer Marrianne Von Graeve-Ward picked fifty grocery bags full of the petals, dried them and put them in scented vials for sale at five dollars each.

UCLA quarterback Tom Ramsey's 1983 Rose Bowl performance earned him a lucrative pro contract with the Los Angeles Express of the short-lived United States Football League. The club also signed Jojo Townsell, Ramsey's "home run" man. Another Bruin who gained financially was Irv Eatman, who also went to the USFL for big bucks by proving he could play offensive tackle, as well as defensive line.

The 1983 Rose Bowl game was not the last championship affair in the Rose Bowl during the 1983 campaign. Three weeks later, the stadium was the scene of the NFL's Super Bowl. The Washington Redskins trounced the Miami Dolphins, 27–17, for the NFL crown. The crowd of 103,667 was slightly smaller than the Rose Bowl game's attendance record of 104,991. But the Super Bowl TV ratings were a smashing record—48.6 Nielsen or 111,500,000 people in 40,480,000 households.

Human Cannonball fired from float

much of its strategy around speedy superstar Anthony Carter because Donahue and his Bruins were fired up, too. UCLA responded by largely stopping the great pass catcher and kick returner.

Also hurting Michigan were injuries which took quarterback Steve Smith and tackle Rich Strenger out of the game.

"The Bruins played near-flawless football," wrote Steve Hunt in the *Star-News*. Junior safety man Don Rogers made eleven tackles, had a key interception and shared player-of-the-game honors with quarterback Tom Ramsey. Michigan tried to bounce back from continued deficits, but three interceptions and one fumble stopped two Michigan possessions inside the 20 and led directly to ten UCLA points.

The Bruins drove for the only touchdown of the first half on their second possession. Ramsey, who finished with eighteen pass completions in twenty-five attempts, completed all six of his passes in the drive, including three to tight end Paul Bergmann. UCLA went 79 yards in thirteen plays with Ramsey sneaking over.

Michigan then moved from its 29 to UCLA's 19, but on first down Smith's pass to Rick Rogers deflected off the tailback's hands into the grasp of UCLA's Don Rogers. UCLA capitalized on Carter's fumble of a punt to take a 10–0 lead at half time on freshman John Lee's 39-yard field goal.

In the third quarter, reserve Michigan quarterback Dave Hall passed 1 yard to

Eddie Garrett for a touchdown. Threatened, the Bruins did not try to sit on a three-point lead but opened up offensively to go 80 yards in thirteen plays with Danny Andrews racing into the end zone on a 9-yard sweep. Both coaches agreed this drive took the game away from Michigan. Then Blanchard Montgomery's 11-yard touchdown return with an interception was the clincher, although Michigan scored before the finish on a short pass from Hall to Dan Rice.

UCLA safety Don Rogers said later that he was pleased by the success of his defensive mates because "our Bruin defense had been kind of a forgotten entity."

Quarterback Ramsey argued that UCLA won by keeping Michigan off balance—which he said was the game plan well executed. Bruin offensive coordinator Homer Smith praised Ramsey as "a fine manager," and Ramsey returned the compliment by pointing out that Smith had called a perfect game—"I didn't have to try one audible."

Thus UCLA finished the year with a 10–1–1 record that also included a win over Michigan at Ann Arbor earlier. Michigan wound up 8–4.

1984
Salute to Volunteers

Donald Judson became president of the 1984 Tournament with the words, "I accept the presidency of this great organization with the pleasure of knowing that fourteen hundred volunteer men and women will be assisting me. The world will share in our year-long labor of love." In keeping with his high regard for those who serve the public, he made "A Salute to the Volunteer" the theme for 1984.

The president of Foss Construction Company, Judson was a lifelong resident of Pasadena, active throughout his life in community affairs. He joined the Tournament in 1958, was made a director in 1971 and was elected to the executive committee in 1976.

Judson recognized entertainer Danny Kaye's lifetime of service to mankind by selecting Kaye for his grand marshal. Much of Kaye's life was devoted to helping the United Nation's Children's Fund. "Voluntarism is not an ego gratification or a process of being used," stated Kaye. "Voluntarism represents the goodness in people. It is really holding out a hand in friendship and in love and help. It is the essence of living together. And I really believe volunteers receive a lot more than they give. It is joy, comfort and a sense of accomplishment."

Mayfield High School senior Ann Colburn of Pasadena was Tournament queen. Her six princesses were Karinn LaVerne Baffa of San Marino, Lisa Marie Bingman of Altadena, Sheryl Lynn Leon and Alison Michelle Moses of Pasadena, Jennifer Meeks of Arcadia, and Ann Jennifer Wasson of La Cañada-Flintridge.

The Sweepstakes Trophy went to the Lawry's Foods float, "Volunteer for Adventure," saluting Marco Polo. Eighty-four-degree heat caused the engines of some floats to break down, as well as other malfunctions. One float, for example, had a spectacular golden eagle whose wings were to flap to a height of forty-four feet; the eagle flapped its mighty wings just once at the beginning of the parade, and then traveled the rest of the route with its head bowed and its wings resting at its sides.

Series Is Squared:
UCLA 45, Illinois 9

With five minutes and ten seconds left to play in the 1984 Rose Bowl game, the

Donald Judson

Despite the reputation of its students for Rose Bowl japery, Caltech—which no longer fields an intercollegiate football team—has a legitimate football history in the Rose Bowl, where no other college has played as many football games. The catch is that Tech never played there on a New Year's Day. It simply used the stadium for all its home games. And, it should be remembered, before the Rose Bowl was built in 1923, Tournament of Roses football games were played on what is now the Caltech campus.

Among the bands in the 1984 parade were units from Australia and Hawaii. The 330-member Hawaiian band, from Pearl City, financed its trip by selling forty thousand barbecued chickens. The Australian band, from New South Wales, marched in the parade with live koalas.

One explanation for Illinois's lopsided loss to UCLA in the 1984 Rose Bowl came from Illinois psychologist Dan Smith. According to Smith, many Illinois players were Californians who participated in family reunions that were emotionally upsetting. The total effect was a major distraction to the team in the two weeks before the game.

Mike White, coach of the embarrassed Illini, had enjoyed happier years than 1984 in the Rose Bowl. He was Stanford coach John Ralston's assistant in 1971 and 1972, when Stanford upset Ohio State and Michigan. Of Illinois's 45–9 thrashing by UCLA, White said, "The only highlight came when the scoreboard went out. We were thoroughly defeated. This is obviously painful to us. It takes the luster off what we had accomplished, but I told the players that I was very, very proud of them."

Danny Kaye meets friends from around the world

scoreboard suddenly read: "Caltech 38, MIT 9." The 103,217 spectators were startled. Until that moment, they had thought UCLA was trouncing the University of Illinois by that very same score.

Two brainy and daring Caltech students, Jan Kegel and Ted Williams, admitted they had rigged the scoreboard and later were charged with a misdemeanor by the city of Pasadena. However, for successfully splicing a remote-controlled computer, as well as other electronic gadgets, into the wiring of the giant board during the quiet and dark-

ness of the previous night, the students were rewarded with classroom credits.

Caltech had much more success than Mike White's Illinois team, which performed far below its Big Ten championship level in sputtering and wilting before the red-hot Bruins, 45–9.

The game was a vindication for head coach Terry Donahue, whose UCLA team had come in with an unimposing 6–4–1 record that included a 42–10 rout at the hands of Nebraska. By contrast, Illinois was an amazing 9–0 in the Big Ten and 10–1 overall; ranked number four nationally, it was a heavy favorite in Pasadena. But UCLA had a picnic on what was now its home field. UCLA's victory did two things. It tied the Big Ten–Pac-10 series at nineteen wins each, and it avenged the 45–14 shellacking Illinois had administered to UCLA in the very first game of the pact in 1947.

Illinois may have enjoyed itself too much during the two weeks before the game when Coach White permitted his team to have "the full Rose Bowl experience"—sightseeing, entertainment and a celebration staged by thirty thousand Illinois fans who came to California to whoop it up. At the Big Ten dinner three nights before the game Bob Hope warned Illinois to be ready: "This won't be an ordinary Big Ten game—like playing Michigan." Ready they weren't.

Donahue smelled the victory before the game even began. "I thought we had a tremendous psychological advantage coming into the game," he said, "the chemistry was perfect for an upset."

Donahue was right. In the opinion of Bob Oates of the *Times,* "Four nervously dropped passes and two interceptions among other misplays took Illinois quarterback Jack Trudeau out of the game before it had fairly begun."

The Bruins' Rick Neuheisel completed twenty-two of thirty-one passes and threw a record-tying four touchdowns, while hitting 71 percent of his passes and having no interceptions as the Bruins piled up 511 yards. The bewildered Illini couldn't figure out the Bruin blocking in Donahue's plan of alternating guards Chris Yelich and Jim McCullough and tackles Mark Mannon and Mike Hartmeier. They joined their fellow linemen Duval Love, Scott Gordon and Dave Baran in dominating the trenches. All-American defensive tackle

Don Thorp of Illinois and his mates up front were blocked out consistently while the secondary, much of it inexperienced, was picked apart by assistant coach Homer Smith's aerial plan, so expertly executed by Neuheisel.

Neuheisel was named Player of the Game and joined fellow UCLA stars Kevin Nelson, Paul Bergmann and Don Rogers in gaining pro contracts. Neuheisel was a walk-on player at UCLA who had been benched earlier in the year because the Bruins were losing, even though he performed well.

Flanker Karl Dorrell caught two touchdown passes, tight end Bergmann one and fleet flanker Mike Young raced in with a 53-yard reception. Nelson and Bryan Wiley ran through the Illini for touchdowns and John Lee added a field goal. All-American Bruin safety Don Rogers enjoyed his second straight Rose Bowl star performance by contributing two big interceptions. The only time Illinois came close was when White's son, Chris, kicked a 41-yard field goal to cut UCLA's early lead to 7–3.

1985
The Spirit of America

If there was anyone who thought that the Tournament of Roses was a tradition-bound fossil incapable of fundamental change, the year 1985 must have been a revelation. Two things happened that year which assured that the Tournament would never again be quite the same.

Kristina Kaye Smith became the Tournament's first black queen, and the Pac-10 Conference finally moved ahead of the Big Ten in the thirty-nine-year-old rivalry when USC upset Ohio State.

An ex-Muir High School cheerleader, Kristina Smith was attending Pasadena City College when she was selected from

Terry Donahue

Warm weather inspired a record number of parade fans to camp out the night before the 1985 parade. They slept in sleeping bags or on sofas or sat throughout the night on chairs or curbs. Two Pasadenans, Harold Ludwig and Mike Eliason, brought 118 chairs for their families, who annually hold a reunion at the parade. Another regular, Frances Friedman, liked to drag an old sofa down to the parade, and then leave it for the city to haul away afterward.

Grand Marshal Lee Iacocca was, of course, best known for engineering Chrysler Corporation's spectacular financial turnaround just when it appeared that the company was about to go under. *Herald Examiner* columnist Mel Durslag suggested that if Iacocca were asked what accounted for Chrysler's turnaround, he would no doubt answer, "We have done it by taking the Pac-10 and the points!"

Queen Kristina Smith and Grand Marshal Lee Iacocca

among several hundred contestants to be Rose queen. She said she didn't feel any different than the young women who had reigned as queen before her, "but maybe, because I was selected, it will encourage more blacks to try out."

Smith's court also included princesses Amanda Hendrickson of San Marino, Andrea Martinet of Arcadia, Stephanie Engler and Christine Gillins of La Caña-da, Suzanne Walter of Pasadena and Karen Sanchez of Temple City.

As president, Pasadena attorney James B. Boyle directed a most successful ninety-sixth Tournament in almost perfect, sunny seventy-degree weather. Boyle's grand marshal was Chrysler Corporation chief Lee Iacocca, who personified the theme, "Spirit of America."

"Patriotism is back," declared Iacocca

James Boyle

grizzly bears, sponsored by Atlantic Richfield, won the Sweepstakes award. The Bank of America's "Spirit of the Eagle" float, celebrating American Indian art with two twenty-two-foot kachina dolls, captured the President's Trophy for floral excellence.

Other prize-winning floats included Rand McNally's "California Here We Come," Honda's "America Sings," Dr. Pepper's "The Old Corner Drugstore" and Eastman Kodak's "Circus America."

In addition to the local and regularly seen bands, groups came from Switzerland, Hawaii and such American cities as Lakeland, Florida; Union City, Tennessee; Owasso, Oklahoma; Midland, Texas; Casper, Wyoming; Auburn, Washington; and Indianapolis, Indiana.

A 1985 economic survey revealed that the Tournament generated $68.1 million in annual economic activity in the Pasadena area. That same year the Tournament presented the city of Pasadena with a check for $1,189,699—which included a half-million dollars for Rose Bowl seismic work and reimbursement for improvements plus policing, rentals and grandstand leases. The future financial health of the Tournament received a nice boost when the Tournament renewed its contract with NBC, giving the network exclusive rights to broadcast the Rose Bowl games through 1990.

after leading a display of floats that showcased the will of Boyle who had said, "We are honoring our country's greatest asset, its people, who are its strength and who contribute to a better country through service and struggle to make their dreams come true."

A patriotic highlight of the parade was the Hilton Hotels float, "Sweet Land of Liberty," carrying the original torch from New York's Statue of Liberty, which was then being refurbished in a project led by Iacocca. Though a favorite with the crowds, the float could not be considered for a prize because it was not completely covered with flowers or seeds. Another popular patriotic float was the Farmers Insurance "Spirit of America" that displayed a forty-foot replica of the entire Statue of Liberty, covered with blue-green flowers.

"Scouting the John Muir Trail," featuring an animated family of California

The Pendulum Swings: USC 20, Ohio State 17

After the Pac-10 Conference had won nine of the last ten Rose Bowl games, and thirteen of the previous fifteen, the Big Ten saw its chance to regain dominance in 1985. Coach Ted Tollner's USC team came into the Rose Bowl with an 8–3 record capped by losses to UCLA and Notre Dame at the end of the season. Ohio State, with a 9–2 record, looked so strong that USC was a decided underdog.

USC's victory over the Buckeyes was therefore a special shocker. Ironically, the game presented USC in a new role—not the running-passing Trojan phenoms of the past, but mass-tackling, savage-hitting physical controllers of their destiny.

It was a "plot switch," in the words of Jim Murray of the *Times*. "It was like Marilyn Monroe playing a nun—the Pac-10 beating you with hard-nosed football is like Babe Ruth outbunting you."

Ohio State tried almost everything to improve its chances: reducing distrac-

USC's 1985 victory over Ohio State was sweet vindication for John Robinson's successor at USC, Ted Tollner, whose first-year record had been 4–6–1 in 1983. Tollner's game plan was to swarm after the powerful but not super-fast Keith Byars and, as Bob Oates of the *Times* put it, "call a team meeting on the line of scrimmage every time Byars tried to run. Lacking cutting ability or explosiveness, Byars's enormous strength couldn't carry him very far."

Rival coaches Earle Bruce of Ohio State and Ted Tollner of USC

Trojan southpaw quarterback Tim Green in action

tions, switching hotels to a more secluded area, shortening its stay in the Southland and introducing a more open brand of football.

During the game itself, Buckeye quarterback Mike Tomczak threw an uncharacteristic thirty-seven passes. USC's swarming defense controlled Buckeye running star Keith Byars after one early 50-yard run while causing Tomczak to throw three interceptions, and opportunist USC quarterback Tim Green directed a near-flawless puncturing of the Ohio State resistance. USC built up an

early 17–3 lead, and Ohio State was forced to play frustrating catch-up with its own mistakes and infractions destroying its hopes. USC lost only one fumble, while Ohio State had four turnovers.

Trojans up front like Jack Del Rio, Brent Moore, Duane Bickett and Neil Hope and secondary opportunists like Tommy Haynes held Byars to 109 yards (59 after his long run) and Tomczak to twenty-four harried completions that never could get the full job done for Earle Bruce's team.

There were some high points for the

An ally of the Tournament of Roses is the Big Ten Club of Southern California, 775 members strong. This club was influential in creating and maintaining the Rose Bowl pact. Originally it successfully campaigned for the relaxation of the Big Ten rule forbidding post-season football participation.

Shortly before each Rose Bowl game, the club sponsors a "Dinner for Champions" at the Palladium in Hollywood that entertains the visiting Big Ten team and more than three thousand Big Ten Followers. The club also sponsors an annual luncheon for the Tournament queen and her court. Once each year club members meet at Tournament House with Tournament officials. Bob Hope usually is the featured entertainer at the "Dinner of Champions," the program arranged by Michigan alumnus, Fred Space.

Bob Hiller, Michigan 1917, was the first president of the club formed in 1933 after a preliminary gathering in the Bay Area in 1925. President during the Tournament's Centennial year was Otto S. Schaeffler of Northwestern, succeeding 1987 president Roger Stoltenberg of Iowa.

At a fiftieth year Club celebration at the Sheraton Plaza La Reina hotel in Los Angeles in 1983, the club honored an outstanding alumnus selected from each Big Ten school plus Bob Hope, Pat O'Brien, Lathrop Leishman and Joe Hendrickson.

USC's Tim Green

midwesterners. Ohio State kicker Rich Spangler set a Rose Bowl record with a 52-yard field goal and tied another mark with three field goals, and teammate Chris Carter erased Don Hutson's pass-reception yardage record by catching nine for 172 yards. But it didn't produce the points that came on two 51-yard field goals by USC's Steve Jordan plus touchdown passes by Green to Timmie Ware and Joe Cormier. Green and Del Rio shared most-valuable-player honors. Trojan tailback Fred Crutcher, whose home was just a few blocks from the Rose Bowl, contributed 72 yards punching the line with fullback Kennedy Pola who had 51.

During the regular season Byars had rushed for 1,655 yards and scored twenty-two touchdowns. coach Tollner's tactics put an end to that. The victory was the fifth straight for USC in the Rose Bowl and it gave USC the all-time national record for all bowl wins at twenty-one, including eighteen in the Rose Bowl. This record was later broken by Alabama's twenty-two bowl wins.

1986
Celebration of Laughter

"Laughter is what keeps us all stitched together in good times and bad," said Frederick D. Johnson when he ascended to the presidency. He selected the theme, "A Celebration of Laughter" and to personify it, he selected humor columnist Erma Bombeck as grand marshal of the parade. "Let's start 1986 with a smile on our face," keynoted Johnson.

An advertising agency executive, Johnson had chaired three Tournament committees—equestrian, float entries and TV-radio—before rising to the presidency. His jubilee year as a Tournament member also marked the twenty-fifth anniversary of the year he joined his advertising agency and married his sweetheart, Barbara.

"We had a wonderful Tournament of Roses," concluded Johnson after the parade and game were over. "I'm 5,000 times happier than I had hoped." He said his only disappointments were that a mild New Year's Eve produced a larger-than-ever street crowd, which in turn led to rowdyism resulting in 481 arrests—and that the parade's world-wide telecast was cut twenty minutes short by the networks for an exchange of messages between President Ronald Reagan and Soviet leader Mikhail Gorbachev.

Johnson's elation over a successful

Tournament was supported by many happenings. The pleasant day, although the weather turned hazy by afternoon, brought out another crowd of a million people along the parade route. The floats were spectacular as usual.

San Marino senior high school student Aimee Lynn Richelieu, the daughter of a former semifinalist in the competition, was queen of a popular court composed of Julene Maree Penner, Christine Helen Huff, Tracey Kay Langford, Shannon Colleen Guernsey, April Louise Lake and Loreen Belle Weeks.

C.E. Bent and Son float builders constructed twenty-one of the sixty floats in the parade, winning seven trophies, including the Sweepstakes winner, which featured the Chinese legend of the monkey god. The float was sponsored by Singapore Airlines and Singapore promotion board. Popular with the crowds was the American Honda entry, which had a clown made of carnations, doing handstands on a teeter-totter. When extended to its maximum height of sixty-two feet, the float set a record as the tallest float ever to appear in the Rose Parade. Another novel float depicting a herd of nineteen giant flowered elephants carrying musical instruments was applauded loudly. Culver City presented the float that best depicted the day's theme; it featured huge caricatures of famous comedians.

The Iowa football team, willing to sacrifice party time for a Rose Bowl win, shunned the usual pre-Rose Bowl festivities and niceties traditionally accorded to the visiting team. Coach Hayden Fry vowed his team would not be distracted—one cause he blamed for the loss his team had suffered in Pasadena four years earlier. But Fry did permit his athletes to attend the annual Big Ten Club dinner at the Palladium, the last taste of victory the Iowans experienced as speaker after speaker, including the state's Governor Terry Branstad, emphasized, "Iowa plays to win—and will win."

The Iowa team also resided in an Industrial Hills hotel, far from all frivolity. The Pasadena Huntington Sheraton Hotel, traditionally the residence of the Big Ten team at Rose Bowl time, had been closed for failing to meet earthquake safety standards. Most official Tournament luncheons and meetings were instead held at the Pasadena Hilton.

A Bruin Celebration of Laughter: UCLA 45, Iowa 28

For the University of Iowa Hawkeyes, the seventy-second Rose Bowl game was not a laughing matter. Iowa came to Pasadena favored to end the dominance that the Pac-10 teams had enjoyed over the Big Ten for more than a decade. Once again, however, the Pac-10 pulled off a major upset. This time the 10–1 Hawkeyes were smashed by the 8–2–1 UCLA Bruins, 45–28, before 103,292 spectators. The victory was Coach Terry Donahue's third without a loss in the Rose Bowl.

The key to UCLA's victory was a red-shirted freshman named Eric Ball. Ball replaced the Bruins' star tailback, Gaston Green, who was injured in the first quarter, and then went on to race through the Hawkeye defense for 227 yards and four touchdowns. With backup quarterback Matt Stevens at the controls while regular signal caller David Norris was sidelined by injury, UCLA completely dominated Iowa to give the Pac-10 its fifteenth victory in seventeen attempts.

Top Iowa running back Ronnie Harmon fumbled four times with UCLA recovering. He dropped a touchdown pass. The Hawkeyes believed they had a

Frederick D. Johnson

As the fifth woman to serve as the Tournament's grand marshal, Erma Bombeck followed Shirley Temple, Mary Pickford, Kate Smith and Dale Evans—who teamed with her husband, Roy Rogers. Bombeck described the Rose Bowl as "the first bowl I've ever seen that I didn't have to clean."

The 1986 Tournament wasn't a lot of fun for the Big Ten. Even its float suffered defeat. The display carrying the Iowa cheerleaders was removed from the parade when someone detected a box aboard suspected to be a bomb. Like predictions that Iowa would win the Rose Bowl, it proved to be just another false rumor.

Chris Baker of the *Times* had this to say about UCLA star Eric Ball: "Ball came from Michigan. He picked UCLA over Michigan because he was tired of seeing the Big Ten lose here all of the time and he was tired of freezing."

Iowa coach Hayden Fry

Iowa quarterback Chuck Long

solid defense, but they were a step behind Ball on his touchdown runs of 30, 40, 6 and 32 yards—which tied USC's Sam Cunningham for the modern Rose Bowl scoring record.

Stevens passed for 189 yards and one touchdown and scored another himself. He fired an errant pass early that Iowa intercepted. UCLA also botched a punting snap. This gave Iowa ten points or the rout would have been more decisive. Stevens was the master thereafter.

"My bad start just made me better," said Stevens. "And I had my friend Norrie giving me confidence by telling me to go back out there and show everybody I was in charge."

Chuck Long, Iowa's superstar quarterback who was second in the national Heisman voting, tried to rally Iowa by completing twenty-nine of thirty-seven passes, but he was intercepted once and sacked four times by the Bruin defense.

Bruin inside linebacker Tommy Taylor told what motivated UCLA. "I've been angry," he told Tracy Dodds of the *Times* in the dressing room after the game. "Every time I heard somebody say that we couldn't stop Iowa's offense or that they were bigger and stronger or that we weren't taking the game as seriously as they were, it just made me angry. When I'm angry that gives me incentive."

Ball, who came inches short of scoring a fifth touchdown, said, "When I saw that Green was hurt and I had to carry on for him, I told him I'd score for him because I knew he was feeling real bad." For Ball, the big day vindicated him for his fumble while trying to score against USC in the last regular-season game, a mishap that gave USC a victory on a late comeback drive. "I was down," said Ball. "I knew I had to redeem myself."

"You have just witnessed the com-

Eric Ball rolls along for UCLA

The 1986 Tournament marked the beginning of the city of Pasadena's centennial celebration, the city having been chartered in 1886. President Johnson of the Tournament presented the city with a check totalling $1,119,484—the first generated under a new twenty-five-year contract combining all city and Tournament income from the festival.

*Arizona State quarterback
Jeff Van Rapphorst*

plete annihilation of a football team," summarized Fry. "They have by far the best group of athletes we have faced this season. We were missing tackles, not because we were out of position but because we couldn't bring them down on the first hit. UCLA was the superior team by far. If they played all season like they did today, they'd be national champs."

Donahue summed it up this way: "Our team played as well as we could possibly have wanted to play. We didn't play anyone as physical as Iowa this year, but we had an edge in speed and quickness. We were awfully good today."

In a final Pasadena football story in 1986, the fourth professional Super Bowl was played in the Rose Bowl, with the New York Giants defeating the Denver Broncos, 39–20, for the National Football League championship.

1987
Ambassador of Peace

Fred Soldwedel, a Pasadena lawyer, took over the presidency of the 1987 Tournament and promptly selected the theme "A World of Wonders" to highlight the international scope of the parade. Soldwedel had been a member of the Tournament for twenty-seven years. A true combination Pac-10 and Big Ten man, Soldwedel graduated from Northwestern and earned a law degree from Stanford.

Few people could have been more appropriate as symbols of international understanding than Pelé, the world-famous soccer great from Brazil, whom Soldwedel named grand marshal of the ninety-eighth Tournament of Roses. Even where people had never heard of roses or American football, Pelé's name was known and honored. An effective ambassador of good will during his Pasadena appearances, Pelé said, "We should have more Rose Parades and less weapon parades all over the world. Roses symbolize peace."

Many followers of Tournament history regarded the 1987 Tournament as the best of many successes. The biggest international television audience and more than one million spectators who lined the Pasadena parade route on the cool but dry morning saw a spectacular parade. Then Arizona State University's underdog football team upset Michigan, 22–15, in the Rose Bowl game.

Celebrities in the parade included Dick Rutan and Jeana Yeager, who had just completed the first-ever nonstop and non-refueled flight around the world in the light plane named the Voyager; Los Angeles Dodgers baseball manager Tommy Lasorda, actor Ernest Borgnine and comic Norm Crosby plus such standbys as cowboy Montie Montana, Lone Ranger Clayton Moore, Iron Eyes Cody, and equestrian favorite George Putnam.

Kristin Leigh Harris, the daughter of a former Pasadena prep football coach, was the 1987 queen. The young Arcadia woman said she always dreamed of being queen after watching the parade atop her father's shoulders at age five.

Joining Harris in the royal court were princesses Mary-Sandra Davis of San Gabriel, Jennifer Lynn Hayes and Alicia Roshan Smith of Pasadena, Andrea Kathlene Milligan, Sandra Lee Waltrip, and Diane Carol Welch of Arcadia.

Eighty-year-old Mary Barnum may have been the oldest parade participant when she drove a team of miniature horses. It was her first appearance in forty-two years. In her previous appearance she had ridden a horse sidesaddle.

For the first time in thirty-one years of participation by Anheuser Busch, the brewing company's float included a mini-Clydesdale. "We wanted to show people our gentle giants with one of

During President Soldwedel's world travels to promote the Tournament he visited Jordan. While passing out rose pins there, he accidentally gave one man his president's pin, which he quickly exchanged for a rose pin. Through a Jordanian interpreter, who was educated at Glendale College near Pasadena, the man responded, "Just think, for a minute I was president of the Tournament of Roses!"

Rodney Dangerfield isn't the only person who gets no respect. The Lone Ranger had to appear in borrowed togs and gun belt when his luggage got lost in an airport on his way to the 1987 Rose Parade.

The high school band from Holland, Michigan, marched the entire 1987 parade route in wooden clogs. Two girls had to be treated for sore feet and several boys admitted their feet were sore, but they said they wore five to seven pairs of socks to prevent blisters. The band's chorus line kicks were a particular hit with the crowds.

Fred Soldwedel

Player of the Game in 1987 was Sun Devil quarterback Jeff Van Rapphorst, who threw for two touchdowns while completing sixteen of thirty passes with no interceptions. Jeff's father, Richard Van Rapphorst, was a particularly happy man. He had been a member of the 1961 Ohio State team that won the Big Ten championship only to be denied a Rose Bowl appearance by a faculty vote on bowl participation.

Sun Devil Coach John Cooper

their babies,'' explained Lotsie Giersch, producer of the company's float. The colt stood in a corral on the float munching hay.

Few Rose Parades have presented more novelty floats. Animated giant rabbits, penguins, pandas, tigers, dragons, dogs and other eye-catching animal creations turned the parade into a colorful moving zoo.

At one extreme the parade featured a brutish King Kong; at the other, a garden of delicate butterflies. The butterflies were on the Sweepstakes winner, ''A Garden Full of Wonders'' built by Festival Artists for the Carnation Company. The butterflies flapped their wings as caterpillars crawled beneath.

King Kong brought the most gasps; he rode hunched over and then rising three stories while holding a screaming woman, actress Suzanne Trimble, in his hand.

The float, built by Festival Artists for the Honda Company, captured the Animation Trophy. Kong was decorated with a half-ton of cocoa palm fiber to resemble hair. Ground onion seed and dried seaweed provided skin texture.

Mechanical failure prevented the Loch Ness Monster on the Baskin-Robbins float from stealing the show from King Kong. The hydraulic system intended to raise the monster's head forty-eight feet high did not function, forcing the terror of the deep to travel the parade route harmlessly cradled in the back of a tow truck.

Bedeviled Bo: Arizona State 22, Michigan 15

While the spectacular Rose Parade floats continued to thrill with their freshness and novelty, the scripts of the Rose Bowl games seemed to repeat themselves. Once again, a highly favored Big Ten team came to Pasadena, only to be dismantled by a lightly regarded Pac-10 team.

A crowd of 103,168 watched Michigan build up a 15–3 lead and then slip into mediocrity. It was Coach Bo Schembechler's seventh loss in eight Rose Bowl tries, as well as the Big Ten's twelfth loss in the last thirteen Rose Bowls and sixteenth loss in the last eighteen games.

Newspaper headlines following Arizona State's 22–15 victory over Michigan told the story:

''New Jeer's Day for the Big Ten''— *Star-News*

''Big Ten Is Bedeviled Again''—*Herald Examiner*

''Sun Devils Keep Curse on Michigan''—*Times*

In his *Star-News* story, Jim Gordon wrote, ''In this uncertain age, it's comforting to know there are still some things in the universe one can depend upon. The moon circles the earth, the earth circles the sun, the Big Ten champions circle the wagons after losing another Rose Bowl game.''

Michigan quarterback Jim Harbaugh directed the Wolverines to two quick touchdowns in the first three Michigan possessions. But after that, he was sacked twice and threw three interceptions. He couldn't escape the quick Sun Devil defense.

An Arizona State touchdown pass from Jeff Van Rapphorst to Bruce Hill that zipped through the hands of Michigan defender Doug Mallory just before intermission put Arizona State back into the game at 15–13. Another touchdown pass to Hill in the third quarter put the Sun Devils ahead and they never relinquished their lead.

"After that we put so much pressure on Harbaugh, he was running for his life," said Arizona State coach John Cooper.

"Jim didn't have any time the second half," moaned Schembechler.

"We didn't play well," agreed Harbaugh.

Randy Harvey of the *Times* came up with this analysis: "Isn't this the way these Rose Bowl trips almost always end for Michigan? The Wolverines come to Pasadena sincerely believing they're the better team, get no argument from the oddsmakers, lose the game and then wonder where it all went wrong. But all the evidence suggests that Arizona State, appearing for the first time in the Rose Bowl game, simply was the better team."

Roger Murray, columnist for the *Star-News,* summed it up as follows: "Actually, the contest wasn't as close as the score suggests. Arizona State's superior quickness became more evident as the game progressed, and the gap between

the teams' skills levels widened.''

Leading Michigan running star Jamie Morris gained just 47 yards and scored once in a losing effort.

Arizona State stars included quarterback Van Rapphorst—who was named Player of the Game, tailback Darryl Harris who gained 109 yards, linebacker Stacy Harvey from Pasadena who made eleven tackles, and pass interceptors Eric Allen, Robby Boyd and Greg Clark.

The analysis of Arizona State coach John Cooper summed it all up: "We were quicker."

1988
A Pearl for Perles

As 1987 wound down with a 508-point drop on the stock market, a Los Angeles–area earthquake and unusually wintry weather throughout Southern California, it all seemed to portend a time for jolting events.

The next major jolt occurred on January 1, 1988, when George Perles's Michigan State football team edged USC, 20–17, in the seventy-fourth Rose Bowl game before a crowd of 103,847. It was an ideal day that brought back sunny weather near seventy degrees to the Southland. The Big Ten Conference victory interrupted nearly two decades of western dominance in the Pasadena game and reduced the Pac-10 edge in the series between the two conferences to 22–20.

The theme for the ninety-ninth Tournament of Roses celebration, a prelude to the 1989 centennial of Pasadena's great festival, was "Thanks to Communications," chosen by Tournament president Harriman L. Cronk, an investment broker, "to thank the media for its contribution in helping to make the Tournament of Roses what it is today and to

Gregory Peck said being grand marshal was an enjoyable substitute to his boyhood dream of one day playing in the Rose Bowl. His father had established a yearly tradition of taking his family on an all-day drive from their La Jolla home to Pasadena to see the parade and game. On one of those journeys, Peck's pet dog strayed away and never was seen again. "My regret today," said Peck, "is that my father was not alive to see me now 'in the best seat in the house.' "

Pelé salutes the crowd in the 1987 Rose Bowl

Arizona State cheerleaders whoop it up

The Harriman Cronks salute the crowd in the 1988 parade

On October 19, 1987, the day Tournament president Harriman Cronk, a Pasadena investment analyst, was announcing the Tournament of Roses court at a luncheon, his capacity to keep his cool was tested. The stock market dropped around three hundred points during the noon hour. "It is a good thing I wasn't in the office," grinned Cronk. "I might have had a heart attack."

The Rose Bowl was designated as a national landmark by the U.S. Department of the Interior. One hundred gardeners from the Southern California Gardeners' Federation replanted and pruned twenty-five hundred rose bushes in the "Lay Leishman Gardens" that beautify the landscape around the bowl under the expert care of "rosearian" Dan Rommerskirchen.

pinpoint communication as a key to peace and happiness."

As grand marshal of the Rose Parade Cronk named Oscar-winning actor Gregory Peck, who was wildly cheered along the parade route as he waved his straw hat to his fans. Peck and his wife Veronique rode in an $8,500,000 Bugatti. This vehicle, claimed to be the most expensive automobile in the world, huffed and puffed like an old Model T when it overheated near the end of the five-and-a-half-mile route. A tow truck had to pull the car to the finish line—a fate of several $50,000 to $150,000 floats.

Two volunteer mechanics were knocked to the ground by a lurching La Cañada-Flintridge float and hospitalized at the start of the parade, and later a horse in the Valley Hunt Club equestrian unit became alarmed by a noise and broke loose into spectators on the curb, injuring four people.

Julie Jeanne Myers, an Arcadia High School senior with dreams of one day becoming another Barbara Walters, was 1988 queen. She planned to study broadcast journalism at UCLA. Her philosophy, she said, centers around compassion for others—"the world would be a better place if people would make more of an effort to communicate."

The princesses were Carrie Gatsos, Kristin Henry and Amy Gordinier of San Marino, Julie Winnaman and Jill Neilson of La Cañada-Flintridge, and Mona Holmes of Altadena.

Riding with President Cronk in the parade were his wife, Phyllis, sons James and David, and daughter Melinda. During their summer visit to communities sending bands to the 1988 Tournament, the Cronks had enjoyed many experiences, including donning Dutch costumes, wooden shoes and all, to help

Player of the Game Percy Snow

scrub the streets of Pella, Iowa, during a fund-raiser for the Pella marching band.

Former astronaut Buzz Aldrin and former heavyweight boxing champion Muhammad Ali joined Mickey Mouse and Bicentennial Ben on the California Bicentennial Foundation's "We the People" float in the parade.

One television negative to Tournament officials was the NBC decision to cut off the last twelve minutes of the parade, replacing the time with the prerecorded New Year's messages from President Reagan and Soviet leader Mikhail Gorbachev.

The Sweepstakes award for the parade's most beautiful float went to Unocal Corporation's "Kabuki Communications Throughout the Arts." It featured two Kabuki characters and a huge Japanese lantern made of chrysanthemums, carnations and gladioli. Surrounded by costumed dancers, the Kabuki performers paid tribute to a centuries-old Japanese theater form.

Once again, spectacle combined with beauty in such floats as Honda's "Greetings Earthlings," featuring extraterrestrials in spinning flying saucers; the Baskin-Robbins float with a performing pink elephant lifting her director, a dancing mouse, thirty-five feet into the air aboard her trunk; and the Fansteel Family of Employees float with a fifty-foot high spacecraft landing with an extraterrestrial bounding down a gangplank.

The tallest float was that of the Casablanca Fan Company, depicting pirates on masts rising sixty-five feet into the sky. In Arco's "Scary Tales," a child was lifted thirty-five feet in the air by a dragon.

Even Giles Couldn't Help:
Michigan State 20, USC 17

While USC didn't win the 1988 Rose Bowl, its mere appearance there established a record which no other school approaches. The 1988 game was the twenty-fifth in the Tournament's seventy-four-game history in which USC played. It has thus appeared in more than one-third of all the games played.

Eighty-one-year-old Giles Pellerin attended the 1988 game, just as he had personally attended all twenty-four previous USC games there. In fact, he was attending his 666th consecutive USC game. If ever a team had a good luck charm among its fans, Pellerin must have been it; however, even his presence didn't help in 1988, as the new Trojan coach, Larry Smith, went down to defeat in his first Rose Bowl game.

The football game didn't equal the parade in creativity and perfection, but it wasn't boring.

Star-News sports editor Kevin Bronson presented the most touching version of Michigan State's triumph. He pictured the late Michigan State coach Duffy Daugherty and the late Reverend Jerome V. MacEachin, long-time Spartan team chaplain, toasting the victory as "the guys upstairs on Cloud Nine." When Coach Perles visited Father Mac in the hospital during his last days in December, the eighty-year-old chaplain told Perles, "George, I'm going to heaven to watch the Rose Bowl with Duffy." Daugherty had died in September.

"Maybe Duffy and Father Mac did some kind of signal calling in the sky," concluded Bronson. "How else do you explain four interceptions and one fumble recovery?"

Yes, USC was intercepted four times. And the fumble recovery spoiled USC's desperate bid for victory after John Langeloh's 36-yard field goal with just over four minutes to go broke a 17–17 tie.

USC drove to Michigan State's 30 when quarterback Rodney Peete couldn't handle center John Katnik's snap. "The ball slipped in my sweaty hand," said the USC center. At least four players kicked it forward until safety Todd Krumm of the Spartans fell on it 7 yards forward. USC was dead, just as it had been when the teams met in the season opener in East Lansing with Michigan State winning, 27–13.

USC outgained Michigan State 410 yards to 276 on New Year's Day, but Perles had the formula for victory— slashing runner Lorenzo White (thirty-five carries for 113 yards and two touchdowns), the accurate toe of kicker Langeloh (two field goals), the capacity

Although the Rose Bowl had been first nine times in television ratings of New Year's Day bowl games, the 1988 game lost in the Nielsen ratings to the Orange Bowl, in which Miami edged Oklahoma for the national title. The Rose Bowl drew a 16.5, its worst in a decade, compared to 20.8 for the Orange. "So what?" commented Harry Coyle, who directed the last twenty-eight Rose Bowl telecasts for NBC. "The Rose Bowl will never be forgotten. It's too steeped in fine tradition. And who knows. We may have a national title game here again."

Nine married couples were counted among the Tournament's active membership list in 1988. They were Christopher and Linda Bateman, Victor and Sandra Eu, James and Jill Hotvet, Frank and Sally Jameson, William and Annette Peters, Richard and Colleen Phegley, Steven and Diane Speer, John and Pamela Tegtmeyer and Steven and Kimberly Van Oss.

John Biggar III

of quarterback Bobby McAlister to complete four timely passes despite being sacked five times, and a defense led by player of the game linebacker Percy Snow (seventeen tackles), that bent but never broke.

Ironically, White was not in the game at the finish when Michigan State won. "Too many banquets," he said. "I was exhausted."

Quarterback Peete of USC deserved a better fate. He gained 54 yards on eleven carries and completed twenty-two passes in forty-one attempts, two for touchdowns to Ken Henry. The latter game-tying catch by Henry in the back of the end zone was so close to the line, NBC announcer Dick Enberg, working his eighth Rose Bowl telecast with Merlin Olsen, shouted, "If he had shined his shoes, he would have been out of bounds."

The victory proved that a Big Ten entry can enjoy Southland hospitality plus entertainment and win on January 1. Perles, once Daugherty's assistant, kept his team near the beach for a week, let his athletes take in all the sights and then brought them to Pasadena to play errorless football. "Men? Men ain't nothin' but big boys," he said. "Hard work is a must, but you need to have fun, too."

Michigan State finished with a 9–2–1 record for the year and eighth place in the final collegiate poll. USC wound up 8–4 and eighteenth.

Michigan State president John DiBiaggio had predicted his school's victory at the Southern California Big Ten Club's dinner three days before the game. "We came out here with one main purpose, to win a football game and restore the dignity of the Big Ten," he said. "I'm here tonight to tell you we're going to do it."

Big Ten commissioner Wayne Duke

enjoyed this trip into the land of Duke Wayne. "It's been tough all these years. I've been commissioner since 1972 and we've won only twice. This victory is most gratifying. I give a lot of credit to George Perles."

1989 and Beyond
What will the second 100 years of the Tournament be like? Even a veteran observer can only guess.

Perhaps the biggest issue centers around the possibility that someday college football will come to a national championship playoff system at the end of the regular season. Many years will pass before this occurs, if ever.

The NCAA passed a resolution in 1988 to drop any further discussion of a national tournament "in the immediate future." That means the subject won't come before the collegiate sports legislators in the next few years.

In an era of renewed emphasis on the educational aspects of college athletics, college presidents and athletic directors hesitate to take any action that will interfere with the educational purpose. A playoff at the end of the season would definitely interfere.

There are other reasons for avoiding a football playoff, including the grueling nature of the game, campus disruption over a long period of time and the reduction of enjoyable and profitable bowl participation to a few. Many conferences like the bowl setup, the Big Ten and Pac-10 Rose Bowl partners, for example. Each school among the twenty conference members receives $500,000 annually from the Rose Bowl game. They will hesitate to threaten that money tree. Because the Rose Bowl game is such a lucrative source of needed income, the Pac-10 and Big Ten schools will constantly lead a movement to prevent a national title playoff.

One factor could change the situation. The increasing number of bowl games may so dilute the television ratings for individual games that the TV networks will pay less for broadcasting rights to the bowls. That could turn schools to a new horizon—the playoff and split of a national title tournament loot.

Look for the Rose Bowl pact to continue as it is, however.

As for the other facets of the Tournament of Roses: The Rose Parade will continue to grow more spectacular. Float builders will dream up more fantastic creations utilizing mechanical and audio inventions. Flowers always will be beautiful.

The parade can't help but get better.

The public loves bands and horses. A proven show will go on and on.

The Tournament of Roses has a tradition and reputation for offering appealing entertainment. The next 100 years should be more exciting than the first century of this festival.

It is very unlikely that Pasadena will ever "sleep in" on New Year's morning.

All-Time Rose Bowl Records

In an event with great future significance to the Tournament of Roses, the Intercollegiate Conference formed in 1895 with seven members: Chicago, Illinois, Michigan, Minnesota, Northwestern, Purdue and Wisconsin. Indiana and Iowa joined in 1899, followed by Ohio State in 1912. The enlarged athletic conference came to be known as the Western Athletic Conference, or the Big Ten. Chicago withdrew in 1946 and was replaced by Michigan State three years later. Wayne Duke announced he will retire as Big-10 commissioner in 1989, after serving eighteen years. Previous commissioners were Bill Reed (1961-1971), Tug Wilson (1945-1961) and John L. Griffith (1922-1945).

The Pacific Coast Conference, which had been founded in 1926, disbanded after the 1958 season—partly because of a regional split over the punishment of schools which violated conference rules. In 1959 a new conference arose known as the Athletic Association of Western Universities (AAWU), comprising California, Stanford, UCLA, USC and Washington. Washington State joined in 1962. When Oregon and Oregon State entered the following year, the conference became known as the Pac Eight— a name it kept until Arizona and Arizona State brought the membership up to ten schools in 1978.

Individual Records—Game

TOTAL OFFENSE

Most Plays, 57
Ron VanderKelen, Wisconsin, 1963
Most Yards, 406
Ron VanderKelen, Wisconsin, 1963 (5 rushing, 401 passing)
Highest Average Gain per Play, 21.6 yds
Bob Jeter, Iowa, 1959 (9 for 194)
Most Touchdowns Responsible for (TDs scored and passed for), 5
Neil Snow, Michigan, 1902
Modern,* 4
Eric Ball, UCLA, 1986 (scored 4)
Rick Neuheisel, UCLA, 1984 (passed for 4)
Sam Cunningham, USC, 1973 (scored 4)
Pete Beathard, USC, 1963 (passed for 4)

RUSHING

Most Attempts, 39
Charles White, USC, 1980
Most Yards Gained, 247
Charles White, USC, 1980
Highest Average Rushing Gain, 21.6 yds
Bob Jeter, Iowa, 1959 (9 for 194)
Most Touchdowns Rushing, 5
Neil Snow, Michigan, 1902
Modern,* 4
Eric Ball, UCLA, 1986
Sam Cunningham, USC, 1973
Longest Run, 84 yds
Mel Anthony, Michigan, 1965 (TD)

PASSING

Most Passes Attempted, 48
Ron VanderKelen, Wisconsin, 1963
Most Passes Completed, 33
Ron VanderKelen, Wisconsin, 1963
Highest Completion Percentage (min. 15 comp.), 78.9%
Charles Ortmann, Michigan, 1951 (15 of 19)
Most Passed Intercepted, 3
Jim Harbaugh, Michigan, 1987 (attempted 23)
Mike Tomczak, Ohio State, 1985 (attempted 37)
Jack Trudeau, Illinois, 1984 (attempted 39)
Steve Juday, Michigan State, 1966 (attempted 18)
Bill Siler, Washington, 1964 (attempted 17)
Ron VanderKelen, Wisconsin, 1963 (attempted 48)
Bob Celeri, California, 1950
Most Yards Gained, 401
Ron VanderKelen, Wisconsin, 1963
Most Touchdown Passes, 4
Rick Neuheisel, UCLA, 1984
Pete Beathard, USC, 1963
Longest Passing Play, 76 yds
Rick Leach to Curt Stephenson, Michigan, 1978 (TD)

*Modern records date from 1947

RECEIVING

Most Passes Caught, 11
Ronnie Harmon, Iowa, 1986
Pat Richter, Wisconsin 1963
Most Yards Gained, 172
Cris Carter, Ohio State, 1985 (caught 9)
Most Touchdown Receptions, 2
Bruce Hill, Arizona State, 1987
Karl Dorrell, UCLA, 1984
Wally Henry, UCLA, 1976
Hal Bedsole, USC, 1963
George Callanan, USC, 1944
Bill Gray, USC, 1944
Don Hutson, Alabama, 1935
Harry Edelson, USC, 1930
Johnny Mack Brown, Alabama, 1926

PUNTING

Most Punts, 21
Everett Sweeley, Michigan, 1902
Modern,* 9
Marty King, USC, 1979
Larry Cox, UCLA, 1966
Len Frketich, Oregon State, 1965
Highest Average per Punt, 52.7 yds
Des Koch, USC, 1953 (adjusted to current stat rules)
Longest Punt, 73 yds
Don Bracken, Michigan, 1981

INTERCEPTIONS

Most Interceptions, 3
Bill Paulman, Stanford, 1936
Shy Huntington, Oregon, 1917
Modern,* 2
Tommy Haynes, USC, 1985
Don Rogers, UCLA, 1984
Bob Stiles, UCLA, 1966
George Donnelly, Illinois, 1964
Joe Cannavino, Ohio State, 1958
John Matsock, Michigan State, 1954
Stan Wallace, Illinois, 1952
Pee Wee Day, Northwestern, 1949
Tom Worthington, Northwestern, 1949
Most Yards on Interception Returns, 148
Elmer Layden, Notre Dame, 1925 (2 interceptions)
Modern,* 67
John Matsock, Michigan State, 1954 (2 interceptions)
Longest Interception Return, 78 yds
Elmer Layden, Notre Dame, 1925 (TD)
Modern,* 68
Russell Steger, Illinois, 1947 (TD)

PUNT RETURNS

Most Punt Returns, 9
Paddy Driscoll, Great Lakes Navy, 1919

Modern,* 6
Rick Sygar, Michigan, 1965
Most Yards on Punt Returns, 122
George Fleming, Washington, 1960 (3 returns)
Highest Average Gain per Return (min. 2), 40.7 yds
George Fleming, Washington, 1960 (3 for 122)
Longest Punt Return, 86 yds
Aramis Dandoy, USC, 1955 (TD)

KICKOFF RETURNS

Most Kickoff Returns, 5
Kevin Harmon, Iowa, 1986
Ralph Clayton, Michigan, 1978
Allen Carter, USC, 1974
Most Yards on Kickoff Returns, 178
Al Hoisch, UCLA, 1947 (4 returns)
Longest Kickoff Return, 102 yds
Al Hoisch, UCLA, 1947
Highest Average Gain Per Return, 44.5 yds
Al Hoisch, UCLA, 1947

SCORING

Most Points Scored, 25
Neil Snow, Michigan, 1902 (5 5-pt.TDs)
Modern,* 24
Eric Ball, UCLA, 1986 (4 TDs)
Sam Cunningham, USC, 1973 (4 TDs)
Most Touchdowns Scored, 5
Neil Snow, Michigan, 1902
Modern,* 4
Eric Ball, UCLA, 1986
Sam Cunningham, USC, 1973
Most Extra Points, Kicking, 7
Jim Brieske, Michigan, 1948

FIELD GOALS

Most Field Goals Made, 3
Kent Bostrom, Arizona State, 1987, 4 attempts
Rich Spangler, Ohio State, 1985, 3 attempts
Vlade Janakievski, Ohio State, 1980, 3 attempts
Longest Field Goal Made, 52 yds
Rob Houghtlin, Iowa, 1986
Rich Spangler, Ohio State, 1985

Individual Records—Career

TOTAL OFFENSE

Most Plays, 94
Rick Leach, Michigan, 1977–78–79
Most Yards, 513
Rick Leach, Michigan 1977–78–79 (452 passing, 61 rushing)
Most Touchdowns Responsible for, 6
Jim Hardy, USC 1944–45 (scored 1, passed for 5)

RUSHING

Most Rushes, 103
Charles White, USC, 1977–79–80
Most Yards Gained, 460
Charles White, USC, 1977–79–80
Most Touchdowns, Rushing, 5
Neil Snow, Michigan, 1902
Modern,* 4
Eric Ball, UCLA, 1986
Sam Cunningham, USC, 1973

PASSING

Most Passes Attempted, 63
Pat Haden, USC, 1973–74–75 (completed 34)

Most Passes Completed, 34
Pat Haden, USC, 1973–74–75
Most Passes Intercepted, 5
Bob Celeri, California, 1949-50
Most Yards Gained, 452
Rick Leach, Michigan 1977–78–79
Most Touchdown Passes, 5
Jim Hardy, USC, 1944–45

RECEIVING

Most Passes Caught, 12
John McKay, USC, 1973–74–75 (269 yds)
Ted Shipkey, Stanford, 1925–27
Most Yards Gained, 269
John McKay, USC, 1973–74–75 (caught 12)

INTERCEPTIONS

Most Interceptions, 3
Don Rogers, UCLA, 1983–84 (52 yds)
Bill Paulman, Stanford, 1936
Shy Huntington, Oregon, 1917
Most Yards on Intercepted Returns, 148
Elmer Layden, Notre Dame, 1925 (2 interceptions)

PUNT RETURNS

Most Punts Returned, 9
Paddy Driscoll, Great Lakes Navy, 1919 (115 yds)
Modern,* 8
Lupe Sanchez, UCLA, 1983–84 (27 yds)
Most Yards on Punt Returns, 149
Ray Horton, Washington, 1981–82 (7 returns)

KICKOFF RETURNS

Most Kickoff Returns, 6
Allen Carter, USC, 1974–75 (118 yds)
Most Yards on Kickoff Returns, 178
Al Hoisch, UCLA, 1947 (4 returns)

SCORING

Most Points Scored, 25
Neil Snow, Michigan, 1902 (5 5-pt TDs)
Modern,* 24
Eric Ball, UCLA, 1986 (4 TDs)
John Lee, UCLA, 1986 (3 FGs, 15 PATs)
Sam Cunningham, USC, 1973 (4 TDs)
Most Touchdowns Scored, 5
Neil Snow, Michigan, 1902 (5 rushing)
Modern,* 4
Eric Ball, UCLA, 1986 (4 rushing)
Sam Cunningham, USC, 1973 (4 rushing)
Most Extra Points, Kicking, 15
John Lee, UCLA, 1983–84–86 (15 attempts)

FIELD GOALS

Most Field Goals Made, 3
Kent Bostrom, Arizona State, 1987 (4 attempts)
John Lee, UCLA, 1983–84–86 (5 attempts)
Rich Spangler, Ohio State, 1985 (3 attempts)
Vlade Janakievski, Ohio State, 1980 (3 attempts)
Chris Limahelu, USC, 1974-75 (5 attempts)

UNUSUAL RECORDS

Most Minutes Played, 180
Bob Reynolds, Stanford, 1934–35–36
Hollis Huntington, Oregon, 1917,1920; Mare Is. Marines, 1918

During the war years of 1943 and 1944, California, UCLA, USC and Washington were the only teams which competed in the Pacific Coast Conference. In 1945 the conference was rejoined by all the other former conference members except Stanford, which returned the following year.

The Pacific Coast Conference consisted of ten teams after the war: California, Idaho, Montana, Oregon, Oregon State, Stanford, UCLA, USC, Washington and Washington State. Montana withdrew permanently in 1950, while Idaho remained—though playing less than a full conference schedule—until the conference disbanded after the 1958 season.

Tom Hansen, former Pac-10 publicity director and NCAA executive, became executive director of the Pac-10 Conference in 1983, succeeding Wiles Hallock, who retired after twelve years in office. Hallock was named in 1971 when Tom Hamilton retired. Hamilton headed the conference during its transitional years after the old Pacific Coast Conference headed by Vic Schmidt disbanded in 1958.

Team Records

TOTAL OFFENSE

Most Plays, 87
Ohio State, 1971 (439 yds)
Most Plays, Both Teams, 158
Wisconsin (84) vs. USC (74), 1963 (853 yds)
Most Yards Gained, 519
USC, 1980 (285 rushing, 234 passing; 76 plays)
Most Yards Gained, Both Teams, 931
USC (519) vs. Ohio State (412), 1980 (137 plays)
Highest Average Gain per Play, 7.5 yds
Iowa, 1959 (69 for 516)

RUSHING

Most Rushes, 74*
Michigan, 1972 (264 yds)
Ohio State, 1955 (305 yds)
Most Rushes, Both Teams, 115
Wisconsin (68) vs. USC (47), 1953 (259 yds)
Most Yards Gained, 429
Iowa, 1959 (55 rushes)
Most Yards Gained, Both Teams, 643
Iowa (429) vs. California (214), 1959 (108 rushes)
Highest Average Gain Per Rush, 7.8 yds
Iowa, 1959 (55 for 429)

PASSING

Most Passes Attempted, 49
Wisconsin, 1963 (completed 34)
Most Passes Attempted, Both Teams, 78
Illinois (47) vs. UCLA (31), 1984 (completed 47)
Most Passes Completed, 34
Wisconsin, 1963 (attempted 49)
Most Passes Completed, Both Teams, 47
Illinois (25) vs. UCLA (22), 1984 (attempted 78)
Most Passes Had Intercepted, 6
SMU, 1936
Most Yards Gained, 419
Wisconsin, 1963 (completed 34 of 49)
Most Yards Gained, Both Teams, 672
Wisconsin (419) vs. USC (253), 1963 (69 attempts)
Most Yards Gained per Attempt, 21.7
USC, 1930 (13 for 282)
Most Yards Gained per Completion, 35.2
USC, 1930 (8 for 282)
Most Touchdown Passes, 4
UCLA, 1984
USC, 1930, 1963
Most Touchdown Passes, Both Teams, 6
USC (4) vs. Wisconsin (2), 1963

PUNTING

Most Punts, 21
Michigan, 1902
Most Punts, Modern Rules, 17
Duke vs. USC, 1939
Highest Average per Punt, 53.9 yds
USC vs. Wisconsin, 1953 (adjusted to current stat rules)

INTERCEPTIONS

Most Interceptions, 6
Stanford, 1936

Most Interceptions, Both Teams, 7
Stanford (6) vs. SMU (1), 1936
Pittsburgh (5) vs. Stanford (2), 1928
Notre Dame (5) vs. Stanford (2), 1925
Oregon (5) vs. Pennsylvania (2), 1917
Most Yards on Interception Returns, 148
Notre Dame, 1925 (5 interceptions)

PUNT RETURNS

Most Punt Returns, 8
Michigan, 1965 (85 yds)
Most Yards on Punt Returns, 124
Washington, 1960 (4 returns)
Highest Average Gain per Return (min. 2), 31 yds
Washington, 1960 (4 for 124)

KICKOFF RETURNS

Most Kickoff Returns, 8
UCLA, 1947
Most Yards on Kickoff Returns, 259
UCLA, 1947
Highest Average Gain per Return (min. 2), 33.8 yds
Oregon State, 1957 (5 for 169)

SCORING

Most Points Scored, 49
Michigan, 1902, 1948
Most Points Scored, Both Teams, 79
USC (42) vs. Wisconsin (37), 1963
Most Points Scored by a Losing Team, 37
Wisconsin, 1963

FIRST DOWNS

Most First Downs, 32
Wisconsin, 1963 (7 rushing, 23 passing, 2 penalty)
Most First Downs, Both Teams, 54
UCLA (29) vs. Iowa (25), 1986
Fewest First Downs, Both Teams, 2
California vs. Washington & Jefferson, 1922

FUMBLES

Most Fumbles, 7
USC, 1955
Most Fumbles, Both Teams, 10
Illinois (5) vs. Washington (5), 1964
Most Fumbles Lost, 4
Iowa, 1986
Stanford, 1972
Wisconsin, 1960
Michigan State, 1954
Most Fumbles Lost, Both Teams, 7
Michigan State (4) vs. UCLA (3), 1954

PENALTIES

Most Penalties Against, 12
USC, 1963 (93 yds)
Most Yards Penalized, 98
Michigan State, 1956 (10 penalties)

RUSHING DEFENSE

Fewest Rushing Yards Allowed, 0
UCLA vs. Illinois, 1984 (17 rushes)

The original Pacific Coast Conference comprised seven teams from 1926 through 1936: Oregon, Oregon State, Stanford, UCLA, USC, Washington and Washington State. California, Idaho and Montana joined in 1937.

The 1987 Rose Bowl game produced a doubly unique score. Prior to Arizona State's 22–15 victory over Michigan, no team had ever scored either 15 or 22 points in a Tournament of Roses football game. Other point totals that remain to be scored are 1, 2, 4, 5, 11, 26, 30, 31, 32, 33, 36, 39, 41, 43, 46, 48 and anything higher than 49.

Six times in Rose Bowl history 7 points were enough to win:
1920 Harvard 7, Oregon 6
1928 Stanford 7, Pittsburgh 6
1934 Columbia 7, Stanford 0
1936 Stanford 7, SMU 0
1939 USC 7, Duke 3
1953 USC 7, Wisconsin 0

*Michigan was credited unofficially with 90 carries in 1902

Index

Page numbers in *italics* denote illustrations

Page numbers in *italics* denote illustrations

Page numbers in *italics* denote illustrations

Page numbers in *italics* denote illustrations

Page numbers in *italics* denote illustrations

Page numbers in *italics* denote illustrations

Page numbers in *italics* denote illustrations

Page numbers in *italics* denote illustrations

Page numbers in *italics* denote illustrations

Page numbers in *italics* denote illustrations

Page numbers in *italics* denote illustrations

Page numbers in *italics* denote illustrations

About the Author

A native of Cokato, Minnesota, Joe Hendrickson graduated from the University of Minnesota in 1935 and soon began writing sports for the *Minneapolis Star*. He later worked on the *Minneapolis Journal* and *Duluth News-Tribune;* he became sports editor of *Esquire* in 1944 and the *Minneapolis Tribune* in 1945. He resigned the latter position in 1954 to work in public relations for General Mills until becoming sports editor of the *Pasadena Star-News*. Nineteen years later, on January 25, 1980, he retired. But, even after he retired, he spent two years as columnist for the *Pac-10 Sports Report*.

He is past president of both the Los Angeles chapter of the Football Writers of America and the Los Angeles–Anaheim chapter of the Baseball Writers of America. He has received numerous awards during his career; his *Star-News* sports section was judged best in California six times and second-best twice.

Joe and his wife Edna are members of St. Therese Catholic Church in Alhambra. They have four children—Larry Hendrickson, Joanne Rahn and Susan Johnson of Minneapolis and Madeline Doyle of Saugus, California.

Maxwell Stiles, who provided Hendrickson with coverage of the early Rose Bowl games, was sports editor of the *Hollywood Citizen News* until his death in 1969.

This new edition of *Tournament of Roses* was edited by Kent Rasmussen, also a former sports writer, as well as author of several books on history. He lives in Thousand Oaks with his wife Kathy and their five children, writes occasionally and works as an editor at UCLA.

Jack French

Frosty Foster

Bill Flinn

Acknowledgements

The author wishes to thank people who helped to develop this story and picture compilation of the Tournament of Roses. Especially cooperative were Tournament of Roses officials including presidents and committeemen, particularly, William Lawson, Walter Hoefflin, Ed Pierce, Frosty Foster, Jack French, Bill Flinn, Kristin Mabry, the late Max Colwell, J. Allan Hawkins and Sam Akers, and Tournament photographer Clem Inskeep. Special thanks also go to the *Star-News* photographic staff including Ed Norgord, Norm Denton, Walt Mancini, Raleigh Souther, John Lloyd, John Emmons, Mary Welkert and Blake Sell; and *Star-News* editorial executives Charles Cherniss, Ray McConnell and Wanda Tucker for helpful consultant contributions. My thanks also go to ex-publisher Larry Collins and current publisher William Applebee of the *Star-News,* as well as loyal *Star-News* associate Dick Zehms. Independent photographers Gerald Chavez, Simon Mizutani and John Dolan also supplied pictures. Jerome Fried and Bernice and Lou Eaton made valuable contributions in the original editing, and Hank Ives did a tricky research task.

For seeing the present edition through production, I am indebted to Richard Cramer and Karen Sinrud of Knapp Communications, as well as Kent Rasmussen, who reorganized the text and edited the present edition with the assistance of Kathleen Patrick Rasmussen and Katie Goldman.